Alive into the Wilderness

An Autobiography
John S. Duryea
with Oso Bartlett

COASTLIGHT PRESS
Palo Alto

Published by
     Coastlight Press
     210 California Avenue
     Palo Alto, California

Copyright © 1985
All rights reserved
Printed and bound in the United States of America

Book design by
     Lyn Smith
Backcover photo and Chapter 10 photos by
     Margo Davis
Typography by
     Lauren Langford

ISBN 0-906288-3-5

Dedicated in memory of my parents
Dorothy Stillman & Robert Francis Duryea

*Aaron is to bring the other goat that is still alive.
And he shall lay his hands on the Goat's head and
confess all the sins of the people of Israel, and so transfer
them to the goat, which is then to be driven off into the
wilderness, to bear their sins away with him into some
uninhabited land.*

Leviticus 16:20 ff

*I am asked if I am not lonesome on my solitary
excursions into the wilderness. One cannot be lonesome
where everything is beautiful and steeped with God.
Every particle of rock or water or air has God by its side,
leading it the way it should go . . . .*

John Muir: Alaska Fragments, 1890

Table of Contents

1. Childhood Years

I am a priest of the Catholic Church.

For thirty-three years, until my marriage put an end to its approval of my ministry, I dutifully served the Church, sometimes with disillusionment and frustration, but more often with enthusiasm, joy, and hope.

I stand excommunicated now. However, I remain a priest. Each Sunday I celebrate the Eucharist for the community which worships with me and find in that communion the same spiritual nourishment that I have enjoyed throughout the years.

The reminiscences which follow are my own experiences as a child, a seminarian, and a priest. These tales are written partly to describe the fulfilling effort of building communities of worship and of leading people to liberty of conscience and partly to give credit to the special role the wilderness played in sustaining my life, my faith, and my work. But they are also written for the sake of understanding the bitter-sweet influence of the Catholic Church in my life and its crippling power over me and others raised under its authority.

St. Thomas Aquinas Church stood just three blocks from my boyhood home in Palo Alto, California. Its slender spire was visible above the oak trees whenever I looked downtown. During the 1920s there were still no other houses built nearby to block my view.

The wide steps of the church rose directly from the sidewalk, and the triple portico was always open, offering welcome. Inside I felt at home. The air was redolent of beeswax and incense beneath the vaulted ceiling; the light was soft, but colorful from the brightly robed saints portrayed in the windows.

In the rose window above the main altar stood St. Thomas Aquinas with pen and scroll in hand. I liked to look up at him whenever I knelt to say a prayer. He had been a great medieval scholar, chosen as patron of this university parish by its first pastor.

St. Thomas Church held an important place in my life. Our family attended Mass there on Sundays, and my mother was the leading soprano in the choir. Although I was still too young to enjoy the learned sermons, I liked the feeling of the place. It did not make God seem frightening or remote.

There was no parish school in Palo Alto in those days, so the religious instruction of the children was entrusted to the Sisters of the Holy Family. Two of these Sisters came on Monday afternoons for catechism class, taught in the parish hall which occupied the basement of the rectory. The older and younger children were grouped into two classes, one on either side of the large room, and the Sisters would drill us in our prayers and in the exact wording of the answers in the catechism.

One Monday afternoon in spring I descended the few steps to the hall and chose one of the folding chairs in front on the right— well away from cross-eyed Mervyn and the other back-row boys who tormented those who knew their lessons. I was eleven, a thin, studious, non-aggressive boy.

My teacher was Sister Mechtilde. Like most Sisters in those days, she had entered the Order when she finished high school, and had not been to college. She was devoted to her teaching role and to her traditional Catholic piety. She was in her early forties, very sweet, but very strict and precise: we were expected to memorize whatever she told us and repeat it verbatim.

On this day Sister read us the Genesis account of creation, on which we would eventually be examined. As she read the story it began to bother me. I could not square it with the geological epochs described in the "Book of Knowledge" that I had been avidly reading at home. Needing this matter resolved, I presented my questions to Sister with child-like candor. She tried gently to allay my puzzlement, but she was not equal to the task. She did not condemn me

2

for my "lack of faith," but simply sent me upstairs to "talk to Father."

"Father" in this case was Father Cronin, a young priest who was a native San Franciscan and an assistant to the pastor. He had recently obtained his doctorate in theology at the Gregorian University in Rome and was full of zeal to assist me. Although I found his erudition dazzling, his explanations reassured me that there was a reconciliation of the scientific and religious views of creation, and that my questions were perfectly legitimate. Father Cronin suggested that I not argue with the Sister, but that I could bring my questions to him at any time.

After my visit with Father, I returned to the classroom just as the other children were leaving. I liked to linger after class and help the Sisters tidy up, especially enjoying the friendship of the pretty and vivacious Sister Tarsitius, who taught the younger children.

Fruit trees were blooming and the warm spring day was making everyone look forward to vacation. Sister Mechtilde asked cheerfully, "Where will you be spending your vacation this summer?" "Oh, we're going to Silver Lake, Sister," I replied. "We camp there every summer, fifty miles beyond Jackson in the High Sierra." Silver Lake was my Shangri-la, my garden of Paradise. I spent half the year planning for our precious three weeks there, the other half recalling its delights. I was happy that she was giving me an opportunity to tell her about it.

Sister's sweet manner did not change as she answered, "I hope you don't miss Mass on Sunday when you are in the mountains. You know, Jack, that it is a mortal sin to do that." I didn't say anything. But I went home frightened and horrified. I wondered how we could get to Mass, a round trip of 100 miles over dirt roads to Jackson, in our 1918 Cole, which was already a decade old. Not to do so would mean having to cut our vacation to one week and return home in time for Mass! The thought was so painful that I was afraid to bring it up to my parents for a day or so. However, when I finally did, I found that Mother was less concerned about Sister's admonition than I was.

We were sitting in our cozy kitchen when I brought it up. Mother was making a baked custard, and Dad had not yet come home from work. "We'll talk to Father Carroll about it on Sunday," she reassured me. (And so she did.) She was not one to leave things unsettled. My parents were enthusiastic about their Catholic faith, but, unlike many Catholics, they were not afraid to approach the pastor or to question the rules of the Church.

The next Sunday after Mass, Mother presented my dilemma to Father Carroll, the pastor. He was a very friendly man. He was always on the steps of the church on Sunday mornings. He would greet us heartily and would laugh with a touch of the naughty boy in his manner. He was Irish born, witty, ruddy, and a great story teller. On the altar he was quite different: loud, learned, and emphatic.

In response to Mother's question, Father Carroll chuckled and assured me that Church laws never bound anyone to do the impossible—such as driving to Jackson for Mass! He agreed that our mountain vacation meant enough to us that we shouldn't hesitate to go there even though there was no available Mass.

We were fortunate in having Father Carroll. Not every priest would have understood as he did that God's love was manifested, at least for me, far more by the glories of the wilderness than by any church service.

The spirit at St. Thomas Aquinas was hardly typical of Catholic life. The priests were not primarily authority figures. They were friends. Although Father Carroll seldom visited people's homes, even ours, he loved a party. My mother, who took great pleasure in being a hostess, held a mammoth New Year's Eve party each year. The church choir was the core group, but it provided a chance to bring many assorted friends together. There were plenty of active games to keep people mixing, and there was plenty of laughter. My brother and I always stayed up for the whole thing. It was one of the best social events of the year, and the priests were always included.

Another event which took place in our home was the semi-monthly "SSS" meeting. This was an invitational soiree which my mother created to talk about religion and the Church. Father Cronin, the assistant, made himself available on alternate Saturday nights to answer questions and difficulties about religion. He would expound on any subject from the saints to the bad popes, from the history of the sacraments to the ceremonial regalia of the Vatican. He loved to talk, and he was familiar with all the latest religious literature. Several of Mother's friends joined the Church as a result of these meetings. I would stay up as late as possible to listen: it was much more interesting than catechism class. There was also a special delight in joining an adult group with a secret ironical name: "SSS" stood for Soul Saving Society.

At that time, most of what I knew about the Catholic Church was contained in the well-informed viewpoints and warm personalities of Father Carroll and Father Cronin. However, the harsher spirit of the Church beyond our parish occasionally became visible when other priests were present. Like most parishes in those days, St.

Thomas had a "Mission," a parish renewal, every year or two. Two priests would come, members of some preaching order, and would present a refresher course in doctrine and morals. Twice daily for two weeks they would pour forth fiery preaching until the last sinner was frightened into repentance.

One evening during such a Mission I was watching from the safety of the choir loft where Mother was privileged to sit. The preacher was Father Hurley, the leader of the Paulist Mission team. I was fascinated by his energy. He would stride onto the altar with a large crucifix stuck into the sash of his black cassock. Genuflecting before the tabernacle, he would whirl around to face the people—so fast that his robe spun out like a ballet skirt—and launch into one of the old familiar hymns, which he led in stentorian tones. His sermon was long and fierce, implying that most of his audience was living in imminent danger of being cast into the pit of hell.

During this oratorical display, I saw an altar boy who had arrived late sneaking softly up a side aisle. Father Hurley stopped dramatically and waited in ominous silence until the boy had disappeared into the sacristy. Then he bellowed, "There's manners for you!" Later on when our family returned home, my parents expressed their disgust with Father Hurley's insensitive behavior. So they decided to protest. The next day on the phone they asked Father Cronin to invite the Paulists to come to our house for the "SSS" meeting after the final service of the Mission.

On Saturday night they came. I was eager to see what would happen, for few people dared to tell a priest that he was wrong. After some small talk, my mother expressed her disagreement with the rigid style of their preaching and their insensitive treatment of a small boy's tardiness. The Paulists were taken by surprise. Father Hurley squirmed in his chair and attempted to defend their conduct as necessary to impress the people. However, they ended up taking their rebuke in good spirit. I felt proud of my parents.

Far from discouraging me, such incidents only served to whet my interest in the Church. I continued to be very active as an altar boy. I often went to early morning Mass throughout the week and was always present for the more special church events. Once, when I was thirteen, Father Carroll took me to visit the Minor Seminary, which was only a few miles away in Los Altos. I loved the priests and could well imagine myself being one someday, wearing the chasuble and cope and other strangely named robes, handling the chalice and other golden vessels, and conducting the wonderful ancient rites of Holy Week. However, I did not like the seminary's echoing corridors and lack of homelike intimacy. The necessity of leaving my family and going into some impersonal boarding school was repugnant. I realized that I was not ready to leave home at this time. So when I asked Father Carroll no questions about entering the seminary, he did not pursue the idea.

Home was the center of my life. Our house was full of friends always coming and going, talking of church and music and the mountains. The house was designed by my father and stood in the old part of Palo Alto called "Professorville," only a few doors away from the home where he himself had grown up, and where my grandparents still lived.

My grandfather Edwin Duryea, a native of New York state, had moved with his family to Palo Alto at the turn of the century. A nationally known engineering consultant, he traveled extensively in his work, but chose to make his home among a group of the early Stanford faculty who were, like him, Cornell men. Roberta, my grandmother, had been the daughter of the boarding house owner where Edwin had lived while attending Cornell University. She was quite young when my father was born. She had the qualities of the American pioneer woman—strong, resourceful, independent. She loved the outdoors, and when Edwin was away on business she would take her brood of five by horse and buggy on camping trips into the mountains west of Stanford and to Pescadero on the coast. She read and loved the Bible, but she never attended church, and she looked with some disdain upon the clergy she had known. She called herself a socialist; she was always well read and held strong opinions about public matters. She was interested in the cooperative movement and was involved in the founding of the Palo Alto Co-op.

My father, the oldest son of Edwin and Roberta, was a quiet man, handsome, tall, and strong. He was always there, and he represented security to us. However, he was never aggressive. Professional ambition was not as important to him as the quality of life.

He was trained as a civil engineer, but had become self-employed in 1929 because of the Depression. Unable to find engineering work, he had succeeded in turning his hobby of wood-carving into a second profession. He would sit by our big front window, wearing his work-apron, whittling away on the figures—mostly animals—which flowed constantly from his active imagination. At other times he would be out back at the work-table, hammering and polishing the bronze book-ends, handles for garden faucets, and other useful articles which were cast from his carvings. He sold very few of his original carvings. Castings were cheaper and, therefore, more saleable.

His art was whimsical and charming, and he knew how to use simple materials and available scraps. His first four carvings came from the cast-off rocker of an old chair. He was happy sketching and carving, but he hated the task of marketing his output and never made more than just enough money.

My mother, Dorothy, was a striking woman, full of vitality and charm, interested in everything and flirting with everybody. Like my father, she had gone to school in Palo Alto and attended Stanford where they met. They were deeply in love from their early college days. Although they were both in the mainstream of Stanford student life, there was never a doubt of their loyalty to each other.

My parents were married in the Stanford Church ten months after their graduation. For a few years, they lived in San Francisco, where Dad was building service stations for Standard Oil. I was born there in January, 1918. However, when I was four years old, we returned to make our home in Palo Alto. The house was built on Lincoln Avenue at the corner of Waverly, where the streetcar ran on downtown and out to the campus.

During my childhood, my mother's singing was always an important part of her life. There was a touch of sadness in her, that marriage had cut short a promising career as a professional singer. However, while we lived in the city she had sung at St. Mary's Cathedral and also at the synagogue. Our Palo Alto home had a living room with a graceful arched ceiling. My father had designed it to be a place of singing.

That room was where the Palo Alto Light Opera Company, which my mother founded, rehearsed for weeks at a time before each production until the airs of Gilbert and Sulllivan Operas became part of my being. And of course, there was the choir of St. Thomas Church.

Aside from music, Mother was not a joiner. She loved to be at home, not so much in the kitchen as at the piano. Whenever I was sick, lying in the sunny bedroom which my brother and I shared, I would listen to her clear sweet voice floating through the house. One of my favorite songs was the Arensky-Koshetz "Valse," whose haunting melody carried me away to strange, sad places.

My mother was the youngest child of John and Emma Stillman, and was raised on the Stanford campus in one of the original faculty houses. My parents and I lived there too for nearly a year while our house in Palo Alto was being built. The campus house had high ceilings and a long staircase leading up from a wide entry hall, which was lined with bookcases filled with fine classic sets, such as Kipling, Dickens, and Shakespeare. There was also a wonderful col-

7

lection of netsukes in a glass case in the front hall. My grandfather had accumulated these Japanese carvings on his Thursday trips to his Club in San Francisco.

My parents named me for my grandfather Stillman. Although I was only four years old when he died, I remember well his gentle, grave expression, his soft white hair and moustache, and the pince-nez he used when reading. During the year I lived in his house, we would sit on the couch in the cheerfully cluttered sitting room upstairs, and he would read to me from his favorite book—Alice in Wonderland. In the afternoon when he came home from the chemistry lab, I would join him at the great rosewood table in the dining room while he ate his milk-toast from a red Chinese-laquer bowl.

He had been born in Rhode Island. His mother, Caroline, had died in childbirth. His father, Jacob Stillman, had then come to San Francisco, sailing around the Horn as a ship's doctor in 1849, leaving his infant son with relatives in the East. Later Jacob returned East to marry again, and, with the baby and his new wife, left once more for California where he fathered two more sons and two daughters. My grandfather graduated from the University of California in 1875, and when Stanford opened in 1891, he was invited to join the founding faculty as a chemist.

His wife, Emma Rodolph, was the oldest daughter among seven children of Dr. Samuel Rodolph, a homeopathic physician who had immigrated from Switzerland in the mid-nineteenth century. The Rodolphs were deeply committed to family unity. Every Christmas, my family would journey to Oakland in our old Cole, crossing the Bay on the ferry, to attend the annual reunion of the Rodolph clan. These gatherings were held alternately at the two large Victorian homes of my uncles, George and Charles Rodolph, which between them occupied a whole block on East 14th Street, then the main thoroughfare of East Oakland.

There were two people beside my parents, one on either side of the family, who were really significant to me as a boy. One was Uncle Dan, my grandmother Duryea's younger half-brother, who came to Palo Alto to stay when I was twelve. He lived in a tiny room in the woodshed behind his sister's house. He called her Bertie. He had · been a third-grade dropout, a messengerboy, and finally a Wells Fargo Express Agent. Uncle Dan had been widowed early in life, and was in rather frail health. However, his spirit was still young and adventurous.

For me as a teenager, he was a fascinating companion. I loved to visit with him in his little room or by the fireside in my grandmother's home, where he told endless stories about his life as an expressman among hobos and railroad men. He shared with me a gentle wisdom that he had drawn from a life of poverty and hardship and ill health and from his multitude of contacts with people of all kinds. I loved to talk with him about the things that were important to me—my faith and the Church and the mountains.

All of my family was devoted to Uncle Dan. He often accompanied my father when he went on selling trips, and, while waiting for Dad, he would do pen and ink sketchings of birds, trees, and roadside scenes. We all loved to hear him describe the people he met. Every incident was spiced with his keen sense of humor. Mother and Uncle Dan would go downtown together and stroll by the stores, looking at things they couldn't afford to buy. Palo Alto was a small town then, and they would always meet friends to visit with. He became "Uncle Dan" to half of Palo Alto.

The other important relative was Aunt Minna. Though tiny, Aunt Minna was a formidable person—stiffed-backed and strong-willed. She took a cold bath every morning, disapproved of many things, and never went to church.

My mother, who was eight years younger, had felt the weight of Minna's dominance as a child, and remained always wary of her anger. Minna had had a beautiful twin sister, Cara, whom all adored. When they were twenty-one, they had gone together to visit an aunt in Chicago, and had been caught in the Iroquois Theater Fire. Minna escaped; Cara was crushed. Minna always felt that the wrong twin had lived.

She went to work at Stanford Library and became director of the Document Department. I often visited her there as a boy, and stood amazed by her knowledge of the location of every obscure document in her domain. She continued to live in the big Stillman house on the campus after her mother's death, which occurred when I was twelve. In the large entry hall was a special stand on which she displayed a Japanese print—different each week—taken from my grandfather's wonderful collection.

We were then Minna's only close family, and we joined her almost every Sunday noon for a delicious dinner around the big rosewood table. Roast lamb was her specialty. She was very generous to all of us, but my fear of her disapproval made it hard for me to realize at that time how intensely she loved me.

None of my relatives had any church affiliation. The Stillmans never spoke about religion; indeed they considered it indelicate to do so. My grandfather loved poetry. Literature and philosophy filled the place of religion in his life. He read Emerson and was a friend of John Muir. My grandmother on the Duryea side was a consistent

9

reader of the Bible, and had a real love for its wisdom, but I never learned what she thought about doctrinal matters.

The fact that my parents were Catholics when I was born was due to my mother's persistent struggle to fill the religious void in her life. She had never been taught even the Lord's Prayer. All through her teens and college years she had hungered for spiritual knowledge. She had first sought help in the writings of Sir Arthur Conan Doyle and the British School of Psychic Research. Her interest in Catholicism had been aroused by the entrance into the family of a charming, glamorous woman who was a Catholic, the young wife of her uncle, Dr. Stanley Stillman. Although Aunt Jo was careful not to impose her faith, her example had an impact. Moreover, she was the first Catholic my mother had met who was not a servant.

My parents joined the Catholic Church in 1915, about a year after their marriage. Living in San Francisco, they received instruction from Father Charles Ramm, Rector of the Cathedral. A child of the Gold Rush, an engineering graduate of the University of California, and himself a convert to Catholicism, he was the perfect teacher for them. Although it was Mother who initiated the whole thing, it was Dad who first decided to accept the Catholic faith.

Their conversion did not put an end to Mother's interest in psychic phenomena, which had nurtured her spiritually in her teens. My dad joined her in experiments—first playful, later more serious—with the ouija board. They always kept detailed notes. Their interest became, by the time I was old enough to be aware of it, a very satisfying and continuous "conversation" with one friend, now dead. He functioned as a channel with certain deceased relatives, most frequently Mother's sister Cara. I watched these sessions with interest, and would have taken part except that the board never moved for me. For Mother in particular, the sessions were a source of comfort and guidance, especially during times of financial anxiety. Although they used "ouija" twice a week, my parents were on guard against anything said by their contact that might have been contrary to their faith; there were, in fact, never any suggestions of evil. This world of the psychic remained always a family secret to be shared only with people who would truly understand. My parents warned me especially never to say anything about it to Aunt Minna.

The day came when my catechism class dealt with the subject of superstition, and I learned that my parents were treading on forbidden ground; I brought the news home. Until this time, Mother and Dad had been unaware of the strictures of the Catholic church, which were intended to protect the unwary against such dangers as hysteria, fanaticism, and diabolical possession. After a consultation

10

with Father Cronin, my parents decided to cease their weekly sessions with the ouija board.

Despite my parents' involvement, quite unusual at that time, with a circle of unseen relatives and friends, our home was not in the least closed or secretive in its atmosphere. Indeed, it swarmed with people! Mother's music, my father's artwork, and our Church community all kept the house busy and full of life. There was always news to be shared about events and plans in the lives of the many people for whom we cared. My mother's friends tended to be a decade younger than she and were unmarried for the most part.

My friends were not of course all adults. Our neighbors included several families with pairs of boys with whom my brother Bob and I played—in our yards or in the vacant lots which still existed in our area. Bob was four years younger than I, and I recall being at one period a relentless tease, but those years passed and we found that we shared most of our interests. We were good friends. We played violin and cello, respectively, spurred on by my mother when our interest lagged. We collected minerals and postage stamps and insects, amassing very creditable collections and studying the literature on them with deep interest. Bob, with the help of a friend, also learned to develop and enlarge his photographs; somewhat later he took up boat building and sailing. He was better with his hands than I was. Of course, we were altar boys together.

Soon after my brother was born, my father brought home our first pet, a small Boston terrier whom we named Tippy for his white feet. A timid, affectionate little creature, he accompanied us everywhere we went, whether it was to the mountains, to the beach, or to San Francisco. He was, above all, Mother's care and love. She was devoted to all animals. Even mosquitoes were immune from her retaliation. And when a column of ants invaded the kitchen, she would pound upon the wall with a hammer until the confused column retreated and she could seal up their hole.

When I was seventeen, we acquired a baby squirrel. A neighbor had found him in the street and had brought him to my mother for care. We named him Nutkin. Though feisty and sharp-toothed, Nutkin became one of the family. He spent much time in the house where he chewed the mahogany moldings ruthlessly. He wore a little leather harness, and went for walks with us, both in Palo Alto and in the mountains.

Of all our family interests, the one which most dominated our thoughts was the mountains. There we went, almost as if on pilgrimage, every summer without fail from the time that I was eight years old. My parents knew the mountains well. They had spent their honeymoon on a horseback trip into the Hetch-Hetchy Valley only a few years before it was flooded for the San Francisco Water System. Also, Mother, at eight years of age, had accompanied her parents on a two-month trip, riding horses from Fresno into the Kings River Canyon.

During the summer of 1926, we took our first family trip to the Sierra. After a little exploring by car, we discovered Silver Lake in Amador County and decided that it was the perfect place for us to camp each year. The altitude was high enough to provide the open granite my parents loved. The lake lay sparkling in a wide basin, with partially wooded shorelines, accessible all the way around its five mile circumference.

In those days, the road through the mountains was very poor, and it took some twelve hours to travel from Palo Alto to the lake. We would start our annual trip, usually in July, leaving home at two or three in the morning. The night drive, with baggage piled and tied all over the canvas roof and running boards, crickets singing in the night, incessant car problems, and of course breakfast in the Mother Lode town of Jackson, was an adventure deeply printed in my memory.

Once at the lake, we enjoyed two or three weeks of paradise. Our camp—always as isolated as possible from other campers—was simple. We really lived outdoors. Dad did the cooking: how I loved the smell of hotcakes frying in bacon fat, golden syrup on sunlit tin plates, hot cream soups in the chilly evenings, and fragrant corned beef hash. Every morning, we would troop around a little nearby bay to our chosen sandy spot to swim and bask until time to go back for a lunch of salad and open-faced sandwiches. This would be followed by reading aloud—Wodehouse, Agatha Christie, the "Tugboat Annie" stories, and Jeffrey Farnol. Mother did the reading in those days. Bob and I would lie on camp cots in the shade of our makeshift tent, with Tippy curled up on a sleeping bag. Dad would sit in a folding chair nearby, carving.

Late in the afternoons, my brother and I would go exploring with camera or butterfly net. The Silver Lake country, especially on our side of the lake, was uniquely perfect for two small boys to explore. Granite ridges, groves of pines, little nooks among the rocks with soft turf and wildflowers, and ledges and shelves of granite leading up toward the high rocky hill above.

There was one special place, just a little farther away, which we made sure to visit at least once each year: the Tiger Lily Glen. This was a swampy flat, densely grown with lodgepole pine, which lay at the foot of a marvelous granite amphitheater. From the bright hot rocks we would enter the forest, dark and hushed, except that some trees creaked against each other when the breeze blew. Lilies, mule-ears, white violets, shooting stars, and other flowers of the moist earth grew thick around our feet as we made our way along the numerous fallen logs. Occasionally a huge hawk or owl arose from its perch as we approached, or a dazzling tanager flashed across a sunny glade. Near as it lay to the lake, the Tiger Lily Glen was ours alone. I passionately loved this bit of wilderness and endlessly struggled to capture its atmosphere in my diary, which I had begun to keep when I was thirteen.

When I was seventeen, we began to seek and discover new areas. We came to love the numerous high valleys along the east slope of the Sierra. Nutkin, our year-old squirrel, accompanied us on those exploring trips of 1936 and 1937. In the car, he had a wooden box full of rags with a canvas top to sleep in; he usually lay on top of it. At night, or when we were busy setting up camp, he had a small collapsible cage. But most of the time he was free at the end of a long chain to climb to the lower limbs of trees where he would sit in a trance with nose raised to catch the informative smells.

When we hiked, Nutkin ran along the trail ahead of us, undisturbed by Tippy, at whom he would glance up curiously from time to time. Best of all, he loved to scramble swiftly up my mother's leg and jacket to perch upon her broad felt hat, leaping airily to a nearby tree when she came close enough. When he grew tired, he would crawl into someone's outside pocket to sleep peacefully with his tail drooping over the edge.

In later years when we went backpacking, Nutkin stayed home with a sitter; but he always went with us to Silver Lake, to which we would return after all our car trips. Although enriched with new memories, we were no less loyal to our own special place.

Towards the end of my high school years, I began to suffer from a painful tension over the future. I would lie awake at night with an urgent need to decide: should I go to the seminary, and if so, where and when? Should I be a parish priest like the priests I knew, preaching on Sundays and conducting the ceremonies of the Church, which would mean attending the regular archdiocesan seminary—a boarding school, even though near home? Or was my vocation to be a priest scientist, teaching in some university?

I was fascinated by what I read of Jesuit Father Bernard Hubbard, the "Glacier Priest." Though a member of Santa Clara University faculty, he still spent half his time in the wilderness of Alaska, and was known for his explorations of the still active volcanic area around Mt. Katmai.

Father Cronin, who was my spiritual advisor, approved of this latter idea, but pointed out that I would have to enter a novitiate of some specialized order. There would be many years of training and education before I could hope for such a career, and I would have to join the Jesuits, or some other teaching order, and submit to the austere training that they required. Their purpose would be to form me to the total service of God; career goals would be subordinated to this purpose. There would be no long vacations to the mountains, and for many years few visits with my beloved family.

Such a sacrifice seemed too great for me. It was rather to the priesthood as I knew it in Palo Alto that I felt called, not to the life of a religious community.

Through this time of uncertainty, Uncle Dan was an ever sympathetic confidant. He listened to my struggles without criticism, and having recently joined the Church, he shared my fondness for Father Cronin, to whom he had addressed his own doubts and questions.

Aside from this undercurrent of anxiety about the future, these were good years. I found life at Palo Alto High School pleasant. I loved to learn, and I got good grades. My most memorable teacher was Miss McCausland, who would read aloud from Shakespeare at lightning speed, but with such enthusiasm that even the most resistant students understood and shared her delight. I took up gymnastics in Physical Education, escaping the tedium of team sports for the quiet haven of the bars and rings, where—in company with two or three others—I became skilled for the first time in a physical activity.

During my teen years I spent most of my time reading: the wonderful historical novels of Willa Cather, the zoological explorations of William Beebe in British Guiana, and the journals of John Muir. I read every travelog in the public library and found in Mrs. Helliwell, the librarian, a constant friend. I was always traveling imaginatively to far-off places, wild and mysterious: Central Africa, Tibet, the far north, and the American West of pioneer days. I revelled in tasting the special "atmosphere" of each place and of other ages.

But in the background always lurked the dreaded need to leave home in order to be a priest. This worry was rendered more difficult by the outspoken and vigorous opposition of Aunt Minna to any word of a religious vocation. Her dream for me was an academic career in the footsteps of her illustrious father— presumably in geology where I had a strong interest. She was sure that my happiness lay there, and that I was being led astray by my friendship with Father Cronin and by my mother's religious attitudes.

As I was finishing high school, I could no longer postpone sharing with her my decision to enter the priesthood, which she would see as a childish fantasy. I dreaded what I knew she would say, "Jack, you're wasting your talents. You should go to college. You need to get away from your mother."

Finally, I went by myself to see her, and we went up the long stairs to the sunny sitting room. Fearing the weight of her disapproval, I clumsily presented my idea of the priesthood. Her words in response were brisk and decisive: "Jack, I'll pay the tuition if you go to Stanford. Take whatever courses you like but give it a chance." I soon yielded to her persuasion, and agreed to try it for two years.

And so in the fall of 1935 as a timid seventeen year old, I registered at Stanford, stating my major as geology. The campus was very familiar to me. I had played as a little child in the spacious arcades of the sandstone Quadrangle. I had known and loved the red tiled roofs, my grandfather's office at the chemistry building, and the colorful mosaics that covered the facade of the Memorial Church. And it was only a few steps from the Quad to where Aunt Minna still lived in the old family home.

I also had a nodding acquaintance with several of the older faculty who were family friends. Professor Rogers in particular, whose field was minerology, had loved to greet me with "Hello, Jack" on the Quad. He always used to fish from his pocket pieces of jade he had found somewhere; I never knew what to say about them. He always asked after my Uncle Phil, Dad's brother, whom he had taught. Another faculty member that I knew was Dr. Blackwelder, head of the Department of Geology. His campus home, always smelling of freshly baked bread, was a pleasant and familiar place where I went to take violin lessons. His wife, Jean, had taught me, in exchange for my mother's giving voice lessons to their daughter Marjorie.

However, in spite of my connections with the university, it was different now. I felt a stranger, alone and confused amid the throng of students who seemed to know what they were doing. And the lofty hall where registration took place was intimidating. I had no sense of belonging.

Father Cronin had assured me that as chaplain for Catholic students, he would be readily accessible to me at Stanford, and I would have the support of the Church through the Catholic fellowship he had developed, which was known as the Newman Club. I joined the Club. This organization at many other campuses brought together Catholic students for moral support and social enjoyment. However, at Stanford it was a pathetically small group, with only one other undergraduate member. It did nothing to dispel my isolation.

Perhaps if I had lived on campus, I would have become involved in the secular life of the university and grown more comfortable; but as it was, I lived at home and remained an outsider. I was so obviously uninvolved that my advisor pressed me to join some group other than the Newman Club. He suggested a political discussion circle called the Walrus Club. However, at the very first meeting, I sensed that it was leftish, if not subversive; again feeling threatened and different, I withdrew.

I was also afraid of academic failure. I had never done poorly in school, but now I was alarmed by the scope of my courses, and tried to protect myself by keeping them to the required minimum. These fears were soon borne out by the constant struggle to make my chemistry experiments come out right. I loved the lectures, but the lab was a nightmare.

The main freshman course, Western Civilization, seemed to be designed for the destruction of my faith. I was not used to the sort of historical writing which dealt with all beliefs—about the Bible, about Jesus Christ, and about the origins of the Church—as simply stories competing with different myths for our acceptance. Within a few weeks, I realized that I was one of only two professed believers in my class, and the only one willing to speak out in defense of my faith. But I was not really prepared for this challenge.

Toward the middle of the year I passed through a period of agonizing doubt. Disoriented, I felt that I was "losing my faith" and with my faith, the whole foundation upon which my life was built. It was horrifying to discover that I could be so easily shaken. I was ashamed to admit my doubts to my parents, and when I finally did so, there was no way to adequately express what I was going through. Neither my supportive home nor the advice of Father Cronin sufficed to dispel my doubts.

I was frightened and alone. Riding my bicycle to campus every day through the beautiful eucalyptus woods, I felt as if were going into the lion's den, and I grew to have a positive distaste for the whole university. In free moments between classes, I would sit alone in the wooded circles of the Inner Quad and dream of the mountains.

Toward the end of the year, my panic subsided. I became more confident in defending what I believed. After Christmas, Western Civ was so arranged that the more successful students were no longer required to attend section meetings. Instead, we met once a week at the professor's home in the evening. Two of the major research papers that I wrote were on matters pertaining to religion in the medieval world.

My choice for a research paper in the spring term was the reality of miracles, and my teacher, Dr. Winther, approved. With the help of Father Cronin's library, I managed to prepare a scholarly paper on miracles past and present on which I got a fine grade. The subsequent discussions were fascinating to me in that the other students always came with the a priori assumption that miracles were impossible. Some other explanation had to be found! They never found one, within the limits of their materialistic philosophy, and I felt thoroughly vindicated. But I was still lonely.

When I preregistered for the following year, I was dismayed to find that the major emphasis in my curriculum was not science but sociology—an area in which I could foresee further challenges to faith. But worst of all was the fact that my friend Dr. Blackwelder, whose course in historical geology was well liked by the students, would be away on sabbatical. The only course in the department open to me would be oil geology.

As the summer passed, I felt increasingly miserable about returning to Stanford. Father Cronin saw this as a sign that my vocation was primarily to the priesthood, and that further delay was pointless. I agreed, but again the decision meant confronting Aunt Minna. I hated to disappoint her; I dreaded to face her disapproval; and I hated myself for my cowardly flight from the religious and academic challenges that the university had involved.

When I told Aunt Minna about this decision, she asked if she might talk with Father Cronin herself. We went together in her little car, her first, which she had bought the year before. It was a Ford V-8, beige with red spoke wheels and a rumble seat. She was cheerful, determined to win Father Cronin to her proposal.

He welcomed us amiably, and took us into the large paneled living room of the rectory. Aunt Minna had never met him or been there before. She sat very straight and tiny in her neat, grey pleated skirt and small black hat. And she came promptly to the point—stating her feelings clearly and with conviction about what would be best for me: I needed to remain at Stanford another year, better yet until graduation; I was too much influenced by my mother; I was too young to make a commitment that I couldn't possibly understand; I needed exposure to the wider academic and social life of the university.

Father Cronin was his charming, erudite self, not flustered by her prim manner and strong feelings. He assured her that the priestly training was academically respectable, and that if I wished I would be free to withdraw from this commitment at any point. He courteously ended, "Since you obviously desire Jack's happiness and this is what he wants, why not let him try it?"

Listening to his convincing argument, I wondered what her response would be. But she simply stood up and extended her hand with a quick smile, "Well, Father Cronin, I guess you win." Then she turned away, and I could see tears in her eyes as she walked briskly to the door. Her brave acceptance was harder to bear than any anger or reproach would have been. Nothing more was said; but it was several months before she could bring herself to visit me at the seminary.

2. Seminary Life

St. Joseph's College, the Minor Seminary of the Archdiocese, sat nestled among the orchard-covered hills at the foot of Black Mountain. Only the top of its tower was visible from a distance. The approach road wound through oak and eucalyptus woods near a creek, and then, upon entering the sacred grounds, became elegantly landscaped, curving up to the foot of a long sweep of lawn, at the top of which stood the building—four stories high with innumerable windows.

In the early fall of 1936, having made the decision to study for the diocesan priesthood, I drove to St. Joseph's with Father Cronin to meet Father Lyman Fenn, who was president of the college. Although classes had already begun by that time, I was admitted without examination, on the basis of Father Cronin's high recommendation. He and Father Fenn had been classmates at the Gregorian University in Rome.

We returned home to tell Mother and Dad of my acceptance. They were pleased to hear the news, although Mother greatly dreaded the separation. St. Joseph's was only ten miles from home, but I would be cut off from my family (except for a monthly visiting day) until Christmas vacation. I felt as if I were going to another country. It was the end of our united family life.

19

Both my parents accompanied me on the day I entered. The marble entry way was as cold and echo-y as I remembered it from my first visit five years before. However, on this day, the echoes came from a well-played piano, which gave it unexpected vitality and a touch of artistic culture that Mother found reassuring. My parents met Father Fenn briefly and were impressed with his immaculate appearance and calm assurance. They helped me bring in my bags and said a tearful goodbye.

Soon I was alone settling into my tiny room on the fourth floor. The size of the room was not important because we were forbidden to use it for anything but sleeping. Our living space was the study hall, together with classrooms, chapel, refectory, and the outdoors. As always, I loved the outdoors, with acres of trees to explore and a wild creekbed cutting through the property. Although we were not allowed to leave the grounds, the dreamy views of the higher wooded hills satisfied my longing for freedom. On the hilltop to the east, beautifully silhouetted at sunrise, stood the Maryknoll Junior Seminary. Its oriental roofline recalled to me that the Maryknoll Order had begun its career with missions in China.

The first evening, when the bell rang for dinner, I was directed to a table near a window, where I joined two other upper classmen. We were called "rhets," from the word rhetoric, a division of the medieval curriculum of studies. Nine students sat at each table. The "head" of mine was Vincent Kelley, who turned out to be the pianist I had heard earlier.

The meal began with a short reading from the Bible, after which we were allowed to serve ourselves. That first evening I made the mistake of saying "please pass the carafe." No one knew the word, and I became suddenly aware—once again, as at Stanford—that I was somehow different. The students, mostly Irish Americans, were not from university towns like Palo Alto, and their interests were not in science and classical music. On the other hand, they knew all about professional baseball, of which I was totally ignorant.

Typically, small groups of three or four would form after leaving the refectory, as the dining room was called. When I joined these groups, the conversation was generally light, about sports or classroom incidents, with a good deal of bantering. I soon learned that my coming had been awaited with lively interest: a transfer from a secular university was a rarity. Most of the students had been at St. Joe's since early high school. They had hoped that I would be a "college athlete" who would beef up one or another of the intramural teams that dominated the recreational life of the seminary. The teams had drawn lots for me, and the winner (the Ramblers) was captained by Walt Albrecht, who was also class president. I was a great disappointment to them.

Nonetheless, Walt became a good friend. He was a powerful, thickset farm boy from the Sacramento Valley. The class called him "Kraut" for his German surname, or "Nobby" for his bald head; he had the thickest, shortest fingers I had ever seen. He was good natured and kindly, not resenting my athletic inexperience, and he understood my love for the outdoors.

Although everyone was kind and even cordial, I felt somewhat left out. Luckily, Vince Kelley was able to ease my discomfort. Like me, he did not entirely "fit in" either. Raised by retired military grandparents, he had sailed a lot, travelled abroad, and played both piano and organ very well. We became fast friends. During the after-dinner free time, before evening study hall, Vince and I would make two or three turns around the roads which encircled the seminary, quietly chatting about our common interests. However, there was some tragedy about his childhood which he never shared.

In time, I discovered other kindred spirits. Tom Donovan, responsive and enthusiastic, a lover of music. Geno Walsh, poker-faced and whimsical, a lover of the mountains. The four of us became regular companions on the after-dinner strolls.

Quite early in the year, Walt and I, and Geno of course, organized an all-day hike. The hills rose directly from the college grounds, and my maps showed that a ranch road followed the crest of the Monte Bello Ridge, the highest part of the Santa Cruz Range. We recruited a large group of rhets, plus one faculty member, and set out one lovely Thursday morning across the fields for Stevens Creek Reservoir, where the Monte Bello road began its ascent.

The going was easy, and we walked in companionable groups, enjoying the ever-widening views of the verdant Santa Clara Valley. Many of the party were without hiking experience; and for all my mountain hikes, I had never before been a leader. Gradually the joviality subsided as blisters formed and cramps began to appear. The picnic lunch on the top was a welcome respite. We could see Palo Alto and the red roofs of Stanford University to the north. And in the distance, the tall buildings of San Francisco and Mt. Tamalpais beyond.

The descent was dreadful: an overgrown trail that plunged down through dense woods that concealed where we were going. Geno and Walt and I took many scouting trips to find the way; but even so we were all home late for dinner, and would have been in real trouble if we had not had a faculty member along to vouch for us. As

21

it was, several of the group were in the infirmary for a few days, recovering from poison oak and general exhaustion. I was a bit lame myself.

This hike was a welcome link to the familiar outdoor world that I loved. Otherwise, during the first months at St. Joseph's I was preoccupied with the experience of regimentation in seminary living and the adjustment to being a part of a religious community. As for the academic life, I found it, compared to Stanford, undemanding and rather bland. I was expecting to study scripture, theology, and church history, but I was disappointed. In addition to a boring English course entitled Rhetoric, I had French and first-year Greek— which I enjoyed rather as I would cryptography.

The philosophy course alone really gave me something new and interesting to dig into: a world of deductive thought drawn from Aristotle and Aquinas. Father Fenn, the rector, taught this course. He was an excellent teacher. Using clear blackboard outlines, he stood before the class with quiet authority, carefully explaining the abstract concepts of scholastic philosophy, which were so different from the empirical data of the sciences.

I also enjoyed the contribution that the students from Maryknoll made to seminary life. Thirty or forty of them came down the hill evey day to share our classes, our library, and sometimes our sports, since they had only dormitories, refectory, and chapel at their house. Although no more mature than our own students, their dedication to a missionary life made them seem to me more noble— almost romantic!

The faculty, whose personalities did much to create the atmosphere of the seminary, included a surprising variety of men. Father Fenn, the president of the seminary who greeted me upon my arrival, remained my ideal that year. I saw him as a superbly disciplined man, cultured, learned and polished. His cassock was always immaculate; when he knelt in prayer before class, his arms hung relaxed at his sides. And he walked with the controlled energy of a tiger. As rector, he was strict; those who broke the rules had to endure not only his quiet, calm rebuke—"You were smoking, Mr. Smith?"—but also the hint of contempt in his gentle smile. Many students, mindful of that dangerous smile, referred to him as "the Gold Tooth." However, my relations with him remained filial and cordial.

One of the personalities which provided endless conversation among the students was a faculty member named Father Webster. The story was that he had joined the Sulpician Order to teach mathematics, but after teaching for one year had retired into a private world of music, vegetables and cats. He wore his black cassock at all times, hitched up at the beltline so that his boots and skinny shins were evident—enabling him to walk through the mud without getting his robe dirty. Most of his time was spent in the vegetable garden, followed by a string of stray cats. The only contact the students had with him was when they were assigned to serve his Mass, which he said in the chapel of the Sisters (our cooks) each morning.

When my turn came to serve him, I was eager to see this strange person at close range. Tall, thin, and deeply stooped, although only in his fifties, he murmured the Latin words in incomprehensible mouthfuls; and the ritual crosses which he made over the bread, the book, and the chalice were wildly sweeping.

The only time Father Webster came alive was at the organ. He played for most services, and often was playing for his own entertainment when we came into the makeshift chapel for evening prayers. With biretta still on his head and long legs and arms moving spider-like, he made the second-rate organ really sing— and not only to the tune of pious hymns. With a little attention, I could pick out tunes from popular musicals and sentimental love songs, such as "Moonlight and Roses," woven together in a magical fabric of sound.

Although there was no science course in the rhet year curriculum, I made friends with Father Bast, the stolid chemistry teacher. Geno Walsh, who also had a deep and constant interest in natural history, had become Father Bast's confidant during the previous year. In a seminary world where science was generally despised, Geno and I were admitted to the fellowship of the "bug room," an unused faculty suite in the administration wing, crammed with maps, books, pickled worms, and such.

The bug room played an important role in making our seminary life livable. In cold and rainy weather, St. Joseph's was a bleak place; there was nowhere else indoors that was cozy and home-like where one could read and visit. It became our clubhouse.

Like me, Geno loved not only the sciences but also the outdoors. He had backpacked as a Senior Scout in the High Sierra. After Christmas, when the warmth and spring odors of the fields turned our minds to the mountains, we spread our maps on the floor of the bug room, reminisced about past trips, and made fantastic plans to explore the most remote wildernesses of the High Sierra.

In addition to our academic life and our social interaction, the seminary also stressed spiritual preparation for the life of the priesthood. Each student was assigned a spiritual director; mine was Father Twamley—"Twa," we called him. He was known for the mechanical regularity of his personal habits. Each morning he would pass our classroom at exactly 11:52 on his way to lunch in the faculty dining room. He walked with measured tread, canted slightly forward, his eyes upon the ground precisely ten feet ahead of him. His teaching methods were similarly inflexible. The textbook, from which he had taught the course called Rhetoric for many years, was annotated with certain predictable jokes, for which we waited with stopwatches on the ready.

As my spiritual director, he met with me each week. At first I enjoyed being criticized and analyzed; it gave me a challenge to meet. Twa thought that I had too high an opinion of myself, and he took pains to point out my faults. "Jack," he said one day, "I think you are the ruthless type. I can see it in the way you walk: long strides, passing everyone else on the way to chapel or refectory . . . You aren't the type for the parish priesthood. Did you ever think of becoming a Jesuit?" At that point, I realized that he was off the track. I knew why I took long strides: I loved walking!

Father Twamley's counsel was not proving helpful in the development of my spiritual life. For him, spirituality meant detachment, whereas in my mind it meant service. When I had thought of the priesthood, it was in terms of bringing to people the faith which meant so much to me, as my parents and Father Cronin had tried to do during the wonderful evenings of the SSS. Many of Mother's friends had gained there the insights which led to their conversion.

But as the weeks passed, Father Twa continued to dig deeper into his theme of detachment. He felt that anything I especially loved must be renounced—only thus could I make space in my heart for God's love and for my acceptance of His will in my life.

Finally, the day came when he suggested a sacrifice that meant too much for me: that I give up going to the mountains! At that point I knew that we had come to a parting of minds. To give up the mountains was unthinkable: they were my ultimate sanctuary, and I was sure that God was there.

The result of this experience was that I never again felt free to share with those who had power over me the true importance and sacredness of the wilderness in my life.

During the summer that followed my one year at St. Joseph's, I was successful in pursuading Geno Walsh to accompany my family on a mountain trip. We had poured over so many maps together all winter: now we could enjoy the real thing.

In July, the usual Silver Lake trip took place, and our camp was idyllic as always, although there were rumors that our chosen

24

sight might be taken over by the Treasure Island Camp. Around the campfires, we practiced what became the theme song of our family and of my own later trips: "God's Wilderness." Starting with this poem by Walter Starr taken from the title page of his "Guide to the John Muir Trail," Mother adapted it rhythmically to the tune of "America the Beautiful;" we sang it nightly until it was well learned.

In August, after a trip home, we set out with Geno to visit an area we had never explored beyond Huntington Lake south of Yosemite. Arriving at Florence Lake, the end of a long narrow winding road, we were disappointed. The campground was littered with dam-building debris, and the trees were few and small. The large lake was flanked on either side by steep walls, quite unlike the gentle shores of Silver Lake. However, we were pleased to find a young man who ran a ferry service with his little motorboat, and would take us to a secluded spot near the head of the lake.

Investing our scanty funds, we embarked in the crowded boat, gliding up the long, still lake toward an array of unknown peaks in the rosy late afternoon light. It was a magical voyage with nighthawks circling overhead, ending at a wide ponderosa flat near the end of a long, narrow inlet. The San Joaquin River roared nearby as it entered the lake, creating quite a current. We were four miles from the road.

The place won Mother's complete approval. "It's so clean and open," she exclaimed, choosing a spot for our tent at the foot of one of the tall pines. We set up a permanent camp as we were used to doing at Silver Lake. A shore trail lay behind the camp, and pack-trains passed now and then with a jangling of mule saddles and a hail from the packers as they headed for Evolution Valley and other remote places.

Almost every day we hiked to one of the points that were reachable within a day, including Selden Pass on the John Muir Trail—a roundtrip of twenty miles—from which Geno could look northward along the route to Yosemite.

Two other seminarians hitchhiked from the Bay Area to the end of the road and were met there by Geno. After spending a couple of days with us, the three of them, burdened with heavy packs, left for the adventure of following the John Muir Trail to Yosemite. It had been a wonderful week: poised at the threshold of the real wilderness, I felt its call. I longed to go on with them!

The next stage in my training for the priesthood lay at St. Patrick's Seminary in Menlo Park, which I entered in the fall of

1937. I was excited about wearing the Roman collar and cassock for the first time; and delighted to be starting new classes which held possibilities of real interest. This was to be where I would spend the next six years in preparation for ordination.

Dad drove me over; it was only two miles from home. The Major Seminary was a massive brick building, surrounded by eighty acres of woods and fields with views of the distant blue hills. We carried my things up the a staircase to my assigned room, which looked out into the tops of the locust trees. Although the room was spacious, with high ceilings and tall dormer windows, the furnishings were austerely simple. However, it was my own to arrange.

After Dad left, I joined the other new arrivals, including many whom I did not know, clustered around the stone steps in the warm summer evening waiting for dinner. Austere looking figures clad in the long black cassocks walked slowly around the circular drive in front of the main entrance reading their prayer books. I met several students transferred from the Minor Seminary in Los Angeles, and exchanged news of the summer with my friends from St. Joseph's. Soon a bell rang, and we hurried in for dinner. The wide corridors were done in fine wood paneling and were lined with etchings of European cathedrals.

My room was on the third floor of the Philosophy Wing, which was the west side of the building; the Theology Department was in the east wing, at the far end of the administration building. I would be in the Philosophy Wing for the first two years, and I looked forward to living and studying in my own private room.

I soon found that seminary life at St. Patrick's was dominated by The Rule—a lengthy document which minutely directed our lives with the aim of "forming our characters towards the Holy Priesthood." The spirit of the Rule was not harsh or dehumanizing like a military bootcamp; however, it had been designed to form respectful and conscientious servants of the Church rather than men of initiative and individuality. Obedience was the instrument of formation.

Every night before dinner, the Rule was read and explained. It had been devised by M. Olier, the founder of the Society of St. Sulpice, especially for the training of diocesan priests, but it was full of petty details that were redolent of the mid-eighteenth century French Catholicism from which it had emerged. For example, we were encouraged to show our respect for the sacredness of our cassock by donning it first in the morning and removing it last at night. (A trick that only Houdini could have mastered!)

We were forbidden to talk above the first floor, where all student rooms were located, unless special permission was obtained from the faculty member residing on that corridor. And even when such permission was obtained, we could never so much as put one foot into another student's room. To do so, or to leave the seminary grounds without permission, entailed automatic suspension.

We were permitted visitors once a month on a Sunday afternoon, and when weather permitted families would form circles with benches on the spacious lawn in front of St. Patrick's. Those were happy reunions, which for me always included Aunt Minna—who no longer held aloof. Sometimes, when they had no visitors of their own, my student friends would join our group. My parents and Minna were glad to welcome them and I was proud to introduce them—linking my two worlds, home and seminary.

Occasionally, when Minna had a chance to speak to me alone, she would ask crisply, "Jack, are you sure you are really happy here? That you still want to be a priest?" Knowing that her concern was only for me, I confidently assured her that I had no doubts.

These official visiting Sundays seemed far apart, so my parents found another way to involve themselves with my seminary friends. On Thursdays, if we were not going out hiking, they would deliver milkshakes to the remote back gate of the Seminary grounds. Orders, given by mail during the week, would be filled at the Peninsula Creamery in take-out containers. Then, at the predetermined hour, Mother and sometimes Dad would drive up Coleman Avenue, a rural lane in those days, and await the appearance of the fortunate students. Then, as we sucked up the delicious contraband through our straws, we would trade news and enjoy a convivial half hour. Mother enjoyed breaking rules as much as we did!

Our Superior for the two undergraduate years was Ed Wagner, a tall, owlish man whose formal bearing hid a keen sense of humor. He was the one to whom we had to go for permission to leave the grounds. On Thursday, our day off, we were allowed to take a hike or go into town for supplies, but the Rule forbade us to "sit down and visit" in any house or restaurant.

Such a silly rule almost demanded to be circumvented! Geno pointed out that it said nothing about lying down; so, from then on, he always lay on the floor when we "happened" to stop at my parents' home. Occasionally, we felt it necessary to report our Rule infractions so that our "sins" would not overtake us all at once. When we did so, Father Wagner would look up with a happy smile of one who has found a treasure, "I suppose you were getting blisters and needed first aid,"—or, innocently—"You must have been getting wet from that shower we had today!" He was playing with us as much as we were with him, and he knew that we knew it.

The classes, as at St. Joseph's, were disappointing, especially philosophy, which was our major subject. Each period consisted of fifty minutes of dictation in Latin, during which we wrote nonstop. With no time to understand or even translate the material, the five minute discussion period at the end was meaningless. I soon decided that I hated philosophy: that it was a useless exercise in abstract thinking without relevance to reality, either in the humanities or the sciences.

This course was taught by Father Redon, the sole surviving Frenchman on this faculty of Sulpicians; we students ironically called him Spike. His age was indeterminate. His short thick hair had been black but was now greying. His dark eyes looked out from death's-head hollows with a gentle curiosity. No one ever saw him without his long black cassock buttoned to the throat over which he wore a short shoulder-cape. He moved through the corridors so smoothly and silently that he appeared to be on small wheels; and his head was always tilted to the right.

An institution dedicated to the production of "good priests" would naturally need at least one "saint"—someone to regard as a model. The Sulpician Order had not succeeded in having its founder, M. Olier, canonized. So we canonized Spike!

Because of his reputed sanctity, many students chose him as spiritual advisor. I did not, for he always seemed to me rather remote; I could not imagine him as a friend, going to the mountains, attending an opera, or even enjoying a dinner party in my home. However, on the few occasions I did visit him, I was fascinated by the austere orderliness of his room. "Ah yes, Mr. Duryea," he would murmur in his sing-song French accent, "I think I have the book you want?" And he would go directly to it, even though his walls were lined with books all jacketed in plain brown paper without labels.

Spike did exemplify quite well the ideal of holiness which the Sulpician tradition held up to us: gentle, serene, detached, pious, orderly, but underneath rigid and uncompromising. Students were always made to feel that they might at any point be found wanting in the required qualities of a priest, and could be dismissed.

Early in my second year at St. Patrick's, my first seminary friend Vince Kelley decided to leave, not for the outside world, but for the monastic life. It was as dramatic and mysterious as his still-unrevealed childhood: "Well, I've decided to enter the Trappists," was all he ever told me. I felt it as a real loss. The plunge into the silence of the Trappist life—the most strict of all Catholic Orders—meant an end forever to our visits, and perhaps even correspondence. It seemed tragedy for one with such a superb mastery of the organ to enter an Order where that skill would not be used. Before going home to San Diego, he went to my home in Palo Alto for a farewell visit, where all my family friends dropped in to wish him well.

However, the drama was short-lived. Only two months later Mother wrote with the news that he was back at our house, aware that the monastic life was not for him. He would not be returning to the Seminary. A few days later, Mother wrote again: "Jack, dear, the week is over, the prodigal is now in San Diego, and I'm in bed, a total wreck . . . People dropped in all day to say goodbye again (very differently) to Vince. Even Andy [Father Carroll] came! He was quite funny, particularly interested to find out that the Trappists do take baths. You boys will be much interested in the details he gave of the life there. I never understood the contemplative life so well before . . . I also do want to know how your cold is. Surely the Infirmarians should know something about medicine. Ye Gods, what a place! Thank God you're somewhere near, so that if something serious happened I could get at you . . . "

Vince was not the only one who left the seminary. I often wondered whether it was the tedium of poorly taught classes and the ever present threat of disapproval by those in authority, or whether those who left did so because they were attracted to other careers. As for me, I was able to find refuge from more frustrating aspects of seminary life in the bucolic serenity of the spreading grounds, full of owls and squirrels and quail. These grounds were to me what Walden was to Thoreau, and I found many woodsy hideouts where I loved to go, often with Geno, especially in spring.

There were certain hours when we were free to wander in meditative silence, which I enjoyed as much as the official periods of recreation. The latter tended to be taken up with endless talk about the faculty and the Rule, lightened by a lot of rough humor. I often preferred the silence and beauty that nature provided.

During my second year on the Philosophy Side, I conceived the idea of living "outdoors" by turning the heat off and keeping my two large windows open all winter. I had a big corner room on the third floor. Owls landed on my ledge outside and screeched; and frost formed on my blankets now and then.

There was ample time to dream of mountain trips; so during the spring of 1939 I was preparing a plan: a first real family pack-trip, starting from Florence Lake, which we had discovered the year before. Geno would not be free to go, but two Palo Alto boys were recruited by my brother to join us. We reserved two pack burros to carry our gear. Bob and I created our own first backpacks—light, fragile, and uncomfortable.

After the two college years, those of us who felt sure of our vocations received in June the first of what were called Minor Orders—a ceremony known as Tonsure, which offically made us "clerics" with all the long obsolete social status pertaining thereto. Several of my friends left St. Patrick's at this point. Tom transferred to another seminary which had just been built near Los Angeles to serve Southern California and Tom's diocese of Arizona. George Coelho, whose whole-hearted laughter often eased the strains of seminary life, simply decided that he didn't want to be a priest. Celibacy was not for him; he had always taken shameless delight in whistling at the girls who occasionally came in view when we were out walking around the grounds. (Vince, we heard, was now pursuing his career in music.)

That summer the time I spent with my family in the mountains was eventful. As we had done for several years, we rented a boat and took our camping gear to a secluded site a half mile south along the shore of Silver Lake. Even so, we had begun to feel that the privacy and serenity which we had found there was being threatened by the increasing number of campers and the development of Treasure Island as a camp for boys.

One day, a man came along the shore, whom we had met casually, a teacher form San Francisco named Dalton. He said that he had an option on two lots (out of a total of six) which the Pacific Gas & Electric company was subdividing on the shore a little south of us. Did we want one of them? The rent would be $50 a year.

We hastened down the trail to take a look: lot #1 (ours!) lay at the foot of a steep granite ridge, against which stood one giant ponderosa pine. The land sloped down gently to the rocky shore, mostly grown with lodgepole pine and a few clumps of willow. We decided then and there to take it, and named it Camp Shadow on the Rock. Dalton had the next lot, and was erecting a tiny stone hut for storage purposes. Unlike the Forest Service, P.G.& E. did not place any requirements on us, other than to refrain from cutting live trees.

The shore trail, an old public easement, ran through all the lots, which were separated from the road by a high ridge of rock, and were accessible only by trail or by boat. The location of our lot was half-way between the two ends of the lake; the island lay a quarter mile off-shore, and across the widest part of the lake, to the east, stood Thunder Mountain. Its dark volcanic cliff rose a thousand feet above the forest at its foot, and was etched by wonderful shadows at sunset.

Although we did not move our camp that summer to our new mountain home, we spent some time there planning where to put a cabin for storage and where the tent would be located.

A week after our Silver Lake outing, we were off into the wilderness. For the first time, we had no pets. Tippy, at age seventeen, had just died, and Nutkin was home with a squirrel sitter. The two-week trip covered a circuit of 145 miles, descending the grand canyon of the Middle Kings and circling back to Florence Lake over Hell-For-Sure Pass.

It was a great adventure, and it remains to this day a marvel to me that my mother, then fifty, not only did it but loved it. Rain began the second day. We had no tents—only heavy oiled canvases that covered the burro packs. On the third day of rain, as we marched over the treeless miles to Muir Pass, we walked in tandem holding the canvases over our heads. We were a soggy bunch, having awakened in the moonlite to find that our little meadow at the foot of Mt. Darwin had become a pool from the drainage of the previous day's rain. But by noon that day the rain was over, and we were spellbound by the series of jewel- like lakes, set in the descending stairs of LeConte Canyon, shining in the afternoon light.

We met few people, but at Grouse Valley we met two old ladies who shared their abundant catch of fish with us. Their husbands were not with them, for they had retired from hiking. At Simpson Meadow we plunged through the waist high flowery fields to the river bank, where a big hearty man emerged from the woods leading a horse for Mother to ride across the Kings.

The lowest elevation on our trip was Tehipite Valley, which we had been warned was full of rattlers. Although we never saw a snake, Mother was determined that we should not camp there but rather climb to the plateau above before stopping for the night. Weary from many miles that day, we began at four in the afternoon the endless zigzag trail to Gnat Meadow, nearly four thousand feet above us. We made it, but darkness was falling as we reached the top, and we trudged along in the heavy forest, breathing dust from the unseen trail. We could smell cattle, and occasionally hear their bells. After perhaps a mile, I began to catch the scent of cool wet grass. Gnat Meadow was fenced to keep cattle out of the pasture: so I had to feel my way along in the dark to find a gate. Greatly relieved we stumbled in and made camp on a trampled spot near the spring. The burros could enjoy green fodder all night. They had become like pets, and had caused us considerable anxiety as they wheezed and grunted up the long climb.

31

A day or two later, after crossing the North Fork, we camped for two nights at Devil's Punchbowl Lake high in Red Mountain Basin. It was a glorious spot in the open granite country we all loved. Dad was particularly glad to have a day of rest. He had pulled a muscle in his back four days before, and must've been in considerable pain. He walked with one hand on his hip, and asked for help when he wanted to sit or lie down. However, he steadfastly followed the advice of his grandmother whom he quoted to the rest of us upon occasion: "Suffer in silence and rejoice aloud!"

The evening meal and campfire were always important parts of the ritual of mountain life, and now that we were rested, conversation was lively. We loved to tease Dad. He was so big and so resourceful that we never worried about hurting his feelings. His calm, strongly chiseled features and his habitual silence suggested the Native American heritage which he claimed to have on his mother's side; accordingly we found various Indian-type names for him. Perhaps our favorite was "Big Chief Slinging Bull"—chosen because of some outrageously inaccurate remark about the country through which we were traveling. But he would smile his broad, close-lipped smile, and shrug off the error as of no importance. Which, of course, was true, for he never failed us when we needed him.

On this particular night, Dad was staring into the fire watching the constantly changing flames as he loved to do; occasionally he stood up to warm his seat. About nine, as we looked across the lake towards the distant northern skyline, I noticed a pink glow that did not belong there. Could there be a fire? It was in the direction of our starting point. Suddenly a greenish beam showed vertically, and Bob thought it might be a firefighting search light. However, it did not move, but slowly faded to be replaced by another. Then it struck me: the Northern Lights! We watched the mysterious sight for a half hour until it disappeared.

There were three more days in the back country before we saw Florence Lake ahead of us and knew that our trip was almost over. It was hard to say goodbye to the burros: they had shared so much of our adventures. Dreams and memories of this high mountain experience and others would provide many hours of delightful conversation for me during the long seminary winter ahead.

In the fall I moved with my remaining classmates to the Theology Wing. We were now graduate students, although no degree had been issued to us. Our curriculum now stressed the long-anticipated professional courses, such as Canon Law, Theology, Church History, and Biblical Studies. However, the quality of instruction was no better. Many of the students put up with it by making fun of the profs or trying to lead them off the track. My refuge was writing my mountain journals, which I did voluminously during the dull classes.

That was the fall when my brother Bob, four years after I did, entered St. Joseph's College. He had worked in construction for a year after high school to test his aptitude and interest in the sort of work Dad knew. However, when he opted for the seminary, I was not surprised. He had shared his thoughts with me during the previous year; he was concerned that his decision would be a disappointment to the family, and that he would appear to be simply imitating me. But when my parents learned of his decision, they accepted it and did not attempt to dissuade him. Now it was my pleasure to share my inside knowledge of seminary life with him.

The graduate division of the seminary was presided over by Father Nevins, commonly called Joey. Each morning at six, we gathered in the Prayer Hall, a big bare room full of folding chairs, for morning prayers and meditation. Joey, who was very short, would arrive just as the last bell rang, sweeping in with his huge black cape dragging behind, and would ascend the three steps to the front platform. There he would kneel, almost hidden behind the massive desk, facing us—his elbows resting on the desk. Then he would unfold a large silk handkerchief, holding it between his hands like a hammock, on which his big red nose would rest. As his eyes darted about checking attendance, we went through the routine recitation of morning prayers. Then followed a 20 minute silent meditation, during which most of us fell asleep, until the bell aroused us and we trooped passively to Mass in the big chapel.

On the Theology side, obtaining hiking permission was more difficult. It meant going with the hike-list and itinerary to the rector's office, a fearsome place. Joey would be sitting behind his wide desk wearing a green eye-shade. His pale blue eyes had a hawk-like coldness as they peered out over his bulbous nose. His greeting was usually a deep-throated "Well?" with a challenging up-swept inflection.

He would generally use the occasion to bring up whatever crimes we might have committed recently; however, he usually gave the permission as requested. For all his gruffness and bullying, he had a soft heart, especially for the sick or lonely or discouraged. He was retired now from teaching courses, but he gave us instead a daily commentary on whatever he liked. His remarks, given in

Prayer Hall before dinner, were awaited with interest for their sardonic wit.

One of the goings-on which he and the other "Sulps" chose to overlook—for our sanity!—was the weekly gathering in "the Pit." The pit was an old quarry at the rear of the property, with a steep drop on the side nearest to the buildings. In the shelter of this little cliff a group of us would gather around a fire on our free Thursday nights to sing and tell tales and let off steam until time for night prayers.

We were an unlikely assortment, united by our love for campfires and by a rebel spirit. Red Regan was the ringleader, loud, profane, and jolly. Geno Walsh and I represented the hiking contingent; I was known as "Big-Jack." Jake DeAndreis was the wistful cynic; Butch Dollard the clown; Speed Hoffman, the innocent young neophyte; Tom Lacey the veteran boys-camp counselor, forever in hot water; and fat Bill Blanchard was known for the foot-long cigar which remained in the notch of a tree when we went to the chapel for night prayers. Other students who passed by would look down at our fire-lit group and make a few cracks before strolling on.

One of the recurring topics of conversation in the pit was our summer assignments to teach catechism. We were required to do this at least once before ordination. Most of us spent a month or two as cathechists in poor city parishes, or as counselors at summer camps. These experiences provided the material for a lot of mirth and also a lot of serious talk. They also helped to slant our vision of the priestly ministry toward work with children and youth.

Our conversations in the pit also concerned the mountains, which meant so much to Geno and me and to Jake DeAndreis. Since my family had begun in 1940 the project of building the little cabin on our newly acquired land, I was anxious to recruit friends to camp with us and help in the building. I only found Geno available, but several of my brother's classmates were able to come.

During the next few summers, Bob and I, together with some of our seminary friends, worked on the cabin, which was to be a place to store the boat my brother had been building in the backyard at home, and to serve as a shelter to use in bad weather. With Dad as architect, we spent long weeks building our stone house, using the native granite rock, roughly squared into building blocks.

When the ready supply of granite was exhausted, we brought up rocks from the lake bottom, and carried well-dried logs down the hill to make trusses for the roof and frames for the doors and windows. The cost was held down to something like $50. Even the

34

shakes for the roof were free—taken from a crushed and abandoned cabin on the island.

We had many a good laugh around the fire in the pit, recalling our struggles to remove gigantic boulders and our constant arguments with Dad about the engineering aspects of the building, borne of youthful ignorance and exuberance. One favorite story was about the time Jake, who went with us the second year, ruined our evening meal. A wonderful pot of baked beans had been cooking all day, buried deep in the hot wood ashes. Offering to be helpful, Jake had taken a shovel to get the pot and had inadvertently—and with disastrous efficiency—scooped the lid off the pot, allowing the sand to run into our anticipated dinner.

There was no one on the faculty who shared my love for the mountains. However, my spiritual director, Father Power, was also the biology teacher. He and I had the seldom-expressed bond of loving science, and his course was for me a refreshing escape from the world of philosophical abstraction in which we lived.

However, he was a bizarre teacher. Nicknamed "the Spook," Father Power was egg-bald, very pale, with china-blue eyes that were usually focused far away. He spoke with maddening slowness, his voice low and hollow; in class it would occasionally rise in a sort of groan when he was trying to make a point. "Mis-ter Thomp-son," he once asked, "What is the most important part of . . . a worm?" Thompson, a sweet simple guy, was totally at a loss in biology. After a moment of silence, he cautiously ventured, "The head, Father?" "No . . . ," Spook groaned (one could almost hear tears in his voice), "the en-ter-on!" In spite of the eccentricity that he showed in the classroom, Spook prepared for his classes thoroughly. He was also very serious about his responsibility as my spiritual director. However, his guidance was quite traditional; he was still very much a Sulpician, and his spirituality reflected Sulpician views of the priesthood. But I found that his training in the natural sciences gave an objective quality to his thinking which made it easier for me to talk with him. He was a kindly man, and with him I felt free to express many of my problems, my hopes, and my ideals.

As in any closed society, the ritual of meals was a dominant aspect of seminary life. We always proceeded in silence from the previous "exercise" to the refectory—a huge well-lighted room, with long tables each seating sixteen men. Eight of us were designated every day to be waiters. One man was assigned to read aloud from a book or paper or to preach. The "head reader" (a position I occupied for one year) would present the introductory scripture, and then give place to the day's reader. The rest of the students were to keep quiet and listen. The whole faculty ate at a "high table" on one side of the room, except at breakfast when a single prof was there to keep order.

Of course, ways were sought to lighten the tedium of these silent meals. And one such way, used when the "Owl" was presiding alone, was the Eel Race. We had learned in biology that there were almost microscopic worms in old vinegar, such as that on our tables. So at the right moment, the end man would tilt the vinegar bottle, and then all eyes would trace the imaginary racing eel up and down the length of the long tables.

Any variation in the routine was welcome. On one occasion the reader, who happened to be my brother, was assigned to read an essay on varves, which are a geomorphological formation of glaciated terrain. Raising his voice above the din of dishes, he announced the title "Varves"—a word which was not only unfamiliar but obviously hard to enunciate. Suddenly the table-bell rang. It was Joey, his head cocked back, pointing a truncated index finger unceremoniously. "What's that?" he demanded. "Varves!" replied Bob. Again a ring from Joey, "Say it again: enunciate."

Everyone had stopped eating; for once there was full attention as Bob, for the third time, in his strong, low-pitched voice, shouted, "Varves!" At this point, Spook intervened: turning to Father Nevins, with a deprecating smile and much waving of his pale hand, he explained the meaning and spelling of this strange word. Bob was then permitted to proceed.

Another change which occasionally relieved the monotony of our schedule was the presence of visitors. Rumors would fly when a stranger appeared at the faculty table for a meal. Who was he? Would he give us a talk? Would he even be important enough to grant us a holiday from classes? One such notable was Bishop Paul Yu-Pin, a political exile from his diocese in China. Another was Cardinal Gilroy from Australia, his cassock trimmed in elegant vermilion piping.

Among the visitors who spoke to us was John C. H. Wu, former Chief Justice of China, now teaching at Harvard. Dr. Wu had grown up a pagan and had been married to a woman chosen for him when they were both children. He delighted us with his tale of their wedding day. Apparently, after they were left alone, he had managed to do or say everything that his wife had been warned would be bad luck. Nonetheless, they had lived a full and happy life, had become Catholics, and had raised thirteen children. Another speaker was

Jim Keller, a Maryknoll priest from New York who charmed us with his supreme optimism. His favorite quotation was: "It is better to light one candle than to curse the darkness."

The only woman who ever spoke to us was Dorothy Day. Joey Nevins had great respect for her and her work among the poor in New York, and he invited her to address us on two occasions. She was a tall, gaunt woman, very simply dressed. Her greying hair was braided around her head. She looked tired as she took her place half seated on the corner of the big front desk to speak to us. Dorothy spoke softly and without emphasis, but her utter sincerity and the innate drama of the stories she told created a hush in the room.

"One day last summer," she said, "I saw a man sitting down by one of the piers along the East River, all alone. He sat on a log, and before him was a wooden box on which he had spread out on a newspaper his meager supper. He sat there and ate with some pretense of human dignity. It was one of the saddest sights I have ever seen."

After her talk, we went to the refectory for dinner. She was even permitted to eat with the faculty in our otherwise completely masculine dining room.

Meeting people like these helped us to gain a broader vision of the priestly ministry, and of course, such visitors provided whole days of conversation for us. We reviewed every word she had said, her philosophy, the story of her conversion and her clashes with the government. These were the occasions when we could look beyond the small world of the seminary and nourish our ideals.

However, it was inevitable that most of the time our recreation chatter was filled with the only material available—the faculty. Unlike sailors and soldiers, we did not have the diversion of talking about girlfriends. There was nothing left to do except complain about or laugh at the faculty. Luckily most of them provided plenty of material for satire and cynicism; as the six years wore on their inadequacies and eccentricities became unbearably familiar.

During the fifth year, there was an opportunity to let off steam: "The Deacon Smoker." The class about to be ordained was traditionally the butt of a crudely crafted play, in which the various personalities in the class were highlighted and lampooned. But this play provided also a perfect opportunity to ridicule the less popular members of the faculty. As it happened, when it was my class' turn to write and produce this masterpiece, I was the director. We got so carried away with our creative efforts that the script could never have been spoken on stage without our incurring the justifiable wrath of the whole faculty. Common sense eventually asserted itself, and a much expurgated version was prepared for the play. The original was regretfully shredded and flushed down the toilet, lest it fall into Enemy Hands.

The following fall, seminary life was considerably altered by the beginning of the Second World War, which began for us with the bombing of Pearl Harbor in my fifth year at St. Patrick's. Although the attack occurred early in the morning, it was during the noon meal that Joey—ringing the table bell for attention—announced the dire news that we were at war. During the remaining year and a half of my seminary life, we followed the progress of world events through our limited access to the radio and through clippings that our parents sent us. Some of the students had brothers who were promptly drafted.

There were a few blackouts during the first year, which we carefully observed without being sure whether there was real danger or not. Otherwise, our lives were only slightly affected by the worldwide upheaval. Permissions to go into town now entailed warnings to be as invisible as possible—particularly not to wear clerical dress—so that our draft exemption would not arouse local hostility. We heard rumors that ordinations would be sped up so that we might replace those called into the Chaplain's Corps. We had very little awareness of the horrors of war or of the concentration camps in Europe.

It was the internment of the local Japanese-American families which brought the war closest to me. On one visiting Sunday, Aunt Minna told me about the plight of Kito Sako, her gardener, and his family, who had been quickly sent to the internment camp at Manzanar, leaving everything behind. She actively befriended them and took trusteeship for their belongings until they were allowed to return.

With the date of ordination advanced to March of 1943, our minds were less than ever on our studies. The content of our courses seemed remote from the problems of the real world and from the work we hoped to be doing. I had no doubt that I could explain the Church's doctrines and conduct the ceremonies with dignity, but I prayed fervently, and I am sure my thirteen classmates did likewise, that I might become a "Holy Priest"— kind and devoted in the service of God's people.

I spent many hours in the dark quiet Chapel during those months, asking myself if my motives were right and pure in seeking to be a priest. Was I really willing to be a victim, if need be, for the conquest of evil and the saving of souls? Was I willing to sacrifice my health, my love of the mountains, or my proximity to my family if demanded by the exigencies of my calling? While many students and Catholic people in general considered celibacy to be the main issue confronting a man about to be ordained, this was not the case for me. I knew that the Church required the permanent renunciation of marriage, together with sexual love and offspring. However, as we had learned, it was not a holy vow, and I accepted it as an unquestioned fact of priestly life without resentment or anxiety.

My dominant concern was more general: was I willing to let God lead me wherever he wished? Like so many others over the fifteen centuries since Augustine had voiced the thought, my prayer was the cautious one: "O God, make me a saint, but not quite yet!"

More intimidating to me than the law of celibacy was the obligation (which became effective with ordination to the Diaconate at the end of the fifth year) of reciting the Divine Office everyday. I knew that for the rest of my life I must—under pain of grave sin—read the long series of official prayers and scriptual readings laid down by Canon Law. I must also do so in Latin, which had been the spoken tongue of the medieval educated world and was still the official language of the Church.

The Office had been designed to be chanted by a choir of monks within the ordered framework of a monastic day, and it was governed by a complex calendar, requiring half a dozen bookmarks for every session. Centuries before, in an effort to upgrade the prayer life of the parish clergy, the Office had been imposed upon all priests and even deacons. However, deprived of its music and its monastic daily rhythm, as well as its communal aspect, it was nothing but a burden. At least this was the opinion of almost all priests with whom I discussed it. The sole exception was Father Cronin, my old friend from Palo Alto. A superb Latinist, he had always found in the Office a source of inspiration and peace. I was not sanguine enough to expect that I would have the same experience. However, if I was to be a priest, I must accept the Office. And I did so.

But we also prayed for more specific and personal blessings—namely that we should be spared the misfortune of being assigned to any of the "salt mines" of the Archdiocese: Petaluma, Stockton, or Livermore—parishes presided over by dragon-like pastors, ready and waiting to devour young and inexperienced assistants. We prayed also against being sent back to school to obtain some advanced degree. In the last few years, the archbishop had been grooming more of his young men for positions in high school teaching or at desk jobs in the increasingly bureaucratic departments of the archdiocese. This was not our image of the priesthood. Our goal was the "care of souls" in some good parish.

In spite of these anxieties, we were universally eager to get out of the seminary. As one visiting priest, ordained two or three years, remarked, "The worst day in the priesthood is better than the best day in the seminary." After so many years there, it was not difficult to believe him.

Ten days before my scheduled ordination, I came down with a strep throat infection. Too sick to stay in my own room, yet barred by canon law from "breaking my retreat" by leaving the seminary, I was put to bed in an extra faculty suite. There I lay, reading and praying, visited three times a day by tray-bearing students. My fever broke the day before the Great Day, and I was driven to the cathedral rectory in San Francisco by one of the faculty.

The cathedral pastor was Monsignor Ramm, the Newman-esque old priest who had instructed my parents for their conversion in 1915 and had later baptized my brother and me. He put me to bed in the room of an absent assistant—on the lumpiest mattress I had ever seen—and the next morning I was dressed for the ordination ceremony in my bedroom and led, shaky-legged, through a secret passage into the cathedral. There, since I was too weak to walk up the aisle, I was given a chair at the side of the sanctuary from which I could emerge on cue to take my part in the ceremonies.

I gazed about from my secure station and watched the arriving throngs. The majestic size of the cathedral was made warm and comfortable for me not only by its richly polished oak seats and pillars, but by memories of childhood when my mother sang in the choir there and the organist was my godfather.

Since the many friends and relatives to whom invitations had been sent knew nothing of my illness, I was acutely conscious that they would not know what to make of my unorthodox role in the ceremony.

However, I was soon caught up in the majestic ritual. The procession of white-robed candidates—my classmates—entered, to the powerful music of the great organ. They looked solemn and holy now, and my heart swelled as I watched them taking their places before the altar. The master of ceremonies indicated unobtrusively that I should step out and join them. Then, in Latin, a priest addressed the archbishop, requesting him in the name of the Church, and on the recommendation of the seminary faculty, to ordain us to the priesthood of Jesus Christ. The archbishop then spoke, admonishing us in formal terms to consider the step we were about to take, and to withdraw at this point, if we were not sure of our intentions. Then we all prostrated ourselves face down upon the carpet while the choir took up the ancient chanted litany petitioning God and all the saints for our strength and our protection.

The red-robed master of ceremonies moved discreetly about, indicating each correct move in the complex ceremony with a bow or gesture. He maintained an unfailingly pleasant smile which reassured the hesitant and kept the action moving. This smile had won him the name of "Happy Harry." Aware of my condition, he led me out once more at the correct moment to take part in the central rites of the ordination: the formal touch of the archbishop's hands upon our heads, and the presentation of the bread and the golden cup of wine. Then all of us—now priests together with the bishop—joined in reciting the prayers of the Mass. At the end we received his embrace and promised him our obedience.

Suddenly it was over, and I found myself maneuvered into position to give my blessing, like the rest of my classmates, to those who pressed forward in reverent joy and pride to receive it. I knew that I was now a priest, chosen from among men to fulfill a special calling in the service of God. I could summon the presence of Christ in the sacred meal of the Mass, and I could forgive in God's name the sins of human beings. I was heir to a spiritual gift passed down from bishop to bishop in unbroken sequence from the age of the apostles! This was March 20, 1943.

3. My First Priestly Assignment

The first two years of my career as a priest were spent at St. Matthew's Church in San Mateo. They were the fulfilment of my fondest hopes. The letter of appointment had been anxiously awaited, but fear was quickly turned to joy when I learned my good fortune: a parish not far from my home in a community of trees and gardens and—best of all—a parish presided over by a priest whom I knew and admired, Father Henry Lyne. I had come to know him because he owned a little sailboat, on which my brother and I had spent an occasional day off while in the seminary. Hence, on the day, two weeks after my ordination, when I arrived with my parents at St. Matthew's, I was free from the painful strangeness of being a completely green recruit in a strange land.

St. Matthew's Church stood at the corner of Third and Ellsworth Streets in the heart of San Mateo. The church and rectory, built entirely of red brick, formed an "L," and the enclosed space was planted like a little park through which one approached the ivy covered rectory entrance. This garden shut out the traffic sounds to some extent and created a little intimacy around the church.

Father Lyne greeted me warmly. He was about fifty, straight-backed, energetic in his movements, neat in his dress. He was good humored and cheerful, quick and decisive, full of youthful enthusiasm. I felt from the first moment that he was in authority and that he fully accepted responsibility for his decisions. He commanded respect without being at all pretentious.

This was the spirit of the house: informal yet dignified. When we sat down to meals, the tabletalk was a feast of news about the community in which we were working. Father Lyne, and also the other assistant, Matt Carolan, whom I had known in the seminary, were truly interested in people, not simply as recipients of our ministry, but as individuals. I would hear about births and deaths, about gifted children and troublesome ones, about couples who were getting married, and about who was taking over leadership of parish organizations.

Abrupt, even impatient as Father Lyne was, he could always take time to fill in the background of some story that was new to me. I felt included from the beginning. Matt and I were not close friends—his interests and temperament were too different from mine. However, we were good teammates, united not only by our interests in people, but also by our loyalty and respect for Father Lyne.

Every night after dinner we would all adjourn to Father Lyne's study for a half hour or so before we went off to the meetings and counseling appointments which filled our evenings. He would stand very erect, feet well apart, in front of the unlit fireplace with his one daily drink in hand. This was the time for conversation to range more widely—to the politics of the church, to my love for the mountains, Matt's love for golf, and Father Lyne's love for sailing. Also, to local civic issues and other contemporary events. I found this time to be a fountain of zest for carrying out our work.

In spite of his high energy, Father Lyne lived a well-ordered life. Every day after lunch, he would shut his door for an hour to rest and to read. Every morning before Mass, he would spend an hour of prayer in the church. He almost never stayed out late, and he took his day off regularly. I noticed that he, like Father Carroll in Palo Alto, avoided visiting people's homes unless there was a real need.

I learned from him, almost without realizing it, what it meant to live a balanced, happy life as a parish priest. He helped me whenever I asked him in all such practical matters as arranging marriages and funerals, and dealing with the sick. However, he did not try to impose his own style by rules or warnings. He listened attentively to my early sermons, offering suggestions and encouragement. He seldom criticized, but when he did so he was clear and incisive. When little oddities of speech or gesture crept into my way of saying Mass, he pointed them out—always kindly. I could not have asked for a better teacher.

Much as I admired Father Lyne, I did not adopt his custom of the early morning Holy Hour. Maybe it was because I could not bring myself to be an imitator. But also it was because I found that an hour was too long to keep my attention on devout thoughts. I believe that my spiritual life took on, at this time, its more or less permanent pattern: prayers generally brief and simple, mainly before and after saying Mass. I never experienced anything resembling mystical delight in God's presence, nor any sense of being guided. Rather, all the insights I gained about myself, my faith, and my work came in the midst of action—during sacramental ceremonies or while hearing confessions, counseling, or reading.

The daily recitation of the Divine Office fitted quite easily into the orderly routine of St. Matthew's Parish. The Latin remained a stumbling block, but I could accept the Office as a time of quiet during which I tried to be open to God's presence. Father Lyne had acquired the privilege of using an abbreviated version, called the "Little Office," and there were moments when I envied him. However, this required the payment of a membership fee in a missionary organization, and at the time, the expense did not seem warranted.

As always, I liked to read, doing so mainly at night or while on duty for housecalls. But my reading did not run to theology or books of spiritual guidance. It was rather about history—there was nothing I loved as much as a great historical novel—about nature and science, and about developments in the public life of the Church. I never hear the strains of Tchaikowsky's *Symphonie Pathetique* without recalling what I felt then as I read Ellsworth's tragic story of exploration in the arctic entitled *Hell on Ice*.

Obviously, the orderly, companionable life of St. Matthew's Rectory was only the background and foundation for the service of God's people for which we were ordained, and towards which I had looked forward during the long seminary years. One way to serve the people was to give them inspiration and instruction, and I hoped to do this each Sunday when I stood before them to preach.

The first time I preached was frightening, and the relief when it was over was immense. I had things I wanted to say, in this case about the special ceremonies of Holy Week. Occurring only once a year, these liturgies were easily forgotten, and I wished to bring to the people the full appreciation of their rich historical allusions and the meaning of their arcane rites. In my inexperience, my talk turned out pretty stilted and academic, but Father Lyne was satisfied. After that first time, preaching was never again so difficult.

Hearing confessions was quite different: being private, it involved no stage fright. But in this role, I was completely alone.

44

Father Lyne could not be there to evaluate my performance. Every Saturday afternoon, and before all morning Masses, I would take my place in the little booth called the confessional. On either side of me was a darkened cubicle where people came to confess. I would hear a soft shuffle and the familiar words "Bless me, Father, for I have sinned." Closing the little sliding door on the opposite side, I would wait to hear what this person would say. It was my duty to pass judgment on his or her guilt and repentance—a lonely and terrifying responsibility.

The people did come: devout old people, who saw sin in the tiniest infraction of any rule; youngsters, who reeled off lists of childish faults in fulfillment of Sisters' weekly admonition; and the adults, who came less often, but whose problems were often heavy—such things as alcohol, birth control, pre-marital sex, and even doubts about God's goodness in the war-torn world.

Probing gently to ascertain the penitent's sincerity and his or her "purpose of amendment," I would often find myself so much in sympathy with the person's dilemmas that it was impossible to demand the clear promise of reform which I had learned was necessary for the forgiveness of sin.

Sin was a concept which was very clear and simple in theology courses. It meant a freely chosen human action or thought which was contrary to the known law of God or the Church. I had learned long lists of sins, great and small, as defined and classified by some theologian in his armchair. But confronted by real people struggling with the complex problems of life, I found these categories completely unsatisfactory.

The consciences of most penitents seemed to be loaded with fear, not so much fear of God as simply fear of sin—and this could become obsessive when sin seemed to be unavoidable. Real moral problems—usually meaning sexual ones—were often too disturbing to express openly; they were dealt with by hiding them among more manageable legalistic faults, such as eating meat on Friday and missing Sunday Mass.

My first funeral occurred within a few weeks of my coming to St. Matthew's. On that drizzly morning in late spring, I drove up to the cemetery in my little '36 Dodge (for which Father Lyne had advanced the money). The small cemetery, owned by the church, was situated on a hilltop about two miles away. The land had been donated by the Parrott family, which had also donated the church building—one of the few debt-free churches in the archdiocese. The cemetery had been surrounded by the gradually expanding town, and could now be approached by a wide, winding boulevard named

Parrott Drive, between tidy upper-middle class homes. However, the occupants of these dwellings had obtained from the city a ruling that St. Matthew's funerals must use the old country road, skirting around their neighborhood, so that they should not be annoyed with the spectacle of these macabre processions.

At dinner the night before, Father Lyne had expressed his annoyance about this regulation. He detested it not because it caused any significant inconvience but because he felt that it was offensive to the religious freedom of his people.

Arriving at the cemetery, I found the weedy grass was sopping and the grave a dark, unadorned, rectangular hole in the turf. There were no chairs, no flowers, no carpets: none of the accessories which undertakers use to soften the reality of burial. The dead man was a derelict found by the police; he was presumed to be Catholic, but a mere presumption did not entitle him to "the full rites of the Church." There had been no rosary at the mortuary, nor Mass in church.

Soon the hearse arrived. I opened my little book of rituals and read, in the ancient Latin phrases, the rite of burial. I sprinkled the already wet grave and casket with holy water. The driver, myself, and Owen Kiley, the caretaker of the cemetery, were the pall-bearers, the mourners, and the celebrant. Then the three of us let the casket down into the hole with the long heavy straps used for such purposes. I went home, leaving Owen Kiley, tall and gaunt, the elderly hard-working father of many children, standing on the wet green hill beside the still unfilled grave.

Father Lyne did not believe that a priest should sit around the rectory waiting for business. Hence, he soon initiated me into the pastoral routine known as "taking the census." This meant visiting the homes of all the Catholic people, ascertaining their relationship to the Church, and when necessary helping them to strengthen or regain it. On a pleasant, sunny morning, he would send me to some distant corner of the parish, where I would walk door-to-door, ringing every doorbell and learning where all the Catholics lived.

I found this a difficult task: I was embarrassed to be intruding into people's lives. Although I met many Catholics who did not attend Mass, there were very few that proved unfriendly. Most were open to receiving my help and encouragement, glad of the opportunity I gave them to have their babies baptized, and to know what parish they could regularly attend. Some even wanted religious instructions for themselves or for their children.

Whenever I encountered Catholics who had left the Church in anger and bitterness, I would cringe under their resentment. Many of them told me of dreadful experiences they had had: of priests who had dealt with them insensitively, enforcing the laws of the Church without mercy. These laws could mean the refusal of a funeral Mass for a person who had a burial plot in the wrong cemetery; or the insistence that the celebration of a "mixed marriage" could take place only in a barren little rectory parlor. The laws could exclude from being godparents or witnesses even the dearest friends and relatives if they happened not to be "good Catholics." And, of course, they condemned the use of birth control for any reason.

Except for the Seminary Rule, the laws of the Church had never been a burden to me personally. Our Palo Alto priests had interpreted them gently. But now I found them standing in the way of my ministry: preventing people whose lives were otherwise exemplary from participating fully in the sacramental life of the Church. I felt this most acutely with couples living in a second marriage which the Church could find no way to approve. There seemed to be nothing I could do for these people.

Father Lyne listened to my distress with real sympathy and concern; he was always kind to the people, but without violating the laws under which we lived. It never occurred to us then that some of these laws were actually wrong and unworthy of our obedience. We were deeply and unquestioningly respectful in our attitude to the Church, her laws, and doctrines.

As a young priest, I felt very responsible to "help" people—to bring everyone into dutiful obedience to the Church. But I soon learned from the census work that there were hundreds of Catholic people in the parish who would have nothing to do with the Church at all. When they showed no interest, it was for me a heavy burden of failure.

Besides its new hilly subdivisions and its old sections where the poorer people lived, San Mateo had its wealthy neighborhoods where impressive gates and fierce dogs made census taking virtually impossible.

One day the reigning dowager of San Mateo, Mrs. Clark, called to invite Father Lyne and me to dinner at the House on the Hill. I had never met her at church, much less on my census tours. Father Lyne was sure that she wished simply to inspect the new priest, and accordingly, managed to excuse himself.

On the appointed day, I drove alone up the long avenue of eucalyptus trees to the hilltop mansion, where I was received with great deference by Mrs. Clark, her two adult daughters, and a male cousin. The whole evening was strange to me. I had grown up among artistic, educated, even learned people. But this was different. It began with an unfamiliar and throat-paralyzing liqueur served in the lofty library, and it continued elegantly in the dining room to the moment after dessert when the ladies adjourned, leaving me and the cousin to such male diversions as coffee, whiskey, and cigars. I had never before dined with only candles in wall braziers lighting the room, nor in a house where there were three grand pianos in the salon where we gathered after dinner. It was a great relief when all the courtesies were over and I could go home to the simplicity of St. Matthew's household.

On the other hand, there were many homes to which I gladly returned whenever I was invited. There was one block on a lovely wooded street where I found three large families, each with a non-Catholic father, who had never had a priest at their door before. They received me warmly, seizing the opportunity to discuss religion in a free and intellectual way—the way my family had done in the days of the SSS. Dinner invitations followed, and we formed lasting friendships. In these, as in many other homes, I experienced a welcome which was out of all proportion to any service I rendered. They saw me simply as a priest, young and inexperienced as I was, and gave me respect which easily grew into affection. Father Lyne was always interested in everyone I came to know.

In the course of visiting homes, I made another contact which was not with a Catholic family at all, but with a well-known Sierra Club mountaineer, Jules Eichorn. He had been one of the young men who had first introduced rock-climbing as a sport into California. My first visit to the Eichorn home was memorable. Sarah, Jules' wife, came to the door holding a baby in one hand. She greeted me with great warmth, and in a beautifully modulated voice that seemed out of harmony with the torn old dress she wore and the chaotic wreck of the front room. The table was strewn with sheets of yellow paper, which Sarah showed me were a manuscript of an article she was writing on the application of vector analysis to logic. Propped above the sink full of dishes was a book of songs in Swedish that she was memorizing. Presently Jules came in from feeding the rabbits, and we launched upon an exchange of mountain reminiscenses which marked the beginning of a friendship which lasted many years.

During my two years at St. Matthew's, I had a boy scout troop to look after. The troop was sponsored by the parish, and Father Lyne assigned me to be its chaplain. As a boy I had felt superior to the scouts: our family had its own outdoor program! Now, once a week I was attending the meetings of the local troop in the church basement to give moral support to Frank, the scoutmaster. There seemed little else that I as a priest could do there. I was not much impressed with the tests and merit badges, but when it came to hikes I was in my element. I arranged to take the boys out a couple of times, following the country road to nearby Crystal Springs Dam.

The junior version of the scouts, the cubs, was cared for by the school Mothers' Club. However, once a month I was required to preside over something called the pack meeting, at which countless awards were given. These events brought together a ghastly, shrieking mass of cubs, always on the verge of tearing the hall apart. After a year, I announced to the den mothers that I would be cubmaster no longer. They must find one among the fathers or disband. They disbanded, and the scout headquarters was duly notified. Unlike Father Lyne, the officials there did not take the matter lightly; I was held responsible for the probable future delinquency of all the cubs.

Life at St. Matthew's had a peaceful regularity about it, which was congenial to my make-up. One day a week I was free, and I left right after breakfast for my home, only ten miles away, where I spent the day with my mother—playing the violin, singing (she loved to teach and felt I had a potentially good voice), reading aloud, and sometimes walking in the hills together. After dinner with Dad, I would head back to the parish unless the presence of friends prolonged the evening.

Father Lyne also took his day off regularly, spending it usually on San Francisco Bay in his sailboat. Matt spent his free time golfing. Vacation times were arranged far in advance so that plans could be made; and Father Lyne was much interested in hearing about our family trips to Silver Lake and about the cabin which we were in the process of building during those two summers of 1943 and 1944.

At the beginning of each summer, all priests were required to attend a diocesan retreat, a five-day event held at St. Patrick's Seminary. Two alternative sessions were offered so that we would not all be away from the parishes at once. In June of 1943, I was not assigned to make the retreat, having been so recently ordained. But the next year I saw my name on the official list and went—quite eager for the change of pace and the chance to meet all the priests who would be there. I knew that, although our seminary retreats had been held in silence, this was not the case with the diocesan retreat for priests. There we were simply expected to consider the desires of those who wished quiet. Hence there was abundant opportunity to meet men we did not otherwise see, make new friends and renew old friendships.

The Archbishop always invited some well-known speaker who, as retreat master, would address us four times a day in a series of coordinated sermons around some central theme. A retreat was supposed to renew our fervor for priestly service and personal spirituality. And being back in the seminary itself was sort of a renewal. It evoked ideals and dreams, free now from most of the heavy atmosphere of obedience and disapproval.

I took copious notes filled with noble resolves and sincere self-analysis. I intended to set aside and observe with strict regularity a time for personal prayer and for meditation; to express my legitimate wishes, rather than feeling unhappy when they were not fulfilled without my asking; to live in the present with full attention, enthusiasm, and humor, rather than letting worry about the future get in the way; and to confront the reality of evil and of unfortunate happenings, so that they could be dealt with decisively, rather then postponing and evading them and thus permitting their bad energy to gain strength. I would occasionally read these intentions over during the subsequent year. I was always amazed to find that I kept having the same problems to solve, and found the same resolutions unfulfilled.

In the spring of 1945 I received an unexpected phone call from the Chancery Office. "Monsignor O'Dowd would like to see you tomorrow morning at eleven." The young monsignor was superintendent of Catholic schools and was shortly to become auxiliary bishop of San Francisco. A summons like this could only mean a change: an assignment out of parish work!

I went to the appointment afraid that I would be tapped for a job in one of the new Catholic high schools—teaching Latin perhaps or algebra!—a possibility about which I had worried before my ordination. I had spent just over two years in the fortunate role of assistant to Father Lyne, and hoped earnestly to remain with him for a few more years. I was resolved to express honestly my preference for parish work.

4. New York: The Three Catholic Churches

Monsignor Jim O'Dowd, the Superintendent of Catholic Schools, had his office in the rambling old cathedral rectory at 1100 Franklin Street in San Francisco, which was still doubling as the Chancery Office. I knew the house because it was the home of the cathedral pastor Father Ramm, the gentle old priest who had baptised me and my parents; I felt comfortable there.

Jim O'Dowd was a hearty red-haired young man, and my feeling about him was pleasantly tinged with the memory of the early 1930s when, as a seminarian, he used to come to St. Thomas Aquinas to help with catechism lessons for the older boys.

He told me his scheme. He wanted me to assume the post of Archdiocesan Director of Music, replacing Edgar Boyle, with whom I had sung on many occasions when he directed the music for great ceremonial events. Jim O'Dowd also felt that the Director of Music should work within the Education Department over which he presided, instead of remaining autonomous. He felt that having been a choir director in the seminary, I was well suited for the job.

The position sounded good in principle, but I didn't want to be the Archdiocesan Director of anything! I wanted to stay in parish work. Fortunately it was not hard to tell him so; he was very understanding.

He said that he had another candidate, and that we should both take a summer session in liturgical music at Manhattanville College of the Sacred Heart in New York. There would undoubtedly be some part-time musical work for me to do while continuing as Father Lyne's assistant. A new Catholic high school was being built in San Mateo.

So on this spring day, with the war still raging, two young priests were assigned to study music for the summer in New York. I expected to return to St. Matthew's in September.

The interesting prospect of going East for the first time was clouded for me by the loss of my treasured High Sierra family vacation. Nor was I eager to see New York. City life, with its barren streets, was never congenial to me—not even San Francisco. I liked open country and trees!

Telling Mother of this development was difficult. She was deeply disappointed that I would be absent from the vacation and she dreaded my having to go so far away. She wanted us all together: it was our annual family outing. She was and always had been very possessive in that way. Her words, "If you're not there, Jack, the vacation just won't be the same," seemed to carry blame. However, the matter was out of my hands.

At the end of June, still feeling a bit guilty about spoiling my family's vacation, I was on the Santa Fe Railroad headed for Kansas City, Chicago, and New York. It was my first time east of Reno! The train trip across the country took four long days, but Joe Martinelli, who had been just been ordained, was a congenial and amusing companion. And there were moments—the Rocky Mountains, the crossing of the wide Mississippi, and the rich green lands of Pennsylvania—when I could really experience the variety of nature's manifestations in our immense country.

The train was crowded with soldiers going East on leave, and the queues for meals were hours long. I made no contact with the men. Their military world was too remote from my experience to provide any ground for communication. I felt distant from them because of a deep-rooted resistance to everything connected to military service, a dislike which I could not explain by anything in my life or that of my family. The military life, even in peacetime, symbolized for me everything I most disliked: regimentation, violence, and the suppression of individuality. I had never volunteered to be a military chaplain, as many priests did during those war years, and I could not imagine doing so. Seminary life had also been regimented, but it paid fundamental respect to the unique and private essence of each person before God.

On the fourth morning, quite early, we saw the towers of New York ahead and knew with relief that the trip was ending. Then the train plunged into the darkness of the Hudson River tunnel, from which it emerged directly into the station. Joe and I stepped down, free at last from the confines of the railroad car.

We were in the echoing immensity of Penn Station. Great pillars supported the lofty ceiling, covered with a fuzz of soot, and the air smelled strongly of coal smoke. Getting our bearings, we headed for an exit, carrying our heavy bags. Soon we were in the smoggy sunlight of the canyon-like street. The temperature was 103, and the sky was a purplish grey, a humid, wretched day. We hailed a cab.

The taxi trip was even more overwhelming than the enormous station. The driver hustled us in, spun the cab in a wild U-turn, and rattled off uptown for St. Patrick's Cathedral, where Joe Martinelli and I were to report. We were required to obtain permission from the Archdiocese of New York to work as priests while staying in the city in return for our room and board.

The cathedral was only a few blocks away. Soon we were standing before the grim grey building which was the Chancery Office, lying in the shadow of the neo-Gothic towers of St. Patrick's. We were dressed in black suits and stiff collars—already wilted, of course.

Timidly entering, we were admitted to a long oak-panelled room lined with desks, each with its black-clad priest, chained to the dreary round of ecclesiastical office work. Directed to two different officials, we presented our credentials. Archbishop Mitty in San Francisco had provided each of us with a railroad pass, a few dollars for food, and a letter of introduction to the New York Archdiocese, asking that we be given places to live near Manhattanville College.

The priest to whose desk I was directed read the letter perfunctorily—he had seen many like it. Remarking that the parishes close to the school were all filled for the summer, he made a few phone calls, and located a place reasonably near. He exchanged a few cryptic pleasantries with "Jack" the pastor, and then informed me that I could stay at All Saints, in Harlem. In return, my duties would be "weekend supply," which meant saying Sunday Mass and hearing confessions.

Saying goodbye to Joe, whose assignment was to Resurrection Parish on the West Side, I was off in another cab, hurtling uptown between endless rows of five- or six-floor apartment buildings, and worrying about how much I should tip the driver!

Before long I was standing in front of All Saints Church at 129th and Madison. Its towering facade was a reminder of the large

Irish population of this neighborhood during the previous century which had required and created this and other fine parishes. It somehow looked alien and forlorn now since these people had gradually been replaced by a predominantly non-Catholic black community. Across the street was a much livelier looking church in an upstairs flat, where a gaudy picture of Jesus was painted on the window. Its sign read HOLY CATHOLIC CHURCH OF ILLUMINATION.

The All Saints Rectory was a sliver of a building squeezed between the church and the next tall tenement. Its street level entry was flanked by heavily barred windows. The hollow sound of the rectory doorbell brought a cheerless housekeeper, who led me through a flagstoned outer "parlor" and then an austere Victorian inner one. Beyond this lay a dark stairwell, cluttered with unclaimed mail, coats, and boxes, which led into the large dining room. This room occupied the rear half of the ground floor. It contained a long table covered with a dirty white table cloth; a few archbishops were framed on the wall, and there was a large window at the far end.

As I entered, the stocky middle-aged pastor was finishing his lunch and smoking a stinky cigar. He introduced himself as Jack, greeting me with rough cordiality, and then showed me around the place with considerable pride. It was an old parish, he said, and it had slid almost into bankruptcy after the departure of its Irish population. The cardinal had sent Jack there to put the place back on its feet, and in financial terms he had done so.

He was a native New Yorker, tough and canny. The secret of his success at All Saints was bingo. Although bingo was outlawed in New York at that time, the police came only once every couple of months. He would close down for a week and then resume the Monday night games. All Saints bingo parties were patronized by crowds of Jewish people from all over the city, and brought in lots of money.

Eventually he escorted me to my room on the fourth floor at the back. It was very large, but only contained a bed at one end and a desk at the other by the window. The floor below was for the two assistants. One had his rooms in the front; the other, who was away on vacation, had the rear. The fifth and sixth floors were vacant, and the housekeeper had the seventh floor. Needless to say, she did not use her rooms much, except to go to bed, since there was no elevator.

It was a relief to be alone and to enjoy the first real rest since leaving home. I was soggy in my clerical suit and limp collar, and it felt wonderful to shower and stretch out on the blanketless bed. When I got up, there was still time before dinner; so I went to the desk by the rear window to write a letter home.

My desk was lightly powdered with soot, and my arm, already sticky again after my shower, was blackened as I tried to write. The narrow space between the buildings was filled with the echoes of boys shouting to each other in words I could not understand as they climbed up and down the iron fire escapes. The view was of dirty brick and curtainless windows; and far below, a dead cat lay in the weeds.

At dinner I met Jerry, the senior assistant, who had been at All Saints for nine years. The younger assistant, just ordained, was away on vacation. After the meal, Jerry showed me the interior of the lofty church, capable of seating fourteen hundred people. It had carved posts at the end of each pew, and a mighty organ, which Jerry delighted in playing, late at night, with all stops open! He said he could remember when the church was quite full for six Masses on Sundays; now there were hardly enough people to fill it once.

Friendly as he was, Jerry exemplified a style of clerical life that was as foreign to me as his wig, which was of an amazing cardinal red color. There seemed to be really no work for him to do during the week, so he spent his days at the racetrack with his brother. Every morning before leaving, he said Mass at the main altar, which was his only daily duty.

Saying Mass at the side altar, I could not fail to notice his strangely mechanical way of celebrating Mass. He seemed oblivious of the half-dozen elderly people scattered through the vast church. His voice rose and fell in a steady whine, like an angry bee against a window pane; none of the Latin words was distinguishable.

After Mass and breakfast, I would set off for my day of classes at Manhattanville College. When it rained, which seemed to be most of the time, I took a streetcar west along 125th Street and another one up Morningside Drive to the school. When it was clear, the air and sunlight reminded me of San Francisco. At these times, I would walk directly across Harlem and up a long flight of stairs in Morningside Park to the top of the hill, which was near the school. The people I passed, sitting on the steps of the old brownstone apartment houses, would tip their caps and murmur "G'morn' Rev'nd."

Manhattanville campus was a quiet, green oasis in the city. It was operated by the Sisters of the Sacred Heart. The school of liturgical music, which I had come to attend, was a special summer program of the College, and was known as Pius X. As soon as I was inside I was surrounded by nuns, choir directors, and clergy from all parts of the country. Pius X was a very busy place, with people bustling from class to class, trying to gain as many credits as possible from the summer session.

55

It was nothing like the seminary, either academically or socially. At St. Patrick's, we were a small, tight community, and the curriculum was undemanding. Here we were so varied in our goals and places of origin, and our time together was too brief for us to become in any sense a community.

Joe Martinelli and I had been given no advice by Jim O'Dowd as to what courses to take. So we simply took a cross section of what was offered, with a view toward our supposed objective, the leadership of the Archdiocesan Department of Music. We learned some skills of teaching music to children, for there would be many such teachers under our direction. We learned how to direct Plain Chant, for the unison singing of chant was being vigorously recommended by the Church for its simplicity and purity of sound, suggesting the purity of spiritual life. And we learned polyphony, the fifteenth century Renaissance flowering of church music. The latter was what I enjoyed most: actually singing the baritone part in the music of such composers as Palestrina and Byrd.

Being at St. Pius X was not sufficiantly exciting to fill the void left by the sterile rectory life at All Saints. There my only duties were Sunday Mass and a sermon and the hearing of confessions on Saturday night. And there were no people! In a church built to hold fourteen hundred, the attendance for all of Sunday morning could scarcely have been more than one hundred.

My sole friend was Joe Martinelli, whom I saw only at school, for he lived on the other side of the city. I felt unsatisfied and essentially alone; not so much lonely as separate. I didn't belong here; I didn't share the values of the priests I had met. It was an experience of isolation that I had never had before. I felt a real need to establish a connection with the religious world that I had known in California. Therefore, quite early in my stay in New York, I decided to visit a place where I thought I would feel at home: Maryknoll Seminary. The spirit and enthusiasm of the Maryknoll community had always attracted me. During my days at St. Joseph's, we had shared library facilities and some faculty with Maryknoll Minor Seminary nearby. We had heard about the great Motherhouse at Ossining, with its rich tradition of missionary zeal, and of the adventures of its graduates in the service of the Church.

So on July 4, a holiday, I took an early train up the river to Ossining. It was good to be out in the country; the trees and summer smells were sweet to me. Hot as it was, I walked all the way from the depot to the seminary, which stood prominently on a hill above the town. It was an enormous brick building surrounded by extensive woods. Nearby stood other buildings, which as I soon learned, housed the convents of the Brothers and Sisters of the Maryknoll Order, and the publishing house of *Maryknoll* magazine.

I was not disappointed in my welcome. I was made to feel at home, and was received as a fellow priest, in the sense that I had known in Father Lyne's parish. I spent all day meeting new people and even some old friends from the Maryknoll house in Los Altos. The feeling of a vigorous religious life was comforting and familiar.

Bishop Walsh, the Superior General of the Order, was there, recently returned from wartime imprisonment as a leader of a foreign religious order in China. I had heard about him at St. Patrick's long before he became a hero of the American Church; the Maryknoll Order was highly respected in the San Francsico area, and he was its head. I was flattered to meet him, and to have him invite me back for Departure Day several weeks later, when the newly ordained priests would be given their assignments to various "mission lands"—Peru, Japan, Guatamala, Tanganyika, Taiwan, and the Philippines.

Encouraged by the lift which Maryknoll had given my spirits, I made plans to use all my spare time in New York to explore other scenes of religious vitality. My weekends were quite free, and I could follow up the names of people and projects which had fascinated me as I read about them back in California.

Toward the end of the following week, I received my first and long awaited family news. I treasured it for the glimpses of life at home and in the mountains. Going up to my room, I sat down at my sooty desk on a steamy hot New York afternoon—so different from the mountain world from which Mother wrote: ". . .Jack, I'm horrified that you had to wait so long for mail. As you know, we agreed I'd better wait until we were up here [at Silver Lake], and I suppose that is the reason. Two letters came from you Saturday, and we read them aloud with interest. It seems so strange that you are there in New York!. . .Darling, you would so love it this year—this beautiful place! I hate to think you can not see all of it. The birds are nesting; one family of warblers we watched grow up have safely left the nest. The birds and chippies are very tame—don't seem to mind us a bit. . .We are getting a spare fixed for the car and. . .[another] tire for the trailer, so we ought to be alright [sic] for the return trip. I do hope the war will be over by next summer!. . .How I miss you!"

I could feel a touch of guilt for not being with them; Mother cared so much about my being there—I was homesick already. But I didn't miss the problems with the car! I could picture Dad always being so patient; we never had a new car, and the mechanical struggles never seemed to end. Moreover, new tires were hard to get during the war, requiring a ration stamp. So he had been buying second-hand fire engine tires which did not quite fit the car. The result was frequent flats!

On my second weekend in New York I took a long subway ride down the length of Manhattan to visit Dorothy Day, founder of the *Catholic Worker*. As the only woman ever invited to speak in the seminary, she had deeply impressed me. Dorothy was a former communist who had joined the Catholic Church some twelve years before and was now the editor of the paper and the leader of a social movement. Her understated accounts of ideals tirelessly pursued and a vulnerable life among the poorest people had given us in the seminary a picture of faith and total service that I never forgot.

I worked my way through a maze of narrow streets in the old part of New York City famous as "the Bowery." I found my way to the chasm of Chrystie Street and located the old tenement building which was the Catholic Worker House Of Hospitality. A long, low room on the ground floor of the building was filled with tables, at which a line of derelicts and drifters was being given a daily meal.

Dorothy greeted me with the serenity of one who meets daily with every kind of person, from raving reds and despairing suicides to officious bureaucrats and idealistic priests like me. We sat in her tiny office, as she talked of her struggle to keep the building from condemnation and recounted her repeated arrests for non-cooperation with the war, even to the extent of refusing to observe air raid drills.

Her conversation was filled with deep spiritual insight. The following quotation, taken from the book *Meditations*, expresses for me the substance of her remarks that day: "There are so many who hate war and who are opposed to peacetime conscription who do not know what they can do, who have no sense of united effort, and who will sit back and accept with resignation the evils which are imposed upon us. This is not working for God's will to be done on earth as it is in Heaven. This is accepting the evils in the world as inevitable and looking toward Heaven as a haven, a 'pie in the sky' attitude. God did not make the evils, but man in his misuse of his free will."

It was a humbling experience to be with her. She did not just talk, or write, about Christian ideals of hospitality, trust in God, and non-violent resistance to evil. Rather, she and the Catholic Worker group around her quietly and consistently lived these ideals amidst the harsh realities of urban poverty.

On the following Saturday, on Dorothy's advice, I took the train to Easton, Pennsylvania, where the Catholic Worker group had obtained a large, run-down farm to use as a refuge for reformed drunks and prostitutes and for the families of men who were in jail for conscientious objection. Having phoned ahead, I was met at the station by Stanley, a member of the group. I perched on a block of cattle-salt in an ancient station wagon for the rattly ride to the farm. Upon arrival at the farm, I found a huge, white stone barn which had now been adapted for dormitories, and contained a large warm, cluttered living space. A retired priest who acted as chaplain to the Catholic Workers and their guests, showed me the farm, where cottages provided homes for a few pacifist families. He commented that these people were great talkers but poor farmers. Then I returned to the big barn, where a meal was being prepared in the communal kitchen area.

I was anxious to meet Peter Maurin, the philosopher and co-founder of the Catholic Worker movement, who was now living at the farm. I had known him from his *Easy Essays*—short versified statements about religion and politics which he had regularly published in the Catholic Worker. Also, like Dorothy, he had spoken at my seminary, where his style, quite different from hers, had caused some consternation. Just as he did in Union Square, he spoke without any attempt at audience contact, loud and didactic—and continued to speak until there was no one left to listen. We seminarians had been too polite to walk out, so the session had gone on all afternoon!

Now I found him sitting before the fire, frail and aged, generally silent. His presence brought home to me the exhausting and unglamorous reality of the Catholic Worker life: an endless uphill struggle to assist the often ungrateful and exasperating victims of poverty and misfortune, and to interpret that struggle to the reading public.

These profound experiences of the Church at work, with its atmosphere of commitment and its searching for honest solutions to human problems, were something I needed to share with others. But I had no congenial companionship at the rectory. Hence I attempted to find a community of interest among the priests at the summer school, again with little success. They were pleasant men, earnest about their studies, and more cultured than Jack and Jerry. However, the closeness I hoped to find was not there. They did not respond to the excitement I felt over my weekend adventures.

I had no better luck with the outdoors. After some attempts to promote a Saturday hike at Bear Mountain Park, I ended up going by myself, and spent one whole Saturday alone in the wet forest. Nature and the mountains were an unknown world to these city priests! In fact, my being from California was perceived as a phenomenon—almost as if I had come from the moon!

Letters from home seemed to come in bunches, with long intervals in between, even though Mother was writing me every three or four days. In one group was a letter from Jules Eichorn, my Sierra Club friend in San Mateo. He was leading a group of teenage boys on a lengthy pack trip into the southern Sierra, and wondered if I could join the group at their camp in Dusy Basin after my return from New York. With gas rationing in effect, I did not see how I could do this, but the thought was very tantalizing. It permitted me to dream of the mountains which I missed so much.

During the vacation of Jim Bergen, the younger assistant, the pastor had replaced him temporarily with a member of a religious order. One night I came home late from school to find Jack proudly showing the visiting priest two enormous fans which he had bought to cool the bingo players; so powerful were they that the fuses blew out immediately. Next Sunday, with the fuses changed, he had the fans in place at either end of the altar during Mass, to cool the priest, of course, but at the cost of enclosing him in a roaring wind tunnel.

Another day, in an expansive mood, he had invited me and the visiting priest to enjoy an evening at his country club. We had walked a few blocks to a rented garage where he kept his car. It was hidden because the diocese did not allow its priests to own cars at that time. As we drove up the parkway to New Rochelle, he regaled us with a steady stream of gripes about the police, the mayor, the cardinal, the Jews, and the Negroes—varied occasionally with some tired, old off-color jokes. At the club we wandered around while he introduced us to people he pretended to be friends with. The evening was totally boring, and although I made no overt protest, my lack of enthusiasm must have been evident. I could not sucessfully pretend that I shared his views and values.

Unfortunately, Jack was not unique. I came to realize that his unpleasant company disturbed me so deeply because his faults were not just those of an individual, but represented a negative side to the Church which was all too common. For example, on one evening I visited Joe Martinelli in the prosperous parish where he lived, and shared with him my feelings of isolation. "It's the same here", Joe commented, with his gentle cynicism. "This place has six assistants—one for each weekday. The rest are just 'off.' I don't know what they do all the time."

"What is the pastor like?" I asked. "He's a handsome white-haired man, well read, very gracious. But he has a boys' camp somewhere upstate where he spends his time. It's his hobby. He drops in here once in awhile."

It was depressing. I felt that much of the Church around me was very sick, and there were moments when its presence cast a heavy pall over my understanding of what it meant to be a priest.

Three weeks after my arrival, Jim, the younger assistant at All Saints, returned from vacation. With his return, I found an ally in the house, someone with whom to share my feelings about the Church. Newly ordained, he had asked for and received an assignment in Harlem, but found himself blocked at every turn. He was frustrated by the attitude of the pastor, who considered any attempt to win the surrounding black population to the faith a threat to his enterprise of white-patronized bingo.

One day Jim took me over to a nearby parish for inspiration. Saint Charles, on Lennox Avenue, which was the hub of Harlem, under the leadership of a dynamic young pastor, had become a real center of religious life in the area. I enjoyed several soul-satisfying hours listening to the three enthusiastic priests talking of their fulfilling ministry. They had succeeded in transforming Saint Charles and its neighbor Saint Aloysius from dying parishes into a joint mission to those without faith. The eager, open-minded, and socially conscious spirit which I encountered there was another world from the moribund atmosphere of All Saints, where the pastor was bored and cynical, heavy with meaningless proprieties and self-important authority.

In my need to offset the depressing weight of this "old church," I continued to explore the other side: the elements in the religious world of New York which were fresh, aware, and humanly sensitive. There was Friendship House in Harlem, a forerunner of the Catholic Interracial Movement, which had been founded by Catherine de Hueck Doherty, a Russian aristocrat, refugee, and convert. There was also a lay Catholic society called The Grail, founded in Holland, which provided a new alternative to traditional religious orders. A community of single women without vows, they had banded together to promote the dignity of women and of the home-craft skills traditionally associated with women, such as weaving and cooking, together with a love of the land, the faith, and simple living.

As I made contact with such people and movements, I found that there was an extensive network of Catholic intellectuals and writers in the city, representing all aspects of the frontier of Catholic thought. This included liturgial reform, Biblical studies, the rights of minorities and the poor, and respect for the contributions which non-Catholic religions had to make to Christian doctrine and practice.

Clearly, there were two "Catholic Churches" in New York side by side. One, represented by All Saints, was run by the diocesan administration and constituted the established, official Church. The other, which was exemplified by the boldly creative and spiritually committed work of Dorothy Day, existed with the cautious blessing of authority but with little or no support—and could be readily abandoned or denied if its voice became too strident.

But there was also a third "Catholic Church," with which I had little contact while in New York. But I discovered it on a Saturday outing at Rockaway Beach.

One week, still hoping for some outdoor companionship among the clergy at St. Pius X School, I arranged to meet a group of priests at Rockaway, a popular resort on Long Island. Somehow our plans misfired, and we never made connections. I spent the day alone walking the length of the long, crowded beach, which was lined with vacation homes, several of them belonging to religious orders. From their porches, elderly sisters gazed benignly down upon the horde of bathers.

Expecting to enjoy the invisibility of an anonymous stranger in a bathing suit, I was amazed to be repeatedly addressed as "Father." I soon realized that this throng of people running on the beach, throwing balls and swimming, were all Catholic! At noon when the Angelus bell rang from the several convents, fully half the bathers stood up and crossed themselves and said the prayer.

Here, for the first time, just being a lone male was sufficient to identify me as a priest. I had never before been in an environment where Catholics, predominantly Irish and Italian, created such a social presence. To me, these people represented a third Church. They were neither involved with the stagnant clerical culture, nor excited by the promise of new things in the Church: they were simply Catholics, sincere in their faith, devout, and loyal.

The Monday after this episode, I had returned from school and was having iced tea in the big dining room at All Saints. Jack came into the room, and with characteristic abruptness, announced, "The housekeeper is tired of cooking for an extra mouth. You'd better find some other place to live." I was stunned and frightened. Virtually penniless, I was in no position to be turned loose in this strange city.

I went upstairs to Jim's room and was relieved to find that to him it was no problem. He had classmates scattered throughout the city, and it took him only a couple of phone calls to find me a place. I felt that Jack was retaliating for my lack of involvement with "his" church. In any case, I was angry and glad to see the last of him.

In a half-hour I was on my way to Saint Andrew's in the Bronx. It proved a much more congenial household, and to my amazement, I found that the pastor was a friend of Father Lyne. My last two weeks in New York were quite pleasant.

However, I ran into Jack once more, and the painful encounter illustrated in a telling way the degree to which those in authority had power to intimidate me. I had gone back to All Saints for some laundry. As I came down the dark, narrow stairs, Jack was coming out of the dining room. Instantly, he turned all his meanness upon me, denouncing me with stinging sarcasm for leaving the house without expressing gratitude to him, and for being an example of the horrible lack of priestly fellowship in the West. I felt too humiliated to respond, and I left All Saints with a crushing sense of failure and defeat.

Despite my interest in and openness to new ideas, and my contempt for the spirit which Jack represented, the authority still held me in its frightening grasp!

This occurred just before the end of summer school. I was eager now to leave the heaviness of the New York scene: homesick for the fresher air and the wide lands of the open West. Joe did not return with me, but was told to remain and to continue his studies. I did not mind traveling alone. My memories and feelings from the summer were a tangle, and the long trip was a needed time for reflection.

Each passing state marked a step toward the moutains and skies and deserts that I loved, and towards my dear family at home. As always, the train was full of men in uniform returning to the Pacific front.

On the third day of the crowded, grimy ride, I was listening to the rumble of the wheels as the train sped across the Arizona desert in the gathering twilight. San Francisco Peak was catching the setting sun, and I felt a swell of joy. I looked out the window as I felt the train braking to a stop. The funny old station of Flagstaff was coming into view. Suddenly the newboys were at the window: "EXTRA!" they cried, "The war is over!"

5. Parish Life at Sacred Heart

It was nearly midnight when the train pulled into the Oakland depot and I climbed down to find my mother and father waiting to take me home to Palo Alto. The delight of being with them and being back in California was heightened by the fact that I now had three weeks of vacation ahead of me.

The days which followed were a re-experiencing of that home life which I had always loved so much: friends and neighbors and relatives coming and going, stories and bits of news exchanged, music and books and the sunny garden. My mother loved having people around and was an informal but ever-enthusiastic hostess.

Unfortunately, my brother was still at the seminary, which had not yet returned to peacetime vacation schedule. Besides visiting him there, I made contact with my clerical world, wishing to shake off the negative feelings about the Church which I had had in the East. In San Mateo, I had a warm and newsy visit; however, I found that a newly ordained priest had taken my place as assistant. This was the time of year when priests were often transferred, and I learned that several of my classmates had been taken out of parish work and assigned to special studies. Tom Bowe was headed for work in the Chancery Office, Jim Maher for teaching, and Harry O'Day for social service. I was grateful to have escaped that fate. But my own future remained a blank. The archbishop, when I called upon him to report that I was home, was very pleasant but non-committal.

Meanwhile, I was eager to get to the mountains during my vacation. Now that gasoline was once more available, I decided to pursue Jules Eichorn's invitation. His wife assured me that the trip was proceding on schedule and that I might meet them in Dusy Basin on August 20. I hated to dash off alone when I had just returned to my family, so we worked out a plan by which I would return at the end of Jules' trip and take Mother to Silver Lake for a long Labor Day weekend.

On my fifth day home, I rose at three in the morning and set off by myself on the long drive to Bishop over the Tioga Pass road. Cars were few and the road poor. Fuel rationing had been so recently discontinued that not all service stations had gas to sell. However, roughly twelve hours after leaving Palo Alto I parked my car at the trailhead in the upper canyon of Bishop Creek.

It was wonderful to be on my way into the high country and in an area where I had never been before. The route to Dusy Basin was through Bishop Pass, which formed a notch in the jagged skyline ahead of me. The afternoon shadows were growing long. Being alone intensified the experience.

Apprehensive now about my rendezvous, I asked everyone I met if they had seen the Eichorn party. One said that they had had sickness and that they had gone out of the mountains. Another, that they had gone to climb Mt. Whitney. A third party said that their camp was in Dusy Basin and would be easy to find. The widely differing reports were unsettling. But I really had no choice about going on. I had driven two hundred and fifty miles and was almost out of food. However, I was too tired to go on over the Pass that night. I ate my last sandwich beside the highest lake, and slipped into my sleeping bag beneath the brilliant mountain stars.

The next morning I found the Eichorn camp in a clump of white-bark pines. But no one was there. A few boxes a food lay about, and some freshly washed clothes were hung on the tree branches to dry. Some large pots stood by the fireplace. I was famished. Having no can opener, I could do nothing with the large cans of fruit and other foods. I found a few potatoes and onions which I cooked in the embers—or rather burned. I also managed to open a large jar of peanut butter, which I washed down with abundant fresh water from a sparkling stream nearby.

I passed that day and another night alone at the camp amid the peaceful beauty of the lakes and meadows. Then on the second morning, I climbed to a gap in the southern rim of the basin, hoping to meet the party on their return from some exploration. For an hour I sat on the crest, occasionally scanning the stark rocky waste of Palisades Basin beyond. Finally I saw them! A tiny line of figures was moving across the immense landscape. A shout halted them and brought an answering call.

In another hour they were with me: Jules and his group of tanned and dirty boys. Jules, wiry, thin, and bearded, greeted me with his customary enthusiasm. As we returned to the camp for lunch he told me of their two-day trip to climb Mt. Sill, the southern-most of the Palisades group of peaks.

With them was Norman Clyde, a legendary mountain man, weathered and taciturn, dressed in clothes that he had sewed together time after time. I had heard about him from Jules, for they were old climbing companions. Norman had gone to the Sierra in 1914, young and recently widowed, and had hardly left the moun-tains since. "A man completely in tune with his chosen environ-ment," as Jules said.

His stiff-brimmed ranger-type hat, his pale blue eyes and jut-ting jaw, his incredible skill as a climber and as a marksman—all these were famous. But above all, his pack. When we got to camp that day, I had a chance to watch him unload his pack, which always weighed over a hundred pounds. He carried five cameras, three pairs of shoes, assorted iron kitchen-ware, but most surprisingly of all, books. He had books in German, French, Latin, Greek, and Spanish—poetry and prose. His pack was his home, and he carried with him all that was necessary for the nourishment of mind and body.

I enjoyed that day with the group, roaming with Jules about the grassy shores of the nearby lakes while the boys fished. Norman stayed at camp repairing his shoes. The following day, I helped them break camp before hiking out over Bishop Pass. The boys then went their separate ways, and Norman headed back into the mountains, his permanent home. Jules rode home with me. We stopped for a day in Yosemite country, so that he could teach me the rock climb-ing he loved so well. I was not converted.

After one day at home, Mother and I were off to the moun-tains, bound for the lovely private spot on the west shore of Silver Lake where we had finished building our cabin the summer before. It was a beautiful little house, complete with fireplace and chimney, nestled into the granite bedrock a few feet above highwater line.

This summer, Mother and I had no need to work. Our few days at the lake were a welcome and needed rest. Most of the time, we swam and lay in the sun on the smooth granite rocks. Now was an opportunity to exchange at leisure my experiences during the trip East. As always, Mother was a very responsive listener, and helped me to sort out my mingled feelings, especially the blend of shame and anger which I felt about Jack, the New York pastor, from whom I had parted with our differences unresolved. And Mother, in her turn, made a good story out of the many and sometimes frustrating guests whom she and Dad had entertained at the lake earlier in the summer and the incessant difficulties with the car.

It was strange to be there without Dad and Bob. However, they came up a few days later for a long weekend. It was a happy, quiet time in which the adventures of the summer faded into the background, and Silver Lake recovered its seemingly timeless place at the center of our lives.

When we got home to Palo Alto early in September, my letter of appointment was waiting. I was assigned to Sacred Heart Parish in Oakland, a place about which I knew nothing. The transfer was disappointing to me. I had loved San Mateo and had been assured I would return there after my New York summer. However, the letter granted me one more week of vacation before I had to report, which I spent at home enjoying it to the fullest.

On a Tuesday afternoon, nearly a month after my return from New York, I crossed the Bay Bridge on my way to this new assignment, an old Oakland parish, whose pastor was Irish and an invalid. I had been unable to glean any further information, and was a little apprehensive. I was taking the place of an alcoholic priest who had been suspended.

Sacred Heart was on Fortieth Street near Grove. Fortieth street accommodated a railroad freight line as well as a street-car track. It was a poor residential neighborhood, with small one-story houses, and an occasional tree. Less barren and less crowded than San Francisco, I thought, but rather run-down. I realized that I was moving into the urban environment I had experienced in New York.

Parking behind the rectory in the schoolyard, I went timidly toward the door. I was greeted by a warm, motherly housekeeper named Mary. She suggested that I go straight up and meet "the Monsignor," whose quarters were at the back of the house. As I rounded the upstairs landing, I passed a tall, lanky priest sitting at an old-fashioned desk piled with books and boxes of printed envelopes. He was using the phone, speaking in cryptic monosyllables.

I found the Monsignor—his name was Bob Sampson—in his brass single bed just inside the door of his room. A bright pink comforter lay askew on the bed, and several days' newspapers littered the bed and the floor all about. The only light came from a bare bulb suspended by its cord over the bed. The shades were drawn, and the dimness was accentuated by rows of black bookcases with leaded-glass doors, filled with dark leather-bound tomes.

The old man rolled his large eyes upward as I came in, extending a soft pink hand. His face was unusually long; his complexion rosy and fresh; his hair thick and snow-white, with long dense eyebrows. He wore a sardonic smile. His first words were, "Glad to meet you, John. I nearly died at two o'clock".

In spite of his hand palpitating feebly above his heart, I found it difficult to take this dire statement seriously. He looked healthy as a bear. He told me that he had served as a young priest under John McNally at St. Patrick's in West Oakland. He was full of stories of Father McNally, who was an Irish pastor of the old school, the kind who found jobs for his people but felt free to denounce them from the pulpit if they were stingy in the collection.

Although Monsignor had retired to his bed a few years before, he assured me that he would not ever resign: he wouldn't give the "new archbishop" the pleasure of assigning a successor! The "new" archbishop, of course, had already been fifteen years in San Francisco, but I knew that he had never been accepted by the Irish "old guard."

Realizing that the old man was a fountain of stories and would likely keep me standing there indefinitely, I managed to escape after a half hour to find the priest I had seen talking on the phone. I needed to know where to bring my things. His name was Frank, and as the senior assistant, he was unofficially in charge of the parish. He showed me my rooms, a study and a bedroom, which were not adjacent to each other. All of our rooms were arranged in a square around the stairwell. I learned that John, the other assistant with whom I would share a bath, was a newly ordained priest that I had known in the seminary. We had called him Butch. He was "off" that afternoon.

After dinner in the dining room, Frank took time to give me some idea of life at Sacred Heart. I gathered that it was unlike St. Matthew's in having no strong leadership for the last couple of years. The parish ran largely on its traditions and precedents. Many of these were long-standing, to the extent that some of the parish organizations were rather resistant to change. However, he assured me that there was plenty to do.

He told me that the area we served covered a compact rectangle of densely populated blocks from Thirtieth to Sixtieth Streets in the northern part of Oakland. There were some three thousand familes or individuals listed in the parish census, which was admittedly out of date. A great many of these people were first generation Italian or Irish, strongly identified as Catholics. An increasing area of the parish was home to a black community which also numbered many Catholics from Louisiana and the West Indies.

I also learned that four hospitals lay within the parish, with another just outside, and these institutions demanded almost daily attention. There were many elderly people in the area, and Frank said that funerals could be expected at least once a week.

After saying Mass early the next morning, I explored the parish plant to see what it had to offer. Besides the rectory and the fine old stone church with its slate roof, there were four other buildings surrounding an acre of concrete play-yard: an old school building now used for meetings, the present eight grade school, a gymnasium, and the convent for the Sisters of the Holy Names who taught in our school. I realized that there was plenty to show for the Old Man's years of work at Sacred Heart, a far more extensive group of buildings than I had known at San Mateo or Palo Alto.

At breakfast, I met Butch, my fellow assistant. Butch was a friendly, good-natured person. He laughed easily, a wide hearty laugh, but although he was a keen observer of human nature, there was no unkindness in his humor. He loved to recount the follies and eccentricities that he saw around the parish. He was amused (but without resentment) by the Old Man's attitude towards the youth of the parish. Sampson did not feel that they should be catered to, and he thoroughly disapproved of dances, which he referred to as "belly rubbing."

Butch reinforced the impression given me by Frank of a very busy, "healthy" parish. In spite of the lack of pastoral leadership during the previous two years, the parish was a smoothly operating complex of services and organizations which fulfilled the principal needs of the people. He said that one of us priests had to be in the house at all times. The phone rang a great deal, and people dropped in constantly with requests for baptismal records, with rosaries to be blessed, and to arrange baptisms, weddings, and funerals. Someone at the door was called a "parlor call." He showed me the three rooms, rather dreary and cluttered, which served as parlors to receive the visitors. Sometimes all three would be occupied at once.

During the first few weeks at Sacred Heart, my duties were to mind the house: to respond to phone calls and parlor calls as they came. Most of those who came to the door were housewives or older people whose needs could be met without consulting Frank or Butch. Some phone calls were about people in the hospitals, others were from young adults wanting to make appointments about weddings and instructions. Still others dealt with matters of parish business that I did not yet understand. When the other priests were out, I would take these messages for them. In the process, I learned much about the activities and history of the parish. I found that Mary the housekeeper was very helpful with her knowledge of the people I was meeting.

Only a month after my arrival, Mary began feeling poorly. She was losing weight, and soon learned that she had cancer. Regretfully, she left us to stay in the care of a relative in Oakland. Father Frank was in poor health himself, and turned over to Butch and myself the responsibility of finding a new housekeeper. We quickly placed an advertisement in the local newspaper and began interviewing applicants. Most applicants could clean and cook, but few had a notion of what it meant to answer the door and phone in a Catholic rectory. A priest's housekeeper had to be a skillful receptionist, aware of the special relationships between priests and Catholic people, and also sensitive to their feelings in times of crisis.

Eventually we found a Catholic widow who seemed to understand our "scene." In our desperation, we promptly hired her, without much concern for her failing eye-sight, or for her complete lack of working experience. Our decision created an agony for all concerned. Burned food, broken dishes, and frequent collisions with the furniture marked her career; and Father Frank quietly poured his food out the window into the bushes. The end came when I found her toasting two cloth pot-lifters, side by side in the oven.

This lady was followed by a cube-shaped Portuguese woman who addressed us as "you guys" and succeeded in making all food taste like linguisa. There were others, but we never found anyone to replace Mary!

These weeks were busy enough without the problem of interviewing housekeepers. It was the time of year when our school was starting classes; Butch and I divided the school between us, and we each taught once a week in the upper classes. Sisters liked to have the children know the priests and to experience a variety in the teaching of religion. Various parish organizations had renewed their meetings after the summer holidays, and one of us priests was chaplain for each organization; this usually meant showing up at meetings now and then and "saying a few words." Several potential converts came in to take instruction, which involved an enjoyable but time-consuming duty.

During my time in Oakland, I was careful to take my day off faithfully. There were plenty of things to tie one down at the parish; however, the statutes of the diocese decreed a weekly day off, and I was not reluctant to comply. I would drive to Palo Alto via East Oakland and the Dumbarton Bridge, a trip of about an hour; during the three years that my brother was also stationed in an Oakland parish, I would pick him up on the way, so that we could ride together.

We spent our days off quietly at home, doing violin and cello trios with Mother at the piano, working in the garden, and reading. Bob often did photographic enlarging, too.

During part of this time, Dad's brother Phil was living at our home. He had been a mining engineer in the Philippines when the war began, and had opted for hiding in the jungle rather than being interned. His four years alone, during which we thought he was dead, had left him undernourished, and he had returned to California to recover for a year or so before returning to the mines. Having learned to be alone, he was almost invisible, and Mother would be startled to find him reading in the front room after many hours of total silence. In 1947 he returned to the Islands, and soon afterward, at age 50, was married to a Filipino woman from Cebu, who became my Aunt Eusebia. They lived in Palo Alto after his retirement.

Early in October, Frank felt much worse and went to the hospital for some tests and rest, turning over to me all his lists and his cases, even the bookkeeping. Butch and I worked out a division of labor, and we managed all right with an occasional assist from a neighboring pastor. Butch was a hard worker, and he was easy to cooperate with because he never took himself too seriously.

The old Monsignor was worse than no help. Every time we went to him with a problem, he got off the subject after only a few minutes, and we were back in the world of old West Oakland for an hour or so. Even when he managed to offer advice, it was obvious that the way he had done things in the past, though it may have worked for him, was out of the question for us. His idea of bookkeeping was to write the income figures in long slanty columns across the face of the big official account book, with no reference at all to the printed columns or headings!

Frank came home in November and was with us again, but was able to do little more than say Mass. He was always worrying about everything, and was acutely conscious of his own symptoms. He often recalled that his mother had died from what he called "pernicious high blood pressure" at exactly his age of thirty nine.

I wished I could have known Frank when he was well. I loved his stories. His favorites were about his first assignment, fourteen years before, with the infamous Father Kiely, the pastor of Petaluma. Kiely was a tyrant with young priests and never hesitated to

71

shout at the people, from the pulpit or in the street, when he felt that they had not fulfilled their obligations. Frank loved to tell of how he got even with Kiely. After the latter was asleep, Frank would sneak outside and make some clattering in the yard, then dash back to his room. He would then wake Kiely and lead him on a long, cold, and often wet search of the premises by flashlight before giving up the chase.

By the time Frank had to return to the hospital in early December, Butch and I had been effectively in charge of the parish for some months, and by Christmas we were reinforced by another assistant, about our own age, named Paul. Three heads were better than two, and without Frank's habitual cautiousness we began to enjoy our feeling of independence.

We made our decisions collaboratively, at conspiratorial sessions late at night, when the Monsignor would not interrupt. It was deeply satisfying to work out our ideas, including our program for the youth, with almost no interference. Butch even obtained from the Bishop's office permission to take funds from Sacred Heart's abundant savings to renovate the gym for a youth program.

Frank, in his hospital bed, was too sick to concern himself with our management of affairs at the church. Visiting him frequently there, we saw his health steadily deteriorating. Frank died on Sunday, January 6, 1946. When I went to tell the Monsignor, he responded "God rest him . . . Oh my heart is terrible today . . . I wonder when the funeral will be."

It was decided by the Archbishop that the funeral should be at Sacred Heart in view of Frank's long service there, rather than in the cathedral. It was my first experience arranging for a major ceremony with the Archbishop in attendance. A temporary throne, an elevated armchair with a green velvet canopy, had to be created for him at the side of the sanctuary.

The influx of priest-visitors began a day before the event. Frank's body was brought to the church and laid in state for the viewing by the people. In the evening, a group of priests chanted the Office for the Dead, which I had not heard before—very impressive in its stark simplicity. Afterward, I remained in the silent church for an hour, considering the mystery of death. I was familiar with funerals, but this was different—a man I had joked with and had recently worked with. Now his life's work was ended, and his spirit had gone to an eternal destiny which I could not know.

The funeral Mass was magnificent: the choir of priests, the impressive eulogy by Frank's friend Bill Reilly, and the throng of nearly two hundred priests in cassock and surplice. Six brown bees-

72

wax candles, each seven feet tall, were placed around the casket. A huge crowd of lay people attended, far exceeding the capacity of the church. I had not realized that he had been so well loved both by the people and by his clerical companions.

The Monsignor did not, of course, attend the ceremonies; however, he welcomed the many visitors with obvious relish and with no perceptible fatigue.

Throughout this time, indeed through all my five years at Sacred Heart, the Monsignor remained the dominant personality in the parish. People came to see him constantly, and he "held court" in his brass bed, regaling all comers with tales of the old days in West Oakland. With priests and lay visitors alike, he was always the entertainer. His stories of St. Patrick's Parish and of various priests he knew were full of caustic humor, and the sharpness of perception of a much younger man. He never repeated his stories, and he never ran out!

When a few hours passed without a visitor, he would get out of bed and drift down the hallway in search of a listener. He never wore anything but faded blue pajamas and black socks; he never seemed to feel drafts, and he never caught a cold. Sitting at my desk, I would hear the soft shuffle of his footsteps, and suddenly his head would appear around the door jamb, tousled white hair followed by his tall, stooping figure. One hand, poised above his heart, would make feeble palpitations as he announced with unfailing regularity, "John, I nearly died at two o'clock." He would stagger into the room and collapse onto the couch, ready for a story-telling session of indefinite length.

In spite of his strong personality and vigorously held views and his disdain for the softness of present-day priests in general, he never asked Butch and me to account for the work we were doing nor did he criticize our style. We realized now the complexity of administering a parish, and began to gain respect for his wide experience. When not too rushed to listen to him, I found his comments to be a rich source of insight into the nobility and the foolishness of human nature.

One of the many factors which contributed to the complexity of life at Sacred Heart was the steady stream of "bums" coming to our door. We were obvious targets, because the church was only a few blocks from the Santa Fe railroad yards. Often we knew that we were destined to meet one of these men from the way in which we were summoned to the parlor. By then, we had a daytime maid named Aldonia Reinhart, a stately young black woman, who answered the door during her hours of work. When she had the unpleasant duty of calling a priest to deal with one of these men, she would warn us by the tone of her voice. Instead of her usual soft and musical "Someone t' see-ya, Fatha", she would speak with an eloquent drawl, "They's a maaaaaan t' see ya, Fatha!"

I dreaded going downstairs knowing, that I would be confronted by another disheveled wreck with a long story, and that any attempt to argue, or to discount his tale, would bring a torrent of scorn, saved up for soft-living, hard-hearted priests.

In dealing with these men and their demands, I experienced an inner conflict and a profound sense of helplessness. On the one hand, we priests were trained to be generous lovers of the poor, as Jesus taught and as the Catholic Workers had shown me by example. On the other, Butch and I knew that every time we gave in to the demands of these men, we were being taken for a ride. They were seasoned liars and usually winos, and they knew how to manipulate our clerical consciences.

Dunstan Miller was a steady customer—every 6 months. I had encountered him at St. Matthew's, and I was sure he was making the rounds of all the parishes. He always pretended he had never met me before. He was a dirty-blond, young-looking drifter who carried a greasy "holy card" of St. Dunstan, his patron saint, to demonstrate his piety. I listened impatiently to his tales of jail, accidents, and hospitals. No matter how I tried to cut in, his tales went on and on. Finally, when he finished, I would give him a little money and send him on his way, relieved to have it over with.

The worst case of all was Pat Murphy, an alcoholic and a former priest. He smelled so that Aldonia wouldn't let him in the door. I would find him leaning against a post on the porch smiling cynically. He never failed to remind me contemptuously that I had only gone to a seminary while he had been a graduate of the Sorbonne University in Paris. When I would tell him that I wasn't going to give him any money because he was just going to drink it, he would launch into a diatribe against the present generation of clergy for their hypocrisy and lack of priestly brotherhood. (Several years later he collapsed on the steps of a Catholic hospital and was carried inside to die peacefully between clean sheets with a rosary in his hands!)

Because our lives at Sacred Heart were so busy with people and church affairs, we all found that the reading of the "Divine Office" took too much time. It consumed at least an hour a day, even at my best speed, and was wholly unsuited to the chaotic schedule of the parish. Like most priests, I put it off during the busy hours of the day, only to find myself faced with the weary prospect of muttering Latin syllables, until the stroke of midnight set me free as it announced the beginning of a new day.

I had occasionally expressed my frustration to the priests who presided over the diocesan retreats. They recommended sublimating this activity by meditating on some pious theme drawn from the texts. However, I could never keep my mind on anything else while I struggled to wade through the Latin words.

Luckily, the Society for the Near East, which granted the privilege of the "Little Office" to its members, announced at this time that only life members would in the future be given this permission and that life membership would be available only through this year. Remembering the value which Father Lyne had placed upon this privilege, I hastened to scrape up the required forty dollars and became a life member of this missionary society. It was probably the best investment I ever made.

The use of the privilege depended upon traveling "in the course of duty." However, it was not difficult to interpret a trip to the cemetery an hour away as traveling, nor to see one's day off as a duty. Accordingly, many of us managed to travel somewhere almost every day. Even so, there were many days when Butch, Paul, and I would find ourselves at eleven-thirty at night walking like donkeys on a treadmill around the downstairs parlor at Sacred heart, keeping ourselves awake until the midnight hour as we fulfilled our obligation of the Office.

Busy as we were with convert instructions, organizational meetings, and visits to the homes of parishioners, we all knew that our essential duty as priests was our role in providing them with the Sacraments. We agreed that none of the other duties, administrative or organizational, should be allowed to distract us, for it was in the availability of funerals, christenings and confessions, and in the dignity of the Mass, that the people really experienced our ministry. In these things we found our greatest satisfaction, and because of them the people honored and sometimes even loved us.

However, there were real pastoral problems, even with the Sacraments: seemingly irreconcilable dissonances between the norms laid down by the Church and the real needs of the people. During those years after the war, some of these were beginning to receive attention in the more daring Catholic periodicals, such as *Integrity*, the *Catholic Worker*, and *Amen*. I would read them whenever time allowed, feeling excitement over the possibilities there might be for real change in the liturgy or in the Church's laws. These magazines reminded me of the freedom and freshness I had felt among the "progressive" Catholic groups in New York.

Of all our pastoral problems, the one I most often encountered was the dissolution of failed marriages. In this matter, a reform was most evidently needed. The marriage laws of the Church were based upon the assumption that once a couple was married, they were bound to each other in a lifelong contract which no court could abolish. However, there were a number of technical flaws which might exist in the marriage bond, and if any of them was discovered, the marriage was considered never to have existed. It was not dissolved, but rather declared "null." In this case, the parties would be free to marry again—for the "first" time. It was the search for such flaws that dominated the work of the Catholic marriage courts. Every diocese had such a court, and every time a divorced Catholic sought to enter into a new marriage, this annulment process was activated.

This procedure impinged upon my life whenever a long heavy envelope arrived from the Chancery Office containing a packet of forms to be filled out. Typically, they would have originated in some distant diocese where a divorced Catholic was seeking an annulment so that he/she might remarry. It would become my disagreeable duty to call upon the former spouse, or perhaps someone else who was presumed to have relevant information, and to "administer" the questionnaire. Sometimes the questions asked were embarrassingly personal. This task was made more awkward by the admonition not to reveal the significance of the questions asked, lest the witness be prejudiced one way or the other. It was foreign to me to be so disingenuous.

Of course I found these procedures most disturbing when they touched the lives of people who had come to me for help. One day after Mass I found a tall, bald man waiting for me in the parlor; I had seen him standing at the back of the church while I was preaching. He was a widower, and was now desirous of marrying a non-Catholic divorced woman; they were both in their late forties. He knew that they faced a problem, but he thought they had the solution: her first marriage had been entered into under a nullifying condition—namely, that there be no children.

I liked him. His forthright manner and determination to solve the problem within the Church were appealing. I thought that I could help him obtain his annulment and immediately set about writing up the case. However, the Chancery Office returned my letter, saying that more proof was needed than just her word. Unfortunately, I could find none to submit, so eventually the annulment was refused.

However, my friend was a persistent man. He decided to move to a different diocese where perhaps the bishop might be more willing to accept the available evidence. He went off on his quest and, whenever he was in town, he would come to tell me how he had been received. He went as far as Arizona and San Diego, receiving responses which varied from encouragement to blunt refusal. This case ended happily for the couple, for they finally found in Fresno a bishop who was willing to grant the annulment. They moved to that diocese, and were shortly married in the cathedral there.

Most couples—there were many—lacked the time, the determination, or the money to pursue their case so patiently through the web of legal obstacles. Some, even though they did so, would receive in the end a negative answer to their plea. As a result, many good people were lost to the Church, and I grieved for them. It did not seem to me that the sincerity or goodness of the couple played any part in the outcome: the decision for or against annulment lay in the hands of some fallible human being, and one who had seldom even met the people involved.

Another aspect of parish life at Sacred Heart that weighed heavily upon me was the care of the sick. We had four large hospitals within the parish boundaries, so that this part of our work was significant. Every third week, I was on night duty for all sick calls, and there were few nights without a call or two. We priests took this duty very seriously, but it was often unrewarding. In this matter, it was not the laws of the Church that created the difficulty: it was rather the entrenched attitudes of Catholic people toward death and sin, and to the role of the Sacraments. Faced with such attitudes, I often felt that the Sacraments were meaningless or worse.

To illustrate, a call would come from a nurse on floor duty at the hospital. As quickly as possible I would be in my car, headed for "Pill Hill" where the three hospitals were. I would hasten to the designated room, only to find in most cases an unconscious patient too far gone to receive communion or even to hear the comforting words of forgiveness. I would unpack my "sick call kit" and begin the recitation of the prescribed prayers from the ritual, ending with the anointing with holy oil.

What was meant to be a beautiful and consoling rite, celebrated amid friends and relatives, became hollow and hopeless in this bare white room; I felt that I must seem as irrelevant as a dinosaur to the nurses and doctors who bustled in and out. Even when the patient was conscious and I took time to read the English translations, the rite did not seem very comforting, because the emphasis was on sin and death rather than on peace and healing. Sometimes, I would alter the words of the ritual to give them a more consoling tone, even though I knew that this was forbidden.

I remember being called one evening to a small Italian home where the grandmother was dying. Numerous relatives sat stiffly in the front rooms, dressed in dark colors; they stared at me with no sign of welcome, as I was led to a back room where the old lady lay unconscious. My escort closed the door, and I was left to do whatever "magic" I was supposed to do! When I came out, I tried to be friendly, but was cut short by the curt question, "How much I pay?" Refusing politely, I left, feeling completely defeated in my desire to make religion relevant at this significant point in the family's life.

Of course, it was not always so grim. One day, a nurse called me to visit a "nice little man" in her hospital wing. He proved to be a dwarf, his toes poking up the covers only a foot or so from his torso, as he sat quite erect in bed. He was eighty-three, although he seemed younger. He was tersely friendly, but cut short the question of religion by saying that he hadn't been to church for fifty years. I dropped in on him each day; soon he opened up, telling of the bitterness he had felt over his dwarfism during youth, his cynical atheism, and later his mellow agnosticism. The day before he was due to go home, he asked for communion, and received it with obvious happiness and peace; the next day he was dead.

The pleasant year of priestly teamwork among the youthful staff of John, Paul, and Butch came to an end with Paul's transfer and the appointment of an administrator for Sacred Heart. Paul's going was a great loss to us. We could not imagine continuing all the projects he had initiated without his buoyant personality and abundant energy.

We were worried about the man who was coming: Frank McCarthy. None of the reports we had been able to obtain about him was reassuring. He was said to be petty, money-hungry, and jealous of his authority. The day when the bad news reached us was September 21. We spent that evening together, Butch, Paul and I, reminiscing about our great year together, recalling how we had progressed from spending a daring $9 on a new sacristy light fixture to spending $9,000 on the renovation of the gym. Butch was at his wittiest, and Paul alternated between hilarity and near tears. We talked of the hypothetical day when the Monsignor would say: "Poor Frank . . . another one gone. I wonder who they'll send here next"—a joke which proved prophetic only fifteen months later.

Frank, the new administrator, arrived in time for dinner on the last day of September. He was a small, nervous man and rather deaf, with a little curl of white hair rising from the center of his forehead. He was very ingratiating, eager to assure Butch and me that his health was good enough to do the work of this busy parish.

Among the available posts, he had chosen that of administrator at Sacred Heart, rather than a full pastorate in a less prestigious parish. No doubt he expected to outlive (or outmaneuver) the Old Man, and become pastor in due time. He made sure that we heard his version of the closing of his previous parish, All Hallows in San Francisco, which had become an industrial area. He did not want us to think that the decision had involved any failure on his part.

It took no time at all to realize that he was perpetually on the defensive. During the next few days, his reputation for bossiness was verified. He immediately began demanding little changes, things that could well have waited until he had been there a while. In the beginning, Butch and I were not the targets of his reforms: they were the housekeeper, the choir director, the nuns, and the church caretaker. He wanted to have the toaster in the dining room; he wanted to have three Masses instead of two on First Fridays; he wanted Butch and me to visit all the school classrooms, rather than specializing in one or two; he wanted us to pick up the mail at the post office, instead of waiting for it to be delivered; he wanted new cruets for wine and water on the altar; he wanted us to mail the offering-envelopes for use on All Souls Day to all the people (no small task!); he wanted to institute a weekly service called a "perpetual novena" . . . and so on. All his schemes involved additional work for someone—never for himself.

It was amazing how fast he succeeded in getting everyone upset. Everywhere I went, I encountered complaints and confusion. What caused the furor was not simply the changes, premature as they were, but rather his fussy manner, his nasal buzz saw voice, and above all his failure to listen to any other point of view. Everybody was on edge, wondering what would come next.

With Butch and me, he tried to be more conciliating. He remarked how smoothly things were running at Sacred Heart. He spoke with appreciation of the facilities, the active organizations, and the large bank account. But he could not resist messing around with everything. I felt that he really resented the fact that we had been able to get along before he came. If either Butch or I indicated that we preferred the way things had been before, he was ready with a lecture on his prerogatives as "Pastor."

Meals became increasingly unpleasant. He would come into the dining room, simpering and bobbing as was his wont, making small talk. However, if one of us made a comment which he could not hear or did not like, his sickly smile would fade and he would lean forward, his hand behind his ear saying "What's that? What's that?" His face would assume a tight, irritated expression, and he would be off on a tirade about whatever grievance we had called to his mind.

Accordingly, Butch and I had small sympathy for Frank when, about two weeks after his arrival, he finally tangled with the Monsignor. The latter had already made sardonic comments to him about upsetting the help. But on this day, the Old Man chose the most vulnerable spot in Frank's fragile ego and let him have it.

Frank came into the next meal greatly agitated. Peering at us through the concentric rings of his thick glasses, he poured out his resentment and frustration at the Monsignor's treatment of him. He had come into the Old Man's room to find him relaxed as usual in the regal security of his brass bed. Without a flicker of welcome, the Old Man had said, "Frank, you should never have come back to Oakland. They're still talking about that house." The long ago episode of the house to which the Monsignor referred was a new story to Butch and me. But Frank poured out his version of it with all the fervor of a decade's worth of brooding.

Frank's tale was this: in the height of the Depression, he had been appointed Pastor of St. Cyril's, a newly created parish in East Oakland. Trying to finance the construction of the church, he had launched an innovative raffle: the prize was to be a new home. Those were hard days, and not enough raffle tickets could ever be sold to pay for the house. As a result, Frank repeatedly had to postpone the drawing. Finally, the archbishop's office had called a halt. Terribly embarrassed and feeling thoroughly victimized, Frank had been shipped off to the "Siberia" of the diocese—the San Joaquin delta. He laid the responsibility for this debacle upon Bob Sampson and the "Tipperary crowd." Frank complained that he had never been accepted by the in-group of Irish-born priests who had controlled the diocese in those days.

Frank talked incessantly and compulsively about this story, which was interesting the first time or two, but not at every meal! He even showed us a suitcase of worthless raffle-stubs that he had been carrying around with him ever since. Realizing his profound resentment of the role Bob Sampson had played in his transfer in disgrace at the time of the ill-fated raffle, Butch and I could never figure why Frank had ventured back within reach of the Old Man's well-known sharp and witty tongue.

Rectory life at Sacred Heart, which had been so companionable, so full of shared work and good humor, had been changed almost overnight into a state of siege. Frank saw himself as persecuted by everyone. Having no way to get back at the monsignor, he took out his frustrations more and more on Butch and me. We learned that he had even complained about us to the archbishop's office, although nothing came of it.

Now that he was in charge, it was necessary, in trying to carry out our parish work, to present questions of policy to Frank and to explain all our plans for his approval. But this was almost impossible to do without confusing and angering him. He just couldn't handle face-to-face contact. There was no doubt that Frank's personality verged on the paranoid. If we were to continue to enjoy our life and work at Sacred Heart, Butch and I would have to work out a way of living with him which did not activate his defenses.

The solution was provided when he had a mailbox installed in the hall outside his room, which was now directly below mine. In this little box Butch and I would deposit messages and questions, neatly typed. From time to time, Frank would pop out of his room, like a gopher from his hole, to obtain the contents of his box. With leisure to read and consider, and without having to relate to anyone, he would write answering notes which were usually affirmative and cordial. We had found the way to deal with him!

It made him feel expansive and generous to say "yes" on paper. Once Butch and I had learned this, we occasionally asked for and obtained an extra day off. We felt that accepting these holidays was justified by the heavy work of the parish and the neurotic atmosphere of the rectory.

Soon after Frank's humiliating defeat by the Monsignor, he had one of the front parlors altered to become his quarters, and he never went upstairs again. The room was in front, which enabled him to peek out through the venetian blinds to see if people coming to the door were ones that he wanted to avoid. He seldom went anywhere.

The only person who appeared to be his friend and confidant was a middle-aged widow who came in from San Leandro once a week to count the collection and do the bookkeeping. "Mrs. Mac," as he called her, was installed in a small dark room adjoining his own, across from the dining room. There, surrounded by money-counting devices and duplicating equipment, she worked all day, while Frank darted in and out like a fast fish in an aquarium tank to harangue her in his oddly nasal voice about whatever was on his mind.

At this time, a third assistant joined us. There was too much work for Butch and me to do in the parish. Moreover, Frank felt that it was a matter of honor to have a staff of three assistants as in the past. The new man's name was John Connery, a soft-spoken Irishman, gentle and slow in his manner. He found no problem in relating to Frank, and chuckled quietly at the poor man's follies.

One Sunday, I was coming in from Mass to get some breakfast, when I heard someone calling from the Old Man's bedroom. I rushed upstairs and found the monsignor lying on the cold tile floor of his bathroom, as helpless as a beetle on its back. Apparently, he had tripped on the sill of the shower stall. He had probably gone to get some whiskey when his regular two o'clock heart failure was coming on. He kept the whiskey—doctor's orders—in the bathroom in a small safe. I helped him back to bed. Still somewhat confused, he kept saying I had hit him with a whiskey bottle.

When Butch arrived, we called the doctor, who ordered him to the hospital for examination. When I came in again, after the next Mass, he was just being carried out on a stretcher, feet first, still in his blue pajamas. He was smoking his curly old pipe and telling the bearers about the old days in West Oakland.

The Monsignor never returned to the house. He occupied the same room in Providence Hospital where Frank Donnelly had died, and which he himself had endowed several years before. Whenever I visited him, I would find him with visitors, pontificating from his bed just as he had done at Sacred Heart, for all comers. His Irish friends, priests and lay people, seemed to be especially loyal to him. Butch and I missed him in the rectory, and Sacred Heart could not be the same without him. (He never did resign as pastor.)

Frank McCarthy had been at Sacred Heart only a year when his health began to fail. He had been feeling sick for some days in early December, and one morning I heard him bumping around his room in a blur of dizziness. I called the doctor, who came promptly, and Frank was taken to a hospital in San Francisco. His absence permitted the atmosphere at Sacred Heart to regain some of its serenity. After only a few weeks of illness, Frank died of kidney failure.

It was only the day after Frank's funeral that the rumor reached us at Sacred Heart that a new administrator by the name of Edgar Boyle was coming. I was delighted. I had known him as director of music for the archdiocese; in fact I had almost succeeded him in that office. He was a big, jovial, outgoing man, the very antithesis of Frank McCarthy.

Two days later he came to lunch with Butch and me, and then went to the hospital to see the Monsignor. He was already full of ideas about what he would like to do at Sacred Heart, and his enthusiasm was infectious. Even though he was bringing with him his own housekeeper and janitor from the parish in Fairfax where he had been pastor, he did not make us feel threatened with another disruption of our work; rather, he said that he wanted to start from what we were doing and build upon it.

Apparently, the Old Man also felt comfortable with Edgar's plans, for when I next saw him he had no sarcastic remarks to make. Edgar had been at Sacred Heart as assistant some years before, and he and Bob Sampson had a mutual respect for each other.

Edgar moved in just a week later on the feast of the Epiphany. He won our hearts immediately with his warmth and openness to everyone. He was eager to learn about the place and people, asking questions constantly. He strode about the grounds with his black cassock flying, meeting the children and the nuns and the trades-people who came to the house. He liked to take long walks around the parish, especially the business district in Oakland along Tele-graph Avenue, making friends with everyone.

On his first Sunday in the parish, Father Boyle gave the annual report—usually a dreary affair, but not in this case. He had a breezy, even boisterous style of talking, and garnished the facts and figures with fanciful humor, tossing compliments to Butch and me, and to the community in general. In that one Sunday morning, he succeeded in creating a feeling of unity, energy, and anticipation that I had never felt in the parish before. It was evident in the com-ments of people as they streamed out of the church when Mass was over. I got the impression that we would all have to work hard, but that it would be fun.

That night at dinner, Edgar and I were alone, and he talked entirely about music. I felt his sensitivity, and his largeness of vision. I was happy that he would be with us at Sacred Heart.

Edgar Boyle had a very serious interest in and love for the lit-urgy, for the dignity and elegance of its language and its symbols, and of course its music. Within a few weeks, he had obtained the approval of the Chancery Office to put a new altar in the church, and an architect was on hand to help Edgar design a sanctuary worthy of the sacred ritual. With the willing help of the Sisters, he began the training of a children's choir; soon there would be music at two Masses each Sunday. He also bought fine new cassocks for the altar boys.

Unlike Frank, whose reforms were fussy and furtive, Edgar's ideas, however extravagant they might seem, were announced with such zest that it would seem petty to oppose them. He wanted to include the people in everything—for example, in answering the prayers of the mass. In those days a "dialogue mass"—with the con-

83

gregation answering a reader who echoed in English the priest's Latin words—was a rare and radical deviation from the usual silent mass. But Edgar dived into the project of preparing the people for dialogue without hesitation.

On Sunday morning he would stand outside the church with a newsboy's bag over his cassock, hawking paperback missals in English, Spanish, Italian, and German, so that everyone would be able to understand the ceremonies and to respond.

Edgar's master plan for the parish included a new school building to replace the two old ones, a parish social hall, and a new rectory. The scheme was so sweeping that it seemed like a pipe-dream; however, the steps were taken one by one for the realization of the plan. Fortunately, the parish had a very large bank account, saved up over many years by the thrifty old Monsignor.

Edgar's plans might have been less attractive if they had not been accompanied by two excellent qualities: a fine esthetic sense, and a real interest in the people, particularly the elderly and the members of minority groups. I loved to see him greeting the old Italian ladies in their own language, bowing low to kiss their hands. He was always "on stage." He loved to throw back his long grey hair with a toss of the head.

He did carry his clowning a bit far at times, especially in the pulpit. The larger his audience, the wilder his fancies! One day he embarrassed a visiting missionary by promising to feed him pickled pigs' feet if the people would be generous enough with their contributions.

When Edgar came, he loved to capitalize on the fact that we three assistants were all named John, and he selected various Saint Johns to identify each of us with. However, Connery was unable to deal with Edgar's volcanic personality: his perpetual motion, perpetual talk, his constant stream of new ideas. "John of God," as Edgar called him, could not stand the pace, and after a few months he collapsed with a nervous breakdown and was given another assignment.

For myself, Edgar's noisiness and foolery were amply compensated by his generosity and enthusiasm. However, as the months passed, it became evident that he too had a darker side. As long as he could be the center of admiration, making people laugh, dazzling them with his versatile antics, all was well: as long as he could sweep everyone with him, he was happy. But any real challenge to the wisdom of his schemes, or any suggestion that people were laughing at him instead of with him, brought out a brooding suspicious part of his personality.

Butch and I, as we began to realize this, adapted ourselves, and were careful that he should never hear us laughing together in such a way that he might suspect he was being ridiculed.

Unfortunately Edgar's bad moods had a very disturbing effect upon me; they aroused old guilt feelings. Whereas Frank had been too pathetic to make me feel that I was at fault, there was something in Edgar that activated old fears—the ones I had felt with the pastor in New York, and the ones that were implanted by the discipline of the seminary. I could not be indifferent to the disapproval of someone in authority.

For example, I began to feel that when I went away, even for my official day off, I was somehow being disloyal to the hard-working team. And when it came to the vacation trips to the mountains, I made my preparations furtively, so that my actual departure could be quick and unobtrusive. I had an irrational fear that at the last minute something would come up to prevent my going. This was really neurotic! Edgar showed an active interest in our vacation plans, and was perfectly open about his own . . . but that feeling was there.

It was the same with reading. No matter how legitimate it was—research for a sermon even—I could not enjoy relaxing with a book as long as Edgar was in the house. He was forever roaming around, and would glance in at my open door as he passed. His look seemed to say: you are being lazy sitting there reading! Only at night, when my door was closed, could I enjoy a good book.

I could not help wondering why I was so susceptible to guilt. Perhaps it was the seven years in the seminary, lived always under the watchful eye of clerical authority figures, who were ready with humiliating and moralistic reprimands, even for such minor infractions as speaking in the hall without permission. I had expected to drop the whole seminary experience with ordination; it was so unlike the warm supportive atmosphere of the church at home. But I had not done so. The scars were still sensitive.

In any case, my time with Edgar was running out. One April morning in 1950 the buzzer called me into the hall, and Aldonia's soft voice announced, "Fatha', the archbishop's office is on the phone." Had I done something wrong? Had Edgar reported me for some reason? However, it was Jim Brown, the Superintendent of Catholic Schools; he wanted to see me the next morning. But I was still surprised to be summoned and felt a bit apprehensive. The only thing I could think of that Jim Brown would want to talk to me about was an assignment for teaching. Suppose it was Latin! I had felt that at the age of thirty-two I had escaped such a fate; I was left in suspense for the rest of the day.

Jim Brown's office was in an old mansion near Golden Gate Park at some distance from the Chancery Office. The building served as headquarters for the Department of Education. Welcoming me promptly into his cluttered, informal office, Jim unfolded his plan to me. He was not asking me to be a teacher, but to be director of a Newman Center. He wanted the archbishop to create a full-time chaplaincy for San Jose State College and he wanted my name to submit to the archbishop along with the request.

This would be the first full-time Newman appointment at this growing college, which had quadrupled in four years with the influx of men supported by the GI Bill of Rights. The need for the appointment had been brought to his attention by a group of San Jose Catholic women, who had formed a committee to clean up the old Newman building (long neglected and little used), and who had come to the conclusion that their work could not achieve any useful end without a priest.

Jim told me that I would probably be given a place to live at a nearby church, where my meals and room would be provided in return for weekend work. It would be up to me and the group of women to raise the money for my salary (officially $75 a month at that time) and whatever funds would be required for our program. He suggested that I might also find a paid job teaching part time at O'Connor Nursing School, which was near the college.

I immediately said yes. I had escaped a desk job or a teaching post, and was being offered a chance to create my own ministry. This was a real challenge. Like a pastor, I would be responsible for a community, free to plan whatever program seemed appropriate. As I carried on my daily work, I would not have to worry about someone's approval or disapproval.

I returned to Sacred Heart full of anticipation to await the official appointment. It came a few weeks later, but would not become effective until September. I had three more months in Oakland.

Butch was philosophical about my leaving, being used to seeing people come and go. Paul, our closest teammate, had already left. The two Franks were dead, Mary Wilson was dead, and the Monsignor had moved to a hospital. John Connery had left, and had recently been replaced by a Lithuanian refugee, Victor Pavalkis. Now I was going too, and he wished me well.

6. On My Own

In early July, not long after the annual clergy retreat, I drove
down to San Jose at the southern end of San Francisco Bay. I
needed to see the facilities of the San Jose Newman Club and to
meet the women who would be my sponsors and supporters there.
San Jose was almost unknown to me. Near as it is to Palo Alto, I had
almost no occasion to go there.

It was a warm summer morning, and the town seemed very
peaceful as I walked along the streets lined with tall elm trees
between rows of old frame houses. Many of the houses near the college had been divided into apartments for students. Among them,
only a stone's throw from the campus, stood a large wooden building
which was the Newman Center. A porch spanned the front, sur-
mounted by a Greek frontal supported by Doric columns.

The door was open. Inside it was dark and cool, musty smelling in contrast to the mellow summer outside. The building contained a large hall with stage and dance floor, two confortable
reading rooms, and a long basement with kitchen, bowling alley,
and ping-pong table. The rugs were moth-eaten, and the fine oak
furniture was covered with worn-out cushions. The ceilings were
high; no doubt the coolness would often be welcome. On one side of
the entrance was a room with a large window looking out on the
street; this would be my office.

Shortly, the ladies began to arrive, and welcomed me warmly. They were society women, all graduates of San Jose State. I had seen many like them pictured in the religious news, both in Oakland and San Mateo, presiding over card parties and pageants. They had been brought together by Mrs. Morgan Dillon Baker, the energetic widow of a local doctor, who was offended and grieved by the rundown state of the building which she remembered from her own college days.

Their first project, for which Monsignor Maher, the local pastor, had gladly given permission, was to clean the outside of the building, which they accomplished by enlisting the help of the fire department. But beyond that they had had little luck. They did not have any avenue of approach to the student community, and Vernon Schirle, the priest whom Maher had assigned to "take care of the Newman Club," had not had the time as a parish assistant to create a real Newman program. So the group of women had gone to the Archbishop with their request for a full-time chaplain.

We sat around a big oak table discussing the history of San Jose, the college, and the building. The building had been erected in 1909 by the Knights of Columbus, at a time when the concept of campus ministry was in its infancy. This was one of the earliest Newman Centers anywhere, second only to Berkeley in California. In those days, San Jose State was primarily a normal school. Its largely female population had used the Newman Center mainly for theatricals and social events.

The women, delighted at last to have a priest, were anxious to discuss the program for the students. However, there was no way to deal with this matter until I had been on the scene for a while, learning my way around the campus and getting the feel of its life. We looked over the interior of the building to see what improvements should be made when possible. We parted after a couple of hours, aware that not much more could be done until fall. They promised that when I came, they would do all they could to support my work, especially by providing the funds for it.

I returned to Sacred Heart somewhat awed by the magnitude of my new job. Not only did I have to make contact with a large student population—my "parish"—but I also had to make the building attractive and useful for our purposes. Even though I did not have a plan of action as yet, I was still excited by the challenge.

My appointment did not become effective until the week that the college opened. I was ready to move, and on September 16, 1950, I drove directly to St. Patrick's Church, where I was assigned to reside. It was just five blocks from the Newman Center—a pleasant walk, but far enough to make my work distinct from that of the parish.

Jim Brown, the Archdiocesan Superintendent of Schools who had invited me to take on this work, had warned me that I must avoid becoming entangled in the affairs of the parish. I was to say Mass, hear confessions, and preach in my turn; and once every three weeks I would have sick call and baptism duty on Sunday. These responsibilities were spelled out, so that the pastor would be unable to keep adding duties which would make me effectively his assistant.

I was met by Vernon, my predecessor at the Newman Club. A friendly, confident man about my age, he was senior assistant at St. Patrick's at this time. He showed me to my room. It was a small one (a guest room) at the head of the stairs. Like all the rooms, it contained a mammoth double bed, occupying over half the floor space. (I always wanted to ask someone why we had such big beds for a bunch of celibates!) Vern had supervised the construction of the quite new rectory, which was comfortable, but lacking in grace or charm. The furnishings were as predictable as those in a furniture showroom.

Vernon also showed me St. Patrick's Church, which was next door to the rectory. The church was shingled on the outside and panelled inside with large sheet metal plates stamped in a floral pattern. The altar was of wood, old fashioned and ornate. The confessionals stood separate from the walls and were too small to allow comfortable legroom. As a whole, the church was quite ugly, but its ambiance was warm and reverent.

Later, at dinner time, I met the pastor, Monsignor Ed Maher. He was about the age of Bob Sampson, but he did not stay in bed. He tottered into the dining room in his seedy cassock with its monsignorial red piping, topped off by a misshapen biretta. Vern had said that Maher was reputed to have been a harsh boss at one time. But now his voice was deep and muffled, his eyes rather blank. As he had grown frail, Vern had become, in effect, the administrator. But the old man welcomed me kindly, vaguely expressing the hope that my new work would prosper.

The third member of the staff was Bill Flanagan, who had just moved out of my room into larger quarters vacated by the transfer of another assistant. Bill had been a classmate of my brother's at the seminary, but he was not one of those seminarians who had shared in the building of the family cabin at Silver Lake. I had never felt much in common with him: he played cards for recreation and chewed a cigar! But I found him to be a pleasant, good-humored companion around the house, easy going in manner, laughing off the trivial interruptions that characterized every rectory and the personality problems that we had to deal with.

Sunday after the Masses were over and we had breakfasted, I asked Vern to show me around the Newman Center. Like all old buildings, it had its peculiarities, such as rather inadequate rest-rooms and strange little cubicles under the stage. Vern seemed eager to share his knowledge and was not jealous of my taking over. But he wanted to be sure that I understood every detail, so that I could continue his high standard of watchful care for the place. No doubt that was one reason why the students had not come around in droves: he seemed all too protective of the property.

On Monday morning, eager to forget about Vern's regime and to make my own plans and independent discoveries in this new environment, I left St. Patrick's after breakfast and walked to my office. The building was, of course, empty and musty as it had been in July, except for my office, where I had brought my books, type-writer, and other equipment the night before. I ordered a phone installed and did a little cleaning.

Then I went out and stood on the sunny street corner, watch-ing the students come and go on their first day of classes. Soon three young men approached me, and rather timidly asked if I were the new chaplain for the Newman Club. They had heard that a priest was to be appointed to work with Newman full time.

Their names were Fred, Tony, and Sal—all with Italian sur-names. They had been elected last May to be officers of the Newman Club for the year, Fred being president. They were eager to see the Newman Club a success, but had not idea how to begin. They were hopeful that I could give them ideas and direction: any support from me would be welcome. Although I knew as little as they did, I found it comforting to sense their commitment to the work ahead.

I learned from them that we could obtain from the college a list of all students who indicated Catholic as their religious prefer-ence on their registration forms, a list which would be valuable in recruiting Newman members. It was almost like being given a par-ish census.

I did not learn much about the three students on that first morning, but I knew that I liked them. They were friendly and respectful, and I thought that we could work together well. They soon went on about their business, and I returned to the hall. But the meeting had given me a point of contact with the work ahead. Newman was no longer just a building, but a group of people, how-ever small.

A little later, I walked across the campus to the "Student Y," a building maintained by the YMCA and the YWCA as a social center for Christian students. There I met the young minister in charge, Jim Martin. He was kind and helpful; he was, I realized, a colleague, the first non-Catholic clergyman with whom I had ever had occasion to collaborate professionally. Doing so was far easier and more natural than I had expected.

I learned from Jim that the college regarded the non-denominational "Y" as the appropriate place for the religious preference files to be kept, where everyone would have equal access to them. However, since there were over two thousand Catholic cards in the file, and I would be the only person who would wish to use them, he permitted me to take them back to the Newman Center for more ready access.

Walking back across the campus, I began to appreciate its beauty. Only two or three new buildings had been added to the original plan of the college, and most of the six square block area had been landscaped in grass and fine old trees. Although I still knew no one and had no identity, except what my black suit and Roman collar provided, I already began to feel, after my visit with Jim at the "Y," that I belonged here. He had said that he was glad that I made contact, and he seemed eager to assist me in finding my way in this new world. I went home with a feeling of fresh energy for the work ahead: I was no longer an outsider looking in!

Soon afterward, a student phoned from the "Y," asking if I would permit the use of the Newman Center for a freshman dance that very evening. The "Y" had no large hall, and the freshman orientation committee had been unable to find any place to hold the event. Unaccustomed to making decisions on my own, I gulped and said yes. I wondered if I were violating any rules. Moreover, the place was not cleaned up yet; I didn't even know where the fuse boxes were or brooms were kept. At dinner, Vernon assured me that I would be sorry: the kids would tear the place apart.

However, I had done the right thing. At eight o'clock students began to arrive in large numbers, along with all the Deans, acting as chaperones. The hall was soon jammed, and no one seemed concerned that it was not elegant or even well cleaned. I met scores of students who said they would be joining the Newman Club; and the Deans and student leaders were most appreciative of my willingness to let the place be used. Clearly this dance had been a providential opening for my work at San Jose State. It established me, and through me the Newman Club, as an integral part of the campus, not just a Catholic ghetto on the fringe of college life.

However, after the excitement of that evening, the next few months were not so easy. The first Newman meeting was attended by some one hundred fifty students, many of whom bought memberships. They danced and played ping-pong all evening. But their involvement was superficial, and in many cases it soon gave way to other aspects of college life—studies, of course, fraternities, and sports. Many Catholic students said they had been instructed before leaving home to "join the Newman Club" as an antidote to religious or moral deterioration. And they did so, but having joined, they did not follow through.

On the other hand, the three men that I had met the first day were constantly there. Newman was their primary allegiance at college, and they were soon joined by a dozen or so others of similar commitment, forming the nucleus of a small but vigorous club. We scheduled social and educational events, and even when the attendance dwindled with the passing weeks, we met regularly in earnest sessions to plan and to dream.

Also quite early in my career in San Jose, I was provided with an activity apart from my Newman work which offered a new challenge: it was teaching. There was a Catholic girls' high school a few blocks away run by the Sisters of Notre Dame. Almost as soon as I was settled in San Jose, they had called me with the request that I should teach the senior course in religion once a week. My text was to be the papal encyclical letters on the principles of social justice, communism, education, and marriage.

As always, I enjoyed a new situation, a new set of people, a new activity. However, teaching this course proved difficult as I struggled to translate the ponderous "Vaticanese" language into terms that would be significant to high school girls. I taught the course for eleven consecutive years, and it became enjoyable for me, and I hoped for the girls too, when I cut loose from the text and dealt with a wide variety of concrete contemporary problems as they came up in current periodicals and in my own experience.

Besides this weekly task (for which I was not paid), I was hired to teach two courses at the O'Connor School of Nursing, also a Catholic institution. The subjects were basic psychology and medical ethics for nurses. The former took a lot of research, since my seminary training had provided very little background in this area. The latter, although more specialized than my moral theology course of long ago, was easier to teach since an excellent textbook was available to use. I really enjoyed meeting weekly with these eager young nurses, and the $10 a week that the school paid me doubled my income.

Except for days on which I had a class to teach, my only routine was provided by coming to the hall in the morning and going home at five. For several months I had difficulty dealing with this lack of structure for my days. Most of the time, I sat in my office, smiling at the passing crowds through the large window, reading and writing and waiting for people to drop in. Some did, of course, for personal and academic counseling, and for help with religious-oriented material in their courses. Some just wanted to relax and visit. Every day I brought my lunch in a bag and ate with whichever students were in the Newman lounge. Many who commuted from nearby towns made use of the Newman Center as a hangout between classes—a cozier version of the student union.

As the afternoons wore on, I would grow weary of my stiff collar and suit, so that it was a pleasure to walk back to the rectory and go up to my quiet room. Away from the late afternoon bustle of the rectory, I would lie down on my big bed for a rest before dinner, a private escape into an article or book, preferably something restfully objective, such as science or the outdoors.

During the whole first year at Newman, I struggled with the question of precisely what my job was as a college chaplain. I knew no one to whom I could turn for a model in this special ministry. It seemed to have three distinct parts. One, familiar from parish life at Oakland, was simply to be available as a counselor for those would seek my help, the way Father Cronin had helped me many years before. This was always an interesting and satisfying part of my work when people came, but there were all too few.

The second task was to build a Newman Club which would provide a "home away from home" for the Catholic students: in a sense, a mini-parish with all the social and educational activities they might wish. The third task was to reach the rest of the campus community in any way I could: to bring them back to the church if they were no longer going to church, or to give them a first contact with the faith.

It was the second of these three which was the focus of my attention during the first year at San Jose State College. Since the Newman Center had no chapel, my program could not include religious services: the students had to seek those in their own parishes. But the effort to provide a club with a strong cohesive core was successful. It grew in size as its spirit became established, and toward the end of the year, there was a hotly contested election for Newman offices. The hall was plastered with signs and mobiles, and Tony, second of my original trio, was chosen to replace Fred as president.

An enthusiastic group was ready to start off the next September in high gear.

I became increasingly fond of the students in the inner circle. They were in a sense my family; I was proud of them, much as I imagined a paternal father would be of his own children, and interested in all their doings. I loved to tell of their activities and to describe their talents, generosity, and humor when I visited my parents and Aunt Minna, usually after Masses were over on Sunday. While driving to Palo Alto for our early afternoon dinners, sometimes at Minna's and now more often at my parents' home, my mind was often full of stories that I was eager to share with them.

About Bill Starrs, the New York street kid who returned to the Church after reading the *Catholic Worker* in the Newman lobby, and went on to marry and raise eleven children while teaching on the Navajo Reservation. . . Shirley Williams and Bobbi Hodge, Diane Reese and Jackie Graham, all energetic and open-minded, lovers of the outdoors, the last two of whom were destined for the convent. . . Sal Giammona, my third president, whose gentle pessimism was belied by his skill and gallantry on the dance floor. . . Fred Vertel, who worked in his father's grocery store, and sometimes brought his Hammond organ to the hall, where he would play all evening any tune that was asked for. . . Audrey Gilpin, Gracie Richardson, and Carol Brown (nicknamed "Brownbird"), who were a witty, light-hearted, and undauntable trio, pitching in on everything that was happening.

As I told my tales of student life, Dad, typically, said little, but smiled a lot. He loved the funny things, like the the time Fred, who had just bought a big old Oldsmobile, brought it down to the club to show it off. Demonstrating how large the trunk was, Fred—who was six foot three—had climbed in and shut the top of the trunk. As we stood around admiringly, we heard a muffled call for help, "I have the keys in here!" We were horrifed. The everybody started shouting directions until he managed to poke the keys out through the upholstery. As I described the predicament, Dad laughed so hard that he had tears in his eyes.

Minna listened attentively to everything I recounted, her slight smile revealing her sympathy for all our youthful activities. This was a time in her life when she seemed to be growing more youthful herself, less inclined to judge, more able to have fun. Each summer now she was with us at Silver Lake, truly happy to be included, yet enjoying the privacy of her own little tent, never needing to be entertained.

It was fun now to share things with Minna, whether in the mountains or at home. When I was talking about the students, she always wanted to get things straight: "Who did you say that was?" she would demand. "Where did you go on that trip? . . . What was that convention for?" I was pleased to repeat when necessary so she could get a picture of what was happening in my life.

After one Sunday dinner and my usual collection of Newman stories, she invited us to see the photographs she had taken on a mountain trip in that summer of her seventy-sixth year. She could hardly wait for Mother to finish dessert; she was always last. Standing up briskly, Minna said, "Let's go into the parlor and see my pictures." She had been on a two-week high country adventure with Joe Wampler, a professional guide, for which she had had a wonderful time outfitting herself with the best equipment. "Look, there's my horse!" she said handing a picture to Mother. "I never rode him, I just wanted to have him along in case." The tight-lipped smile with which she told her tale showed intense delight in the accomplishment, and in being among the initiates of the truly High Sierra.

Mother responded to my stories of San Jose State in her usual social way: "Jack, you should bring some of the boys and girls for an evening here. I'd love to hear Fred play, and meet all of them." I took her invitation to heart, and we had several evenings of music and conversation at my home. Always the hostess, Mother greeted everyone warmly, made sure the fire was lit and food available; then she would withdraw to the kitchen, where she could still listen to the sound of music and laughter without interfering. Under Fred's versatile hands, the piano came to life, and we had lots of singing, led by Jackie's strong soprano. I loved bringing my two families together.

Surrounded by interesting and active young people, I found that the days were becoming filled with energy and promise. Music and good talk and people coming and going had always been an important part of my life at home. Now laughter and activity filled the cavernous old Newman building. I felt happy and at home at the Newman Center.

With my hearty encouragement, hikes began appearing in our calendar. We visited such places as the redwood forest of Muir Woods across the Golden Gate and the lava formations of Pinnacles National Monument south of San Jose. These outings were always a social success as well as a chance for me to teach people about the plants and rocks of the area.

In May of that first year we held a mammoth barbeque in the Mt. Hamilton foothills at a ranch belonging to Mary Costa, an aunt of one of our members. The picnic site was in a grove of oaks beside a lovely clear stream, where a small dam had been built to make a swimming hole. Mary Costa and her two nephews had made a little screened kitchen house and slab dance floor in the middle of the grove, and picnic tables were scattered about. There were also several horseshoe pits and a nearby field for playing ball.

The barbecue itself, managed by Sal Marvaso, was delicious. He loved to be cook and to yell directions at everyone! The stream was filled with squealing, freezing swimmers; a baseball game was organized; and small groups wandered off to explore the ranch roads in the hills. Everyone agreed that it was a great day: a tradition was born. Each Memorial Day the Newman Club had the exclusive use of the picnic area, and a long row of cars bumped over the hill and down the dusty road to the shady grove. The place was all ours, except for a few cows who gazed at us as we passed.

Such outings provided me with an opportunity to talk about the High Sierra, to share with the young people my specially remembered campsites and the lore of the glaciated rocks and cone-bearing trees of the mountains.

In my enthusiasm, I invited a few of the Newman faithful to visit Silver Lake during the summer, when I would be there on vacation with my family. As the time approached, I saw that my parents were anxious to preserve their privacy, so I decided to have the students camp on a large island a quarter of a mile from my family's camp. This had been the site of Camp Treasure Island for Boys for several years before the wartime gas rationing caused its failure. Since then, the place had been unoccupied, and the buildings were collapsing.

The island was perfect for the students. They enjoyed a sense of possession and the adventure of having to go and come by canoe or boat. Those of the group who returned to school in the fall shared their mountain experiences with other Newman members, and it was decided to incorporate a Silver Lake trip into the program for future years, scheduling it right after graduation so that everyone could take part before leaving for the summer.

One of the hard things about Newman work in the early years was that I knew no other priests in campus ministry with whom to share ideas and problems, and from whom I could draw encouragement. But in the spring of 1952, my second year, I found the answer to my isolation when our Newman Club was invited to attend a state convention. By that time we had a strong club and were eager to go and to compete for honors.

This meeting, and the other conventions which followed it, brought together the most active and enthusiastic student leaders from many universities and colleges up and down the state. They took me to many campuses I had never seen—Chico State and Fresno State in the north and south parts of the Central Valley, the University of California at San Diego, and also the University of Nevada at Reno—and entailed lively days of meetings and social events.

There were lectures on eveything from liturgy to fundraising to inter-faith relations. Much of the time, the students were absorbed in amending constitutions, and they were forever producing idealistic resolutions on social issues, which were seldom consulted until the next annual meeting. Intense regional politicking went into the choosing of new officers for the student federation.

What mattered to me was not the agenda, but the great young people and delightful priests who attended these conventions. Friendships were formed which carried on from year to year, and reciprocal invitations were extended where the distance allowed. Unfortunately, Stanford, our nearest neighbor and one of the major universities in California, was conspicuously absent from these gatherings.

In 1955, the national convention was held at the University of Colorado in Boulder, and we decided to take part. The trip, my longest drive up to this time, was spiced by the fact that Father Dwyer, the chaplain at Sacramento State, also went with a group from his school. We drove together and stayed together. There were ten of us from California, and we had a wonderful time. It was my first experience of the Rocky Mountains and the desert of the Great Basin. The week-long conference was a feast of interesting talks and stimulating people, including chaplains from Vermont and Louisiana, Texas, and Chicago, some of whom had been many years in the Newman movement. They were the most exciting group of priests I had ever been with, open to all kinds of fresh and new ideas and even aware of the larger world outside the Catholic Church. I found great companionship with them.

The third part of my campus ministry—after personal counseling and the lively growing Newman Club—was the effort to reach the vast majority of students who were, at least in name, Catholic, but who seldom or never approached the Newman Center. This task corresponded to the census work in a parish, or to the missionary work of the Church. I felt a pastoral duty to reach these students,

97

but they obviously did not feel a need of my service. Clearly, if I was to be of any help to them, I must first be known as an approachable person and one who would take their questions seriously. I tried to achieve this by appearing on campus whenever some event provided an excuse: a lecture, a concert, or a theatrical performance. I wanted to be seen and known as a priest whom they could like and respect. To be identified, I always wore my clerical suit.

In this effort, I found increasing support and assistance from the non-Catholic clergy who were also working at San Jose State. We shared the same hopes and the same frustrations. Only rarely did we sit down for deep theological or personal sharing, but we worked well together under the consistent and amiable leadership of Jim Martin, the Student Y Director. The "umbrella" of our ecumenical cooperation provided the legally acceptable framework for the college administration to sponsor religious programs, and the major focus of our efforts was an annual "Religion in Life Week."

During this week we were able to use college facilities, college speakers, and college publicity, and to offer a slate of "religious experts" to address living-groups or classrooms at their invitation. I loved being one of these "experts!" As many as twenty separate and diverse invitations came my way in the course of such a week. It was exhausting, exciting, and satisfying, uncovering the enormous curiousity about religion in so many students whom I otherwise never saw. There was no way to be fully prepared for these many short-notice invitations; I had to rely on general background and wit—a challenge which was in many ways the high point of the year. Academic expertise and precision were much less important than spontaneity and honesty.

We found that it generally did not pay to bring into our pro-gram any clergy from the "outside." They did not know the college world and only looked ridiculous. One year, Diane, the bright-eyed, purposeful girl who was our representative to the ecumencial plan-ning committee, had obtained as keynote speaker for the week a priest who was a superintendent of Catholic schools, a hearty, ath-letic man with a Ph.D. from University of California at Berkeley. She was worried about having a small turnout for this event. That even-ing, after dinner at St. Patrick's, the visitor and I entered the room to find the usual devout and loyal members of the various religious clubs. However, we were soon glad the crowd was small.

The speaker began by saying that he planned to address mod-ern moral dilemmas in the light of religion, but within minutes it was painfully apparent that he was simply giving a Catholic sermon. The hall grew very quiet. The concluding applause was politely brief.

People dispersed quickly, permitting the speaker to "hurry back to the city." I realized that Newman work gave us a different consciousness than that of most priests, however well educated.

Although most of my attention was focussed on the various phases of campus ministry, I also had weekend work to do at the parish where I lived. In the beginning, I did just the minimum; but as the months passed, I began to know the people, a large, loyal community not unlike the one in Oakland, and to enjoy meeting them outside of church on Sunday morning. This time was a welcome link to the old days of parish life. Most of the people saw me simply as a member of the staff, and greeted me accordingly.

As always, I truly enjoyed preaching. I also realized that what I said from the pulpit was a way to reach the many students who lived in that neighborhood and were not accessible to me through the Newman Club. I tried to present to all my audience interesting and unpredictable material, rather than the familiar rounds of Catholic doctrine and scriptural commentary, which were everywhere the regular Sunday morning menu. I liked to use articles I had found on current happenings in the Church and about social issues of the day. My favorite periodicals were *America*, published by the Jesuits, and *Commonweal*, a lay-edited magazine.

Living at St. Patrick's gave me an unexpected and enjoyable glimpse of another aspect of priestly work: a rural parish. St. Patrick's had at one time embraced much of the Santa Clara valley when it was all orchards and farms. As the population had grown, new parishes were created to serve the neighborhoods, but some rural parts remained, and one of these was Almaden, a tiny community set in the hills sixteen miles south of San Jose.

There was a little chapel there, St. Anthony's, and the clergy of St. Patrick's took turns saying Mass there at nine o'clock every Sunday. It was a pleasant drive through the apricot orchards. St. Anthony's was a typical country church, sitting on a weed-grown slope in the shadow of a mountain, and was heated by a wood stove in winter. There, a small but extremely faithful group of people gathered for Mass. Half of them were named Pfeiffer. They would linger and visit after Mass, as the sun came over the hill and warmed the dewy grass outside. I loved my Sundays there. The atmosphere was much like my beloved Sierra foothills near Jackson.

In 1951, I received notice from the Archbishop's office that my room at St. Patrick's was needed for someone else, and that I must move to another San Jose church, named (like my Oakland parish) Sacred Heart. I was annoyed that this new location was almost a two-mile drive from the College, but it proved a very pleasant place to live.

My brother, who was now a chaplain in the Air Force stationed at Kwajalein in the South Pacific, had been there on his first assignment in the mid-1940s, and through him I knew Charley Hardeman, the pastor, who had grown up the oldest of twelve children on the sand dunes of western San Francisco before the 1906 Earthquake. Charley's presence in the house was more like a grandfather than a pastor. Indeed, this parish house felt more like a home than any other that I had been in. Before meals, he would always smoke his cigar and read the paper as we gathered in the dining room, which was full of good smells and cheerful chatter coming from the kitchen.

Charley's easygoing manner in the house was in sharp contrast to the tough, no-nonsense attitude he showed with the people. For example, he might look out the window and spot a dissheveled individual approaching the rectory. He would suddenly exclaim, "Katie, let me take this one," and he would go to the door with battle in his eye. He had been earning money by the time he was nine, and as a result, he had no patience with "bums."

Katie, the housekeeper, was the mother and wise-woman to all the priests who ever lived there. I found that, without being bossy or intrusive, she took care of whatever needed doing at Sacred Heart, from the mending to the money, and from cooking to counseling. Her loyalty to Father Hardeman was boundless. When I got to know her well I learned her story. She had been a farm wife in South Dakota and was widowed suddenly by an accident. She had come west with her two remaining children and found a job in the town where Charley was then pastor. He had asked her to be his housekeeper, and when he was transferred to San Jose he suggested that she come too and bring the daughter who was still with her. By the time I knew her, the daughter had married Charley's nephew, and was living a few blocks away. Katie's presence made the rather small rectory a cozy home, and I was happy there.

Although my primary attention was on my work at the College, the time I spent at Sacred Heart was sufficient to make me aware of the special quality of this parish. It was in a largely Sicilian neighborhood of small houses surrounded by flourishing truck gardens. The women, always in black, walked ten feet behind their fierce-looking husbands on the streets but never stopped talking to them. Although these women came to church, the men, if they came at all, stayed outside. These people gave very little money, and it was reputed that their hostile demands and failure to cooperate had driven several previous non-Sicilian pastors to heart attack, nervous breakdown, or resignation.

But Father Charley let them know that he was different. Shortly after his arrival in the parish, he called a meeting and announced that the people had better not try anything with him because he knew that many of them were not legally in the country. He might not be Sicilian, but he was going to be too tough for them to drive out.

There was an annual ritual among these people of creating home altars to St. Joseph on the nineteenth of March. I first encountered this custom one day when Mrs. Roster had gone over to her daughter's home for a visit. Alone in the house, I answered the phone and heard a woman's voice. Without introductions, she demanded, "Fath', today you bring'a twelve altarboy to bless'a my altar!" Her tone permitted no excuses. Wondering what to expect, I managed to find one boy. Together we went to her house a few blocks away, where we found the most amazing edifice filling most of the front room.

Spread out on several tiers of the altar were statues, candles, and crucifixes, and around them, mounds of Italian breads and confections, baked fishes, and fresh and candied fruits, most of which looked as if it had been prepared some days before. The lady insisted that I bless this array—she was not particular about how it should be done—and that we then help consume it. At this point, I saw the reason for wanting twelve altar boys! We nibbled what we dared and quickly departed in peace.

In spite of Sacred Heart's homelike atmosphere, it was still too far from the campus. I had prized the convenience and freedom of walking to and from Newman Hall whenever I wished. In addition, the area around St. Patrick's was like an extension of the college, with boarding houses lining the streets for blocks, from which many students walked to church for Sunday Mass. Living there meant being in the middle of the college life. Accordingly, I wrote letters now and then to the Archbishop asking for reassignment to St. Patrick's.

In 1956 after more than four years at Sacred Heart, I was granted my request to return to St. Patrick's. Vern had meanwhile been replaced by Jim O'Malley, whom I found very congenial; and Bill was now acting administrator to the old Monsignor, who was increasingly feeble.

Instead of my little guest room, I was now assigned a regular suite across the hall from Jim. I no longer closed my door to read before dinner, but listened to the calypso beat of Harry Belafonte's records, and sometimes went over to Jim's room to enjoy the friendly warmth of his personality. Without perhaps appreciating fully what my student family meant to me, Jim gave an interested and uncritical ear and was glad to talk about the people he was working with and his own ideas for talks and sermons.

Perhaps the last person that ever came to the old Monsignor for convert instructions was a professor of German at the college. He came every Thursday in the late afternoon for these lessons, and then stayed to dinner! We found him entertaining, with his poetry, his strong opinions, and his insistent questions. For a while, until we became aware what was happening, he even had us all running errands for him. But it was too much of an invasion, and we began skipping dinner on Thursday nights.

In spite of the congenial atmosphere of the rectory and also in spite of the thriving Newman Club that we had developed, there were still problems to be dealt with. One of these was money.

One of the problems of having little money was the maintenance of the old Newman building. In order to eke out my meager income, I sometimes rented the facilties for wedding receptions. On some of the more riotous occasions, it took me hours of messy, tedious work to clean up—far more than their deposit would have paid for if I had hired a janitorial service. A solution seemed to offer itself when a near-starving student asked if he might live in the Newman basement in return for cleaning. There were several tiny cubicles, intended originally as stage dressing rooms, barely sufficient to hold a bed; in one of these he was installed. Later, another student who needed a cheap room was similarly housed, and I began to worry about what city codes I might be violating.

One day Willi, the professor who dined at St. Patrick's, came to ask that I provide a room at Newman for still another needy student. He had somehow learned about the illegal cells in my basement and thought rather presumptuously that one of them would be just right for a Greek whom he was sponsoring to study here. I remonstrated that I could not take another person, and Willi went away. But a few minutes later a truck arrived and unloaded a bed at our front steps: it was destined for "Nick." While I was arguing with the driver, Nick arrived strolling down the street, and cheerfully addressed me in what he assumed to be English. Since neither of us understood the other at all, Nick smilingly accepted my unwilling hospitality and moved in. It took two months to dislodge him, after many visits to the professor. But as it turned out, Nick became a good friend for the several years he remained in California.

Financial insufficiency had plagued me though all the years in San Jose. There was never enough to pay my full salary, or to subsidize students going to conventions, much less to renovate the ancient building and its furnishings. From my contact with chaplains from other dioceses, I knew that it did not have to be that way. Some of them received generous allotments for the work of their Newman apostolate, on the reasonable theory that Newman Clubs could not be self-supporting. The Women's Guild struggled valiantly, but their efforts netted no more than $2500 a year. As the Club grew in the scope of its activities, the inadequacy of the funding became ever more obvious.

At one point I made an appointment to see Archbishop Mitty, in the hope of a small subsidy. Like a mighty corporation president, he occupied the big office at the end of rows of closed doors, protected by a phalanx of priest-secretaries. Entering, after a long nervous wait, I met his cold grey eyes and found no comfort. Without waiting for a word from me, he remarked in his nasal voice, "I believe, Father, that you owe me $76,000." Needless to say, my planned appeal died on my lips. He pulled out a file showing me that the mentioned sum had indeed been loaned by the Archdiocese to the Knights of Columbus for the building of Newman Hall nine years before I was born and had never been repaid.

My only defense was to hand him my balance sheet for the past five years, carefully prepared to show my annual income and expenses in a half-dozen categories. He read it with lightning comprehension, then smiled and stated in his flat voice, "Obviously, you can't pay it." The rest of the interview was pleasant as he inquired about my work. However, he gave me no money.

There were other matters besides money which demanded contact with the Chancery Office. I needed various permissions to carry on my daily work. In Oakland, I only needed to deal with the Office over marriage problems, but now there were other things. In those days, clearance from the Archbishop was required in order for a priest to address any non-Catholic audience! Because of our ecumenical programs on campus, I often needed this permission. And to obtain it, I had to make the Office understand the special interdenominational spirit of a secular campus.

As these programs grew, it was impossible to seek a new permission for each speaking invitation, because of the necessity of being available to speak at a moment's notice. After several phone calls and letters, I finally won the "general permission" which I needed and felt immensely liberated by it. I could now say yes to all the invitations that came my way without having to worry about contacting the Archbishop's Office.

Now that I was not in the regular pattern of parish life, I kept encountering situations where the needs of the people conflicted with the demands of Church Law.

One day a young lady came in to discuss her wedding. She was a sorority girl, and the only Catholic in her house. She had picked four sorority sisters, all non-Catholic, as her bridal attendants. I wrote to the Office for her, seeking permission for this exception to the rule. It was denied, to her dismay. The advice the Office gave was to "find some nice Newman Club girls" to attend the bride, which obviously did not satisfy her. The Office didn't seem to understand that having strangers in her wedding party was out of the question. More phone calls resulted in the advice "use your own judgment," which I did.

A similar problem arose about the *Index of Forbidden Books*. At that time, the Index included a great many books that every college student had to read. The Law required that I obtain clearance from the Archbishop for every book and every student. Luckily, most people never thought of asking permission, but even the number of students who did so was sufficient to make the paperwork involved burdensome. Again, I assaulted the Chancery Office with my letters until someone got tired of me, and again I received a "general permission."

Dealing with the official Church and handling the finances were constant problems. But these administrative matters could not destroy the enjoyment I had in my youthful and enthusiastic Newman community. Moreover, the connection between my work with the students and my own lifelong love for the mountains was becoming stronger each year.

One of the great Silver Lake trips was held in June, 1955. On the last day of exams the Newman Hall was seething with preparations. A mound of groceries waited to be picked up by Walt in a borrowed truck. The complex task of finding rides for everyone at the right times had been accomplished, and the results posted on a chart. My car was the third to leave. My riders inluded a cheerful gnome-like fellow named Ray who made puns constantly; Barbara, a tall, strong girl one year out of the local Catholic high school; Charlotte, a graduate student in her twenties from Missouri; Jesse, a sardonic poker-faced Chicano from the Central Valley; and Annalee, a tiny, rosy girl who had never been in the outdoors before. Conversation remained lively in spite of the hot drive. School was out! We felt free and happy.

Through the mountains I gave my tour-guide commentary on the familiar, lovely route. We stopped for a relaxed country-style dinner at Cook's Station, twenty-five miles short of our goal. It was only 7 p.m. when we parked by the shore of Silver Lake and stepped out into the pure, pine-scented mountain air.

Two other cars were parked there. In a few minutes we set out along the shore trail. The occupants of the other cars were waiting outside at the stone cabin—Camp Shadow on the Rock, as our family called it. I unlocked the Dutch door, and we carried out the Old Town canoe that had been stored there all winter. The island lay only four hundred yards offshore; so, before returning to the cars for more baggage, I ferried the first few students to the island, leaving Joe and Hank in charge there to set up camp. Some people hiked back and forth to the cars carrying armloads of equipment, while I took two people at a time to the island. It was getting cold and dark by the time we were all at camp and the mountain of sleeping bags and food had been carried up from the shore.

Two fires were burning. Several students were already in their sacks. However, the evening was not over for me. A pair of car lights at the road bend high above the lake flashed on and off, signaling new arrivals. So I hopped in the canoe to pick them up.

In a moment I was out on the calm surface of the lake. The canoe, empty now except for me, moved swiftly over the slick dark water, which was broken only by the sparkles of light where I drew my paddle out of the water. The black silhouette of Thunder Mountain stood up against the starry sky. It was satisfying to be alone on the moonlit lake, quiet at last, able to feel the mystery of the mountains.

By the time I arrived, a carload of students and a truck loaded with the bulk of our food had reached the parking place and were waiting at the shore. Rejecting my suggestion that they sleep by the car till daylight, they insisted on completing the move immediately. So, I took one load back, and then crawled into my sleeping bag, dead tired. They worked till 4 a.m., as I learned later; and one girl was lost for an hour with her arms full of clothes and bags. Luckily it was a brilliant night, though cold.

The next few days were a time of blessed contentment. The sun was warm, the breeze soft and fresh, the lake deep blue. Wildflowers were just coming out, and the robins were singing their nesting songs. I loved to awake to their singing in the morning. We all spent much time on the rocks sunning, with an occasional brief, icy swim. Each day there were new arrivals to enliven our companionship, including two affectionate couples who made a separate camp in a nearby glade. Some eager groups went exploring, sometimes to check out the little store at the north end of the lake, or to take short hikes on nearby trails. Those remaining on the island helped by providing the ferry service. I remained on the island most of the time, content to play the role of host and dispatcher as they came and went. On the third day, Ted arrived with his motorboat, which greatly increased our collective mobility. In the evenings, after excellent meals cooked on three Coleman stoves by a horde of willing workers, we would sit around and sing by the fire, to the accompaniment of Carol's uke, the "green machine."

On Sunday I had to break the serenity of camp life with a business trip back to the Bay Area. Up at 5 a.m., I roused the camp with some help and celebrated Mass for the sleepy-eyed group. I used an improvised table in an open rocky area at the top of the island, as the rising sun poured through the pines and gilded the meadow where our camp lay. The students stood or sat on the uneven ground wherever they could see and hear.

Wearing my lightweight traveling vestments, I stood behind a rough table made of boards from the old boys' camp and gave a short sermon about the presence of God in nature. I wanted to make religion relevant to their wilderness experiences of the last few days. My theme was that nature worships God just by being what it is and that we translate that unspoken worship into language by our prayers. Then, taking the bread and wine from the table, I continued the offering of the Mass, using the tiny gold chalice given to me by the old Episcopal priest who had married my parents. At Communion time, the students picked their way among the bushes and logs to be accessible as I went to place the consecrated bread in their mouths. The spiritual closeness we felt was almost tangible.

After a quick breakfast, I left, along with three other people whose vacation was at an end. Ted ferried us to the car, where we met yet another group just arriving: Fred and his friends, who had been delayed a day while completing their fiber-glass canoe. They proudly lifted it down from the car and placed it in the water, where it sat like a feather on the surface. I had never seen anything like it before. It was almost transparent and proved to be almost as unsteady as it looked.

For Charlotte and Jess, this trip home was a farewell; both had finished college. We reminisced during the ride about the numerous events at Newman Club in which they had particpated. Reaching San Jose, I left them at their lodgings and quickly headed for Sacred Heart Church. The noon Mass was already in progress. Entering the rectory unobtrusively, I showered and changed and shaved in preparation for two weddings I was scheduled to perform.

The first marriage ceremony would have been simple, except that the organist had not been notified. After an awkward wait, we proceded sans music. As soon as it was over, I went on to St. Clair's Church in Santa Clara for the second wedding.

After this ceremony, I went to the rectory to make the usual entries in the marriage register. The Jesuit pastor, a massive, bear-like man with filthy fingernails, questioned me ponderously about my Newman work. When I told him my work included taking a group of students to the mountains from which I had just returned, he hinted broadly that I must have had a hard time handling the "moral problems" of a mixed group in the wilderness. Recognizing that he would have no comprehension of the spirit of the trip, I simply said I had no problems and left it at that.

As soon as I could escape, I headed for San Francisco to attend the welcome dinner for newly ordained priests, held at the the center built for Catholic sailors in the rundown South of Market district. As secretary of the St. Patrick's Seminary Alumni Association for that year, I felt it my duty to be present at the annual event, although large clerical parties were never to my liking. As it turned out, the evening was hilarious, largely thanks to Butch, my former companion at Sacred Heart in Oakland, who carried on a continuing charade of finding a hobo outside the hall who claimed to be an alumnus.

At 9:30 I managed to slip out, although I felt somewhat guilty for leaving so early. As soon as I was in my car, I was mentally back in the mountains. I headed for San Jose, where I got three hours of needed sleep, then picked up four new campers to take back to Silver Lake with me. Without the stimulus of their conversation, I could never have kept awake. However, it was only 7 a.m. when I tooted my horn from the special road-bend visible from the island. Ted was waiting with the boat when I parked the car.

Even back on the island, there was no time to catch up on rest. There were other newcomers to be greeted, including Ron ("Big Red"), who was loud enough to compensate for all who had left. Everyone was busy making preparations for the overnight pack trip which was to climax our stay in the mountains. During my absence, Audrey and Gracie had worked out the menu. There were twenty-two students who had decided to go on the hike, but it was a chaotic scene, and I was not sure who and what were going along until breakfast was over and we were actually on our way.

Four cars were required to get all of the hikers (plus return drivers) and their baggage to the trailhead, which was at the summit of Carson Pass. An hour after leaving camp, we were waving goodbye to the four drivers as we stood in the warm morning sunshine by the road on the brink of our adventure.

A picture was taken to record the start. Packs varied from a brand-new Kelty to an old canvas dunnage bag over the shoulder; clothes ran from bathing suits to arctic gear. Then off we went, up the winding trail to Winnemucca Lake. Before long Round Top Peak, heavily snow covered, came in view across the upland meadows.

It did not take long for our large party to divide itself into sections—the jackrabbits, the tortoises, and the regulars. I found myself trying to be in all three groups: to encourage the slow ones, to keep the speeders from losing the way, and to enjoy the company of the larger middle group. There was a fellow named Bob in the party who belonged to San Francisco City College Newman. He was very solemn and rather inarticulate, but ever cheerful and willing. I appointed him rear guard, and he proved to be utterly reliable.

We had lunch near the snowfields, and some of the group went glissading, to the delight of all. We then crossed a ridge and descended several hundred feet into the cirque where Fourth of July Lake lay. Long after camp was set up at the forested lower end of the lake, Bob arrived with the slower people. The sandy shore was peaceful, and the golden afternoon light came warm through the trees bringing out the strong forest smells. We lay around; a few swam—modestly, in their jeans; some fished. Gracie found a lovely ribbon snake, which frightened the usually imperturbable Norma out her wits.

Dinner was a disappointment. The rice was the kind that doesn't swell much, a fact unnoticed by those who planned the quantity. Salt and butter had been forgotten. And the fishermen had caught nothing. However, there were no recriminations, and the campfire was happy and companionable. As the moonlight cast the misty spell of its silvery light over the encircling cliffs and the calm dark lake, I sat up chatting with one fellow for a long time. Most of the campers were in bed, but we had no desire to close our eyes.

At breakfast time we found further deficiencies in the menu. There was no spatula to turn the hotcakes, no grease for the pan, and no syrup, jam, or sugar to put on them. Boiled raisins were offered as a substitute, but they did little to enliven the scrambled batter which passed for pancakes.

With the adventure of a trail-less route ahead of us, we packed quickly and started around the lakeshore towards the gorge which would offer the first stage of our hike back to Silver Lake. I led the way with gusto, and eventually all, even the most timid ones, were at the top of the long snow-filled cirque. Soon Silver Lake could be seen in the distance, looking fresh and cool as it shimmered in the afternoon light. From the ridge, I let everyone take his own pace down the clear trail toward camp.

When we arrived, we found that a volleyball game had been set up to pit the the Mountaineers against the Flatlanders—which was won (not surprisingly) by the latter. There were many Mountaineers with sore feet and achy muscles that night.

After a great dinner—anything would have seemed great after our trip!—we sat around fantasizing about how to convey the spirit of this week to the Newman Club and its new members when we reconvened in September.

As we broke camp next morning, everyone pitched in to carry the remaining supplies and bags of clothes down to the shore. It was apparent that many people who had been only casual friends a week before were now enjoying working together. We were united in permanent bonds by shared adventures and quiet conversations. This mountain experience (and others) did more than anything else to create, a strong cohesive Newman community.

After returning to St. Patrick's as my residence, I found that Monsignor Maher's aging was much more evident. He seldom left his room and depended heavily upon Bill Flanagan for everything. His death came quietly from no definite cause.

His place as Pastor and Dean of Santa Clara County was quickly filled by a man who had been the founding pastor of a new parish in Vallejo. Two of my friends, when newly ordained, had served under him, and they had liked his energy and organizing ability. We were, therefore, basically optimistic about his coming. But my immediate impressions were not good. He had an unctuous, fawning manner when he was trying to be pleasant, which made me distrust him. And he was just too big! Standing over six feet six— five inches above me—he was made even bigger by his full redpiped monsignorial robes and biretta, he seemed to fill the house. Moreover, his head was large and sat directly on his shoulders, so that his heavy jowls spread over his collar.

The real trouble was that he was very insecure. He felt under attack a great deal of the time, and his supposed attackers varied from day to day: the undertaker, the organist, the Mothers' Club president, the police. At the table, he would sit hunched forward over his food, glaring around, and fulminating over his latest outrage. Since no response was possible without taking direct issue with him, we all kept quiet and left the table as soon as possible. One could imagine him as a dictator, issuing random sentences of execution against all supposed enemies.

It was no longer a pleasure to go home at night, for it was impossible to be in the house without feeling the weight of his unhappy presence. However, I made sure that he understood the official immunity that I enjoyed. As I left the house after dinner to go back to the Newman Center, I would let him know my program: "Monsignor, I have a conference this weekend, so I can't be here for Mass." Not wanting to stir things up more than necessary, I would add, "I'm sorry if it is an inconvenience, but it's part of my work." He would growl a little and stare belligerently as I turned to go.

Unfortunately, besides the tensions at St. Patrick's, the fall of 1960 was a time of stress for me as I tried to find a solution for the financial problems of the Newman Center. The Women's Guild had continued through the years to hold benefits, such as card parties and fashion shows, raising perhaps $2,000 a year. In the early years this meager sum sufficed to pay my tiny salary and to take care of the buildings; program costs came from student membership dues. However, as the Club grew and the building aged, this sum became ever more inadequate for supplies, improvements, and travel expenses; and the women became increasingly embarrassed by the size of my salary. Something had to be done. They consulted the new Dean about having a drive, and he assured them that he "was right behind them."

Joined by their husbands, they began meeting to plan the campaign and gather names of likely donors, alumni for the most part. I attended their meetings as much as possible to show my interest and appreciation, but I did not want to get directly involved. One reason was that I didn't wish to take time away from my work with students, but I had also heard plenty about fundraising from other priests, and it sounded like an activity that would be totally alien to my nature. So I was more than happy to have the Guild undertake this project, and I put my faith in their ability to succeed.

However, I became concerned as I watched the lists of potential donors. If the ones I did not recognize were as unpromising as the ones I knew, I saw small hope of substantial results. Many were names I knew either from St. Patrick's or Sacred Heart, people who had little money or had never displayed any interest at all in my work at the Newman Club.

As I feared, they decided at the end of two months that they could not handle a campaign of this scope. No viable plan had been developed and no money had been collected. So they asked me to find a professional fundraiser to show them how to do it. I agreed, realizing that I could not avoid getting drawn into the fundraising effort.

I found them the name of a man who had recently conducted a similar campaign for a parish in the East Bay. We wrote to him, and on the appointed day, Mr. Farley arrived to look over the facilities and to discuss with the Guild his plan of action. He seemed very confident. Our goal was a modest $50,000, and he assured us that four to six weeks would suffice. He would stage the campaign, train Guild members for their work, process the pledges, and call upon major donors. The Guild could follow up afterward by collecting the pledged amounts. His salary would be $500 a week—about what I made in a year!

In late October he came to town, taking over a large part of the Newman basement for his office. He hired a secretary and put in another phone. Meetings with Guild members were held and charts were drawn up. More and more more names were collected from everyone, names of all those who might conceivably be interested in the welfare of the Newman Center, obviously the alumni, but also rich, elderly dowagers and prominent businessmen. Farley indicated that my role was only to go after the "big ones." The Guild members would do the rest.

But my misgivings, which began with hearing his salary, increased as the days passed and the pledges brought in were few and small. Farley began to realize the ineffectiveness of his team and to push me to do more and more. He would arrive early, and after a few minutes in his lair downstairs, would march into my office with a list of prospects to call on. Using my car (it took weeks to get the reek of his cigarettes out of it) we would set out on a daily round of calls.

It was a painful process. We called on many wealthy doctors, ranchers, and lawyers. My expectation that they would be indifferent to my Newman cause proved quite accurate. Most of them gave nothing. Only a few, mostly Protestant businessmen, were generous. But these weren't the only people on Farley's lists for me to see. He pushed me to the limits of my available time.

Some of the homes to which he directed me were those of people whom I had known as students. They were young and poor. And

111

although I could count on their interest in the project, I was embarrassed to ask them for money. Even with Mr. Farley constantly at my side, I could barely muster the courage to say why I had come to them. As could be expected, most of them, with their house payments and babies coming, were in no position to make a pledge.

It was a miserable two months. I dreaded the arrival of my "slave master" every morning. My general distaste for salesmanship soon grew into a real horror of asking people for money. I found myself hating Farley and the Guild—and even the Newman Center itself!

The Christmas holidays put a merciful end to the torture. With eight weeks gone, and $4,000 paid to Mr. Farley, we had netted only about $15,000. He laid out a plan for me to continue the drive after the New Year, but I knew in my heart that I would never do it. In fact, I swore to myself that I would never again do such a thing for any cause whatever!

It was an immense relief to ease back into my primary work, which was with the students, and soon after the holidays I plunged into it with renewed enthusiasm. The Newman Club became, once again, my own place—away from Tom Byrne, the new pastor—where I could enjoy the activities of my young friends and could await with eagerness the opportunities each day would bring.

In the late 1950s, the Federation generated a more seriously academic cooperative effort, a series of "Newman Schools of Catholic Thought." These were held in early summer, in a couple of centers around the country. They sought to provide a week-long intensive curriculum on current religious and philosophical matters. I was a faculty member and organizer of several of these—one in Los Angeles at Mt. St. Mary's College, one at the CYO Camp at the Russian River, and one at the Asilomar Conference grounds near Carmel. These weeks were more satisfying than any of my courses in the seminary had been.

As with all whose lives are governed by the academic calendar, I found a pleasant and reassuring rhythm in the events which recurred each season: the existing contact with the new-arriving students every September, some of whom would become Newman members and my friends and fellow hikers; the retreats and conventions and other regional gatherings; the election and training of Newman leaders, and the planning of new programs together; and of course, the weddings and graduations and mountain trips that came at the end of every academic year.

Life was full of people, some who were difficult and troubled, naturally, but many who were able students and devoted friends,

My mother
Dorothy Stillman, 1913 Stanford grad

My father
Robert Francis Duryea, 1913 Stanford

My parents at Lake Eleanor, Yosemite
Park, during June 1914 wedding trip

JD and mother, 1919, San Francisco

*John "Jack" Duryea and Bob jr.,
with Tippy, at Stillman campus home*

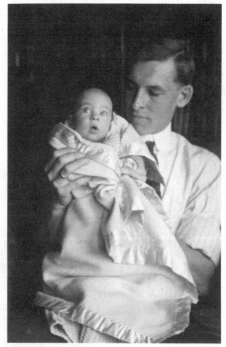

*JD, Bob jr. and Dad at Fanshell
Beach, Carmel, c. 1924*

JD with dad, 1918

JD, Dad and Bob jr. en route to
Santa Cruz; Los Gatos, near old
Linden Hotel, 1925

JD, Bob jr., and Mother at patio
gate of our Palo Alto home,
c. 1923

Jack and Bob jr. by the
pond in our Palo Alto
back garden, 1934

My class picture, Palo Alto High School, 1933 (JD at right end of row 2)

Dad carving bas-relief of "Wild White Horses of the Lord" (Kipling), c. 1940

Duryea cabin, Silver Lake, Amador Co., begun 1940, complete 1944

Mother and Dad on ridge above our Silver Lake camp, c. 1955

Mother and Dad and JD by our campfire, Silver Lake camp, c. 1965

Dad's art works

JD about to enter major seminary, in cassock and biretta, taken at our Palo Alto home, fall 1937

Aunt Minna, 1940-1950?

Newman Club camp at Treasure Island, Silver Lake; Duryea cabin in background, c. 1954

JD saying mass at Newman camp on island in Silver Lake, c. 1958

San Jose Newman Club camp at Silver Lake; using Duryea canoe, 1954-55

Newman Club group climbing Thunder Mountain, during Silver Lake camp, 1954

JD with Msgr. Stanley Reilly, wedding of
Frank Hill and Jane Davidson

A Stanford wedding, 1961
Simon and Therese Sze

A Newman Center wedding, Stanford, 1969
Tony Silvestri and Teri Hanzelka

A wedding, late 60s; Newman Patio, Stanford
Newman Center

A wedding in St. Ann Chapel, JD officiating with Robert McAfee Brown, 1969

A wedding at St. Ann's, 1968

JD in new tie-dyed vestment, in the Newman gardens, late 60s

Yosemite wedding, 1984

Student and her visiting family, after mass at St. Ann's, 1965

San Jose Newman ski trip, c. 1953

San Jose Newman backpackers, approaching 4th of July Lake, 1954

Members of St. Ann community (Paul Pitlick and Frank Koch) marching with the farmworkers to Sacramento, 1967

Renovating the bus for the trip to Michoacan, 1962

Stanford Newman group by the Stanislaus River, spring backpack, March 1972

JD taking pictures, Yosemite back country, August 1974

Stanford Newman group, spring backpack, March 1972; it began to snow

JD at the Newman Center, c. 1973 or 74

Brother Bob and wife Lu

Bob and John Duryea with parents, at their Golden Jubilee, 1964

Eve, 1976

people I was proud to know. Some who had been my Newman leaders a few years before, such as Tony, whom I had met on my first day in San Jose, and Bob Keller, who had been a Newman vice president the following year, were married now. I enjoyed visiting their homes, and baptising their babies.

However, as this cycle repeated itself again and again, I began feeling that I was stale, that I had no new ideas to try. Several of my priest classmates—we all met annually for a reunion on the day of our ordination—were now pastors in the Bay Area. Walt, who enjoyed the seniority advantages of a small diocese (Sacramento), had been a pastor already for a number of years. Perhaps it was time for me to move on, out of Newman work. I took the pastoral qualifying examination so that I would be in line for some worthwhile place.

Still another year went by with no sign of a change. Then it came, in June of 1961, as sudden and unexpected in its timing as it was surprising and gratifying in its substance.

I had returned from a week with the San Jose Newman group at Silver Lake, content in the prospect of a hot shower after the work of closing camp and the long drive home. My peaceful mood was suddenly shattered when the mother of one of the girls in my car ran out of the house with the news, "Father O'Malley announced at Mass this morning that you have been transferred!"

I was stunned. I didn't know whether to be terrified or pleased. She had no idea where I was going, so I hurried home to St. Patrick's to open the letter I expected to find waiting for me and to learn my fate. Fumbling through the pile of mail on my desk, I found the official document and tore it open. I was relieved and excited. My new post was to be the Newman Center at Stanford University!

I did not know much about life in that great university where I had been a student myself. Neither the chaplain nor the students from Stanford appeared very often at regional Newman events. The few Stanford students I did meet at conferences seemed smug and distant.

Yet I had wondered occasionally how it would be possible to make Newman work effectively there. I had grown up close to Stanford, where my grandfather had headed the chemistry department and where my parents and all their siblings had graduated. As a timid freshman in 1936, I had joined the Newman Club and struggled to find in it the moral support I so much needed at that point in my life. The feelings of alienation that I experienced at that time had cast a shadow which even twenty-five years had not dispelled. Now I would have the challenge of bringing my style of ministry into an environment so filled with past associations.

Not knowing what to expect, the day after receiving my letter of appointment I made a quick trip to visit the outgoing chaplain, Jack Tierney. His wish to become a pastor had been granted, and he had been assigned to a newly created parish in Marin County. During my short visit, he briefly told me about the history of the place and showed me where things were, but I also wanted to know about the people and the program of Newman at Stanford. In answer, he just referred me to the files. I left him feeling rather let down. He told me nothing that generated enthusiasm for the work ahead.

The next week was taken up with the diocesan retreat, which was held at St. Joseph's College in Los Altos. Never had I been so anxious to get it over with! Moreover, the retreat itself was dull. The weather was unbearably hot, and as the retreat master suffered, his wit and eloquence declined day by day. I asked the priests who knew Father Tierney for information about Stanford Newman. But I found little encouragement and almost no information. As always seemed to be the case, Newman work didn't interest them. However, they did say that money wasn't a problem there.

When the retreat was over, I wanted to hurry back to San Jose, but Stevens Creek Road was full of traffic, no longer the country lane between orchards that it had been when I was in the seminary. I had only hours left before being due at my new assignment in Palo Alto.

There was so much unfinished business in San Jose: so many people to see and to thank and to console, and so many notes to leave for my successor. After eleven years, many relationships were suddenly going to change; deep friendships would have to be maintained across a distance, and the work at San Jose would have to continue without me. I quickly called a few members of the Guild, the officers of the Newman Club whom I could reach, and some of the people I had just been with in the mountains. After packing frantically, I drove up the Bayshore Highway to Palo Alto.

Arriving with a carload of baggage, I parked on Cowper Street by the arched gateway into the Stanford Newman Center. The building was an elegant Spanish colonial residence, set among stately oaks and deodars. A long brick walk curved up to the arched entry, where a wrought iron gate stood open. Within was a patio, from which an outside stair led to balconies above. However, the patio fountain was dry, and the garden looked rather neglected. The heavy front door was not locked, and I opened it quietly, somewhat awed by the silence of the place. Inside was a spacious hallway, from which arched doorways led into other rooms, furnished with massive oak tables and benches and a few couches.

I climbed the front staircase looking for life, and heard water running. A bedroom door stood open. Father Tierney was shaving. As I waited for him, I looked into his adjacent sitting room. It was ugly and dark, with the furniture all pushed back against the walls as if no one lived there, and it was plastered with wedding photos—scores of them.

Soon he emerged from the bedroom, slipping his coat on. "There's a wedding for you at two," he said, and was gone. He was on his way to a new assignment. I was left in an empty hall, wondering what I was to do next, for I was now chaplain of the Newman Club at Stanford. Only a week before, I had no idea that I would be here.

That Saturday afternoon after arriving at Stanford Newman Center, I went out to the chapel to prepare for the wedding that was scheduled for two o'clock. The couple were Chinese students who were as unfamiliar with Newman as I was. However, the ceremony was very simple and went off to their satisfaction.

The next day was Sunday, with Masses to say and new contacts to make. I stood on the plaza outside the chapel until the last minute before Mass so that I might meet people as they came. I was surprised to find that the congregation was made up mostly of adults from Palo Alto. They welcomed me warmly and told me that they were regular patrons of the Newman chapel during the summer months, when Father Tierney allowed them to come. It had been his custom to send them off to their own territorial parishes as soon as the students began arriving for the fall term.

They were not able to tell me much about the work that lay ahead of me, but I did learn something more of the history of the facilities. The Newman Center itself had been the home of the author Kathleen Norris, her husband Charles, and their family. In the late 1940s it had been purchased by the Archdiocese for a Newman Center at the urging of Father Munier, who had replaced Father Cronin as assistant at St. Thomas Aquinas while I still was in the seminary. Munier was part-time Newman chaplain until in 1948 Father Tierney was appointed, shortly before my own appointment to San Jose, as the first full-time chaplain.

Soon after that, Claire Booth Luce decided to give a chapel in memory of her only daughter, Ann, whose tragic death had occurred while she was a Stanford student. The relationship of Mrs. Luce to

115

Stanford, and the building of the small but expensively decorated chapel of St. Ann on the grounds of the Newman Center, made national news when it was dedicated in 1952. The chapel had become a source of community pride, and buses frequently stopped to allow groups of tourists to look at the unusual stained glass windows.

In spite of the beauty of St. Ann's and the Newman Center, their location in Palo Alto, two miles from the university, interfered with their effectiveness as facilities for student work. Like the priests at St. Thomas in earlier years, Father Tierney found it difficult to get them to come so far from their snug academic ghetto even for Mass, much less for other events at Newman.

My first weeks at my new assignment, and indeed that whole hot summer, were a quiet time, well suited to gathering other information and impressions. My parents and many old friends came to visit, to inspect the place, and to make suggestions. Professors and graduate students, some of whom had been dissatisfied with the previous regime, came to look me over and to offer advice. San Jose friends came too, to see my new situation and to ask questions about how they might continue the program we had developed at State.

I thoroughly explored the grounds and buildings to assess their possibilities, cleaning out basement rooms and closets. The gardens needed a lot of work too. Although there was a gardener on contract, he did little but mow the big lawns and rake the leaves; so I did a lot of outdoor work in my spare time.

The most frustrating thing was the sparseness of the files: there were long lists of names, but very little to indicate what had been done and what plans were made for the year ahead.

I loved rearranging my room, making a cozy desk area in the corner by the balcony window, where the morning sun came in, and a comfortable visiting area with couch and chairs at the other end. I took down Father Tierney's vast collection of wedding pictures and boxed them for him to take away. In their place, I put up some of my mountain photos. The afternoon light on Upper Evolution Valley and a violent storm in the Lyell Fork Canyon above Yosemite were among my favorites.

As I had heard from Tierney at my first visit, several rooms in the house were rented to students. They were away when I arrived, because it was a weekend, but I met them at dinner on Monday night. Although they ate fast and talked mainly of sports, I found them to be a pleasant group. All were male graduate students at Stanford for the summer quarter.

116

I formed no strong bonds with these students, but I quickly found a good friend in our cook, Fern Brown. She had a room off the garage, where she had lived for several years. She assured me that life in the house would be much more lively when the fall term arrived, but her description of the "boys" made me think that Jack Tierney's choice of residents ran to "jocks" rather than scholars. It did not sound like the type of serious-minded community which I had known and enjoyed at San Jose State.

The first intimation of a really supportive group at Stanford came from an unexpected source. A married graduate student, who lived at the International House on campus, came one day to enlist my interest in a Christian Family Group which he and his wife had helped to organize among the married students in the English Department. Father Tierney had cautiously consented to the forma-tion of the group during the previous year. I enjoyed an evening with them and learned from them many things about life at Stanford, and about their perceptions of the Newman Club program. They felt that its emphasis fell too heavily upon rescuing the younger stu-dents from the assaults of unbelief and too little upon making a mature and respectable contribution to the academic world from the rich cultural heritage of the Church. They were the first people I met in my new community who seemed truly aware that the Church could be a positive force for good, rather than a fortress for the pro-tection of a set of beliefs.

Another group which welcomed me with open arms was the association of non-Catholic ministers who served the campus, which at Stanford called itself the "Clericus." One of the members telephoned the Newman Center about a meeting and cried in a hearty voice, "Glory be to God!" when I said that I would be glad to come. He was delighted that a Newman chaplain was finally joining their group. I was eager to find in this group a source of information They weand companionship as I had in San Jose. But I was disap-pointed. supposed policy of exclusion by the official university chap-lain, which they felt stood in the way of their work.

As a private institution, Stanford was not required by law, as San Jose State was, to remain aloof from all religious activities. However, Mrs. Stanford had created her own rules, one of which was that the Memorial Church, a magnificent building at the center of the campus, must remain at all times strictly nondenominational. Most of the campus community regarded this rule with cynical amusement, since the chaplain was clearly denominational—Angli-can—and the art and style of service there were very high-church. But Chaplain Minto himself took the matter very seriously and saw the presence of denominational clergy anywhere on the campus as an invasion of his territory.

Meetings of the Clericus were frustrating to me even when they stopped their political maneuvering and began talking of religion itself. They used a lot of Protestant theological jargon which seemed to me as remote from real life as the language of scholastic philosophy I had learned in the seminary. Sometimes they got caught in their own abstract verbiage and the whole discussion would come to an embarrassed halt because no one understood what the previous speaker was talking about. These colleagues were nonetheless sincere and kind people and became my friends.

Toward the end of summer, finding that my ties with the clergy were not bringing me any hope of closer relationships with the university, I began making my own contacts with various campus officials. I made appointments to visit the deans, and even Wallace Sterling, the university president. All were delightfully cordial and informal, and welcomed me to the campus as grandson of Dr. Stillman and as having in my childhood known David Starr Jordan, the first president. Many of them knew my Aunt Minna, who after retiring as document librarian, remained a beloved figure as she continued to work in various campus libraries. As a result of these meetings with the academic community, I did not share the feeling of exclusion which pervaded the meetings of the Clericus.

With the opening of the fall term, changes in the resident community at Newman demanded my attention. A group of students who had been living at Newman the previous year returned at the end of September, together with a few who were new to the house. They were different, in some subtle way, from the sort of students who had formed my community at San Jose State. As Mrs. Brown had implied, I found them something of a party crowd, and the conversation over the dinner table was mostly about football and other sports.

Unfortunately, I did not find in them the companionship I needed and hoped for as I started my first year of Newman work at Stanford. They did not appear very serious as students, nor did they seem serious about being at the Newman Center. I did not feel that they were seeking anything from me other than a place to live. The extent of our religious interaction was simply Mass on Sunday. Although they were a pleasant group, I could not feel close to them.

They must have felt a dissonance between their values and my expectations, for several moved away when the opportunity arose. But I did not have a problem keeping the house full. There were always students looking for rooms, especially such inexpensive ones, with a good cook to prepare the meals.

With each student who moved into the house, a new personality and new interests were added. They included Robin Nowinski, a big, blond athlete, always working out, who became a sensitive and loyal friend; Gabe Pinheiro, a wiry, dark grad student in Spanish, who eventually entered the seminary; Denis Tsao, from Hong Kong via St. Louis University, who was studying aeronautical engineering; and Angel Aguirre, a softspoken Puerto Rican who presented himself as a born loser, but who won everyone's heart; and John Antush, tall, clean-cut, an English major who, with a room near the kitchen, became a confidante for Mrs. Brown.

The dinner hour was increasingly enjoyable to me as the students lingered at the table to debate the merits of their various fields of study—particularly the contrast of the sciences and the humanities. When Gabe and John spoke in defense of human culture and the arts, Denis would be sure to point out: "Don't forget that we scientists know a lot more about the humanities than most of you humanists do about science." Philosophical debate of this kind was an integral element of student life, and it was satisfying to watch the community develop as these students got to know one another.

Naturally, once the summer was over, I was eager to get a Newman Club started, but I realized I should not burden members of the household with responsibility for it. I only hoped that the spacious house would provide the opportunity to bring students together as a community. In the beginning I could only take advantage of the contacts with students before and after Mass to find leaders for my Newman Club. But I only found a handful who showed any interest. I asked some of them to serve as "officers;" they were all graduate students.

Together with my few leaders, I developed a little program of social events and lectures to bring students together. Announcements were made at Mass, and ads were placed in the Stanford Daily. We found students in some of the dorms who would form ride-pools so that everyone could come to Newman more easily.

During the first few weeks, we were able to generate a modest amount of response, including some from members of my household, to our Newman Club program. However, the attendance diminished rapidly. The spurt of effort during the first few weeks was followed by almost total apathy. The leaders soon became busy with their academic work and disillusioned with the struggle to create a club. It was a time of discouragement for me, too.

In my concern to accommodate students who lived on campus, I decided to hold classes and discussions on religious subjects at some campus location, and I found that the Bowman Alumni House would permit this. The directors of Bowman did not feel that they were bound by the campus policy of excluding denominational activities. Much as I valued these courses as a symbol of offering an academically respectable program, the number who attended them was small.

None of the things I thought I had learned at San Jose seemed to be working in this new environment. At San Jose there had always been a large enough crowd that our program at least appeared to be successful, even though there were many we did not reach. But here there was no such crowd to make us feel we were accomplishing anything.

I was painfully conscious that I had not found a way to make my ministry to students effective here. The Newman Club had no image at Stanford. There were indeed some students who cared deeply for their religion, and some of them even came daily to Mass, but they expressed a general distaste for the clubby model of Newman which prevailed, of course, at most American campuses. Since all I could expect of most students was that they would attend Mass, I realized that this brief contact must be exploited to the full if these students were to retain their relationship with the Church. I decided to make sure I met them as they entered and left Mass, so that they would understand that I was accessible and interested in helping them in any way they might need me.

During this first difficult year, I was able to meet Mrs. Claire Booth Luce. I was eager to see this well-known woman who had done so much for the Newman Center at Stanford. She returned to Palo Alto, as she had done each year, and a special Mass for her was said in the Chapel on the anniversary of her daughter's death in early January.

That morning, she was already in the chapel, alone, kneeling very erect in the front row when I entered to prepare for Mass. Without having had an opportunity to know her, I wanted to fulfill whatever expectations she had for this event. Slight, and perfectly coiffed and dressed, she participated in the Mass with quiet dignity.

Afterwards, she stayed to visit with me, and I had a chance to tell her of my plans and hopes, to which she listened with careful attention. I took her on a little tour of the public rooms downstairs before sitting down in the library. Glancing at the worn couches and drapes, she remarked in a clear incisive manner, "Now that I have completed the chapel, I would like to see the house looking better.

You should get an interior decorator to make some plans, and send me an estimate." I was thrilled to hear that she was still willing to contribute to the Stanford Newman Center.

Shortly, I escorted her to the dining room where she was to have lunch with a group of students as she had requested. I had invited a few girls to come down from the campus to join our male household for this occasion. Mrs. Luce entertained the young people with elegance and grace, telling them of her work in government and diplomacy. They were happy to meet this public figure whom they had known only as the donor of our chapel.

In a few weeks I found an interior designer who took a lively interest in the project, which included new couches, carpets, and drapes in all the public rooms, as well as a fine round table for the breakfast room. Although Mrs. Luce had been only concerned about the decor, I included in my plan some minor structural changes—another bathroom and a storage room for the kitchen. The total came to a startling $50,000! I sent her the estimate with some trepidation, but Mrs. Luce promptly approved the project in its entirety.

During the early spring of this same year, I was contacted by leaders of the San Jose Newman Club. The rumor had reached them that the club at Stanford was small and not well organized, and they wanted to help me. They felt that the model of Newman organization we had developed in San Jose was worthy of being shared with other clubs, and they were willing to send a team to train leaders at other neighboring colleges. By this time the nucleus of interested Stanford students had grown somewhat, and we invited San Jose's team to meet with us at Guthrie Hall, one of the women's dormitories on campus.

I attended the meeting and listened to their enthusiastic presentation. They described an elaborate structure of organization, involving many officers and committees. I empathized with their feeling of success—after all I knew almost every one of them!—and I realized how effective this model could be in their large and active Newman Club. Appreciating their good will, I felt sad that we could not make use of what they offered.

The Stanford students were cordial and polite, but their skepticism was evident in their reserve. They didn't ask many questions, and it was obvious to me that they saw this model as trivial and irrelevant. To my surprise I found I was beginning to share their feeling. The San Jose model was too complex a structure for the accomplishment of a simple spiritual objective: the creation of a deep individual relationship with God through the Church.

121

During the first year one event took place which was an unqualified success. Teri Risberg, one of our members who had spent the previous year in France, had participated in the famous Chartres Pilgrimage: hundreds of students annually converging from all over France. With her urging and planning, we developed a pilgrimage of our own: we would journey some fifteen miles from Arroyo Seco in the Salinas Valley over the mountains to a place of religious significance—the San Antonio Mission. Because the Mission was within the Hunter Liggett Military Reservation, permissions had to be obtained to camp on the reserve; drivers were found to move the cars to the Mission for the return home. I was delighted to be with the students in any activity that involved the outdoors.

Unfortunately, we started without deciding at exactly what point we would leave the cars and begin hiking. As a result, when the lead car plunged onward over the almost impassible jeep-trail along the arroyo, the rest followed. The road was barely one car wide, and sometimes was blocked by boulders which had to be rolled out of the way. Turning around was out of the question, so the next few miles were a test of patience and ingenuity, as well as driving skill.

Soon all of the passengers climbed out and began to walk. Cars and hikers kept passing one another. Before long someone had a flat tire, another car was almost out of oil, and we all realized that there was no gas to be had for many miles. But we all stuck together, sharing tires and cans of oil with those who needed them. Eventually, the road improved as we approached the reservation and the cars were driven on to the mission.

In the late afternoon we hikers descended into the serene beauty of the Jolon Valley, with its great oaks and drooping lichens and spring flowers. We made camp and had a cold dinner, as no fires were permitted on the reservation. Later, we sang songs in the moonlight.

Next morning the group continued the remaining miles to the Mission in time for Mass with the Franciscan Brothers who were in training there. We then drove home to Palo Alto. As always happens with adventures, the memories of car troubles—rolling boulders out of the road and trading gasoline and tires—were later shared and laughed about. As happened after the Silver Lake trips from San Jose, friendships took on a new dimension.

Later in the year I took a few of my faithfuls to attend the state Newman convention, which was held that spring in San Jose. I wanted to have the Stanford group participate in a regional activity, rather than remaining isolated. Although they took part in the meetings, they told me when we got together for the final assembly that much of what happened seemed rather pointless. The granting of awards, which San Jose Newman had taken very seriously, brought only amusement to the Stanford group. One chaplain went to the extent of giving twenty awards to members of his group for all manner of fairly insignificant accomplishments, lavishing praise upon each one of them. It seemed almost childish.

Another activity originating during that first year, one which had lasting impact on the developing Newman community, was an inter-cultural service trip to Mexico in the summer of 1962. The source of this idea was Richard Mielbrecht, a new transfer student who had spent the previous summer vacation on a similar trip.

Richard told us at Newman that the Mexican branch of the Christian Family Movement had backed the project, providing materials for the building of a community center in a slum area of Mexico City called Actipan. The work had been successful, even drawing into it a number of upper class Mexican youth who rarely had contact with the world of poverty.

Richard was very eager to gather a group to go this year to Zinapecuaro, a mountain village in Michoacan. There the group would make friends and assist the villagers with practical skills. A number of Stanford students responded to Richard's idea and began systematically planning for the expedition. An old school bus was bought for $50, which stood outside the Newman Center for two months being slowly recommissioned and decorated.

To me, the scheme sounded wildly impractical, considering the distance, the cost, and the inexperience of the students. However, I had to take Richard's enthusiasm seriously, since his previous venture had been with Mario and Estelle Carota from Aptos, whom I had come to know during my San Jose years. They were remarkable people who had adopted and raised more than a dozen children with the slimmest means of livelihood.

At one point, Mario even visited us at Stanford and listened to our plans. He felt that they were workable, and he was full of enthusiasm for the project. I felt that if he thought it could be done, it was indeed possible, for everything that Mario did was well thought out and highly motivated.

However, as the summer approached, some of the group began to have second thoughts, realizing that they had neither the time nor the money for this venture. A few dropped out, feeling sad and a little guilty about it, but the trip did take place during that summer. I did not go myself: I was not free to be absent from St. Ann's for the two months of the expedition.

Although it was not possible for me to be away from the church on weekends because the schedule of Masses continued throughout the year, I did manage to enjoy the usual vacation with my family at Silver Lake. But Mother, who was now seventy-four, did not feel strong enough that year to take a pack trip.

I still longed to get into the back country, so, after the summer term, when the graduate students in my house were less busy, I suggested that we go on a five-day backpacking trip together. None of them knew the High Sierra, but they were strong and eager. Therefore, I chose a fairly demanding circuit in northern Yosemite Park which I had long wished to take: starting by the quiet river in Tuolumne Meadows, we would follow it for twenty-two miles through its deepening canyon all the way to Pate Valley; then, climbing the north wall of the canyon, we would return along its rim to our starting point. It would be about sixty miles; there would be one hard climb on the third day, coming up out of the canyon.

As it turned out, the late summer river was one long series of gorgeous blue pools set among the shining granite rocks. We met almost no one, and the weather was perfect. However, the trip proved harder than my group expected. The last two days, which I had described to them as "plateau country," involved crossing many side canyons into which we had to descend and then climb out on the other side.

The men were quite exhausted, and it took me a few months to live down my reputation as a slave driver, especially with Mike Cowley, who became the chosen head of the Newman household that fall. In spite of the hardships of the trip, it served to launch a tradition. Backpacking eventually became as much a part of Stanford Newman as Silver Lake had been at San Jose.

The old bus returned at the end of summer from Mexico, but it barely made it. Only one person and the driver endured the last leg of the trip; the rest had flown home to spend the rest of the summer with their families. When all reconvened at Stanford at the end of September, the participants claimed that they had learned a lot, and they had established an inter-cultural relationship which they wished to maintain.

As I began my second year at the Stanford Newman Center, I noticed that an important change was occurring in my own life. The distinction between my professional life and my personal life was breaking down. The mingling of business with pleasure had been discouraged in my seminary training: a priest should be always and only a priest when "on duty." But now I was taking more and shorter intervals of time off, instead of one full day a week.

124

I could visit my family any time, they were only three blocks away. And when I was there, I could run back to Newman in a few minutes if I was needed for any reason. Moreover, I found great delight in introducing my family to the students, and vice versa. I no longer had two lives, private and priestly, but one.

Being in Palo Alto where I grew up, I also found that many people who had no connection with my Newman work liked to come to my Mass and hear me talk. It seemed silly to make a distinction between the Stanford community, with whom I was assigned to work, and those who simply chose St. Ann's as their place to worship. Father Tierney, I knew, had drawn the line firmly, insisting that the latter group stay away except in summer. But such rigidity was foreign to me: as far as I was concerned, whoever came was welcome.

7. Moment of Opportunity: Vatican II

The academic year 1962-63 coincided with the opening of the
Second Vatican Council, an event which had an immense impact
upon religious life at Stanford, as it had almost everywhere in the
Christian world. The personality of Pope John himself, the pre-
conciliar fact-finding work which raised many important issues, the
journalistic coverage of the key bishops and cardinals in both progressive and conservative camps all kept the Catholic Church in the
focus of public attention.

With the unexpected openness and spontaneity that Pope
John had brought to the Church, almost anything seemed possible.
Bishops and archbishops who usually concealed any private opinions behind the dignity of their office were openly disagreeing with
one another on the floor of St. Peter's. And most amazingly of all, the
press was able to bring this information to the world without having
it filtered through the evasive language of Vatican diplomacy.

I had never expected such an event to occur. It was like a new
beginning of the Church for me. I was very hopeful that long-awaited
changes would finally take place, especially with the liturgy, which
was the subject of discussion at this time in Rome. Progress that I
had worked and hoped for during my years as a priest seemed about
to be implemented on a large scale. I felt excitment watching the
Church at a moment of opportunity—becoming relevant to the mod-

ern world—and not knowing from day to day which way the debate would swing.

I hastened to the breakfast table every day in October to get the newspapers and to find out what was happening. As the other students came in, they asked for the latest news, and we enjoyed discussing the various personalities of Church leaders and the various positions that they took. Breakfast was no longer quiet and sleepy, but full of lively talk.

With the whole world watching the progress of events in Rome, and with the possibility of old conflicts and stubborn theological positions being abandoned, the ecumenical relations at Stanford were transformed. There was a new mood on campus among the clergy, seminars were held on matters being discussed in Rome and on relevant books, such as Kung's *Council, Reform, and Reunion*. Faculty as well as denominational clergy participated.

At these seminars, I met Robert McAfee Brown, who had recently joined the Department of Religious Studies at Stanford. He was a well-published author in theological matters and was slated to represent the American Presbyterian Church at the Vatican Council in 1963. He was a very effective speaker. His clarity of expression and the energy of his voice and gestures did much to make our meetings as exciting as they were companionable.

There were also a number of regional meetings, involving primarily the members of the faculties from Santa Clara University, St. Patrick's Seminary, and the Graduate Theological Union in Berkeley. I attended some of these, as did some Stanford faculty members. These meetings were like a Vatican Council in miniature, with the representatives of various churches struggling over such long-taboo subjects as inter-Communion and clerical celibacy.

University Chaplain Minto, in accordance with the ecumenical spirit, also invited the denominational representatives to meet regularly with him to work out the areas in which we might cooperate in our common ministry. With this encouragement, the Newman president, Tom Fox, promoted a weekly luncheon on campus for casual social activity among Catholic students. These luncheons were held in the building known as the "Clubhouse," formerly Stanford Women's Club, a convenient old building which was used by all sorts of groups and organizations.

During the wonderful time of openness that followed the first session of the Vatican Council, the university invited Archbishop McGucken to speak in the Memorial Church. A graduate of UCLA, he had been bishop in Sacramento for a few years and had become Archbishop of San Francisco with the death of John J. Mitty.

He telephoned me personally to say that he would like to come early and have dinner at the Newman Center so that he might see our well-known facilities. I was delighted with the opportunity to meet the "new boss" and to enlist his interest in my work. I assumed that with his own university experience he would be interested in campus ministry. And of course we all hoped that he would prove to be a strong leader for the "new Church" which was emerging from the Council.

He arrived while I was saying Mass, and when I came in to the house, he was being entertained in the front room by some of the students. Loud-voiced and friendly, he was a large, impressive man. Shortly, we went into the dining room for a good meal that Mrs. Brown had prepared. We had a pleasant visit, and he seemed quite open to what we were doing and what I hoped to accomplish. But at times, he looked restlessly about. Finally, he rumbled, "Is it permitted to smoke in this monastery?" Obviously, I let him smoke! Then I realized that no one had thought of offering him a drink either; in fact, there was probably nothing but beer in the house.

Soon after dinner, I drove him out to the campus and parked behind the Memorial Church. Naturally he was asked to talk about the first session of the Council from which he had just returned. He did so, but it was rather disappointing, considering the eagerness with which his audience was waiting for hope and vision. He was cautiously optimistic but vague about what changes he considered possible or desirable. He had felt the euphoric spirit of freedom in Rome, but he was at pains to state that the Church could not change its basic positions. "A lot of exaggerated things—ha ha!—were being proposed by the liberal theologians . . ." he said, in a pompous, booming voice.

In spite of Archbishop McGucken's lack of enthusiasm for change, the great Constitution on the Sacred Liturgy, which was the major product of the first session of the Vatican Council, proved to have far-reaching effects. Pope John had chosen liturgy as the first subject to be dealt with because it was where the assembled bishops all shared experience.

Sweeping reforms were allowed, but the local authorities were given the responsibilty to introduce change gradually so as to avoid shocking people whose religious lives were tied to the old way of doing things. Even among the clergy, these changes would likely be difficult, for in the seminary we had been taught that the slightest voluntary deviation from the prescribed words and motions was a sin!

Not only were vernacular languages to be introduced, but the whole Mass was to be given a different tone: more communal, more flexible, more personal. The dialogue Mass, which Edgar Boyle had introduced in Oakland during the late 1940s, was still a novelty in most places at this time. Everything was still said in Latin, and for most people in the average parish, these traditions were as beloved as they were immutable, and the changes were very disturbing if not disastrous to them.

But for me, who had been interested in these matters for many years, this period of gradual transition was a time of anticipation and delight. It was the dawning at the end of a long night.

To deal with the numerous questions of procedure, schedule, and music which the Council reforms were going to raise, I began to hold meetings with students and other interested people at the Newman Center.

One of the first changes we made, which was not even asked for by the official announcements, was one of atmosphere rather than liturgy. Art Lange, one of the students, had asked rhetorically at a meeting, "Father, why do you have to duck into the sacristy like a rabbit into his hole at the end of Mass?" Instantly recognizing his point, I considered other ways to handle the conclusion of the Mass. Next Sunday, I walk down the aisle with the people instead of going out the side door into the sacristy to remove my vestments. Taking off my chasuble as I went, I enjoyed my conversation with the departing congregation without the need to hurry around to join them. How natural . . . and obvious!

Another change we introduced involved the newly revived ceremony of the "pax" or "kiss of peace." This rite, a symbol of Christian love, had long been confined to a formalized bow between monks in the monastic liturgy; now the peace greeting was to be extended to the laity. The problem was what symbol to use. The official decision in our diocese was that it should be a handshake. I was to greet the people from the altar before Communion with the phrase "Peace be with you" and then approach a few of the people nearby to shake hands, wishing them well. They would pass the greeting on from person to person around the church.

But it struck many of us that between family members and close friends a handshake was ridiculous. So we decided to replace it with whatever gesture the people felt appropriate. As before, I would walk to nearby members of the congregation, but now I would greet them with an embrace or a handshake depending upon how we felt about each other. Many of the young people passed the greeting in the form of a hug or a kiss.

The Bishop's office apparently considered this to be close to immoral, at least in church, and I received a warning call directing that we desist. I knew I could not ignore the directive from the Bishop; on the other hand, I did not want to become an autocrat with the people by suppressing our new custom. So I simply informed them from the pulpit of the Bishop's objection. They complied, but not for long. When they revived the "dangerous" custom, I ignored the violation, and we did not hear from the Bishop again.

Another change which resulted from the Vatican Council involved music. Although St. Ann's, like most churches, had a choir, it normally sang at only one Mass each week, and the congregation did not participate in the singing. The Vatican Liturgical Constitution stated as an objective the participation of the community in the music. To do so, it ordered that modern forms of music and instruments other than the organ could be used. Accordingly, musicians in the United States were beginning to produce church music to the accompaniment of guitar or banjo.

When these permissions were announced in our diocese, we enlisted some singing members of our community to lead, to play, and even to compose. However, their experience and confidence in leading were insufficient to develop strong congregational participation. The people's singing was timid and barely audible.

Father Bob Giguere, who had been coming to St. Ann's to say Mass on Sunday for some years, offered to help in providing musical leadership. Being a member of the faculty of St. Patrick's Seminary, he told us that seminarians were now being permitted to go out on Sundays to assist in neighboring parishes. He was in a perfect position to recruit and also to transport some of these volunteers, who were most eager for the implementation of the liturgical directives.

Under the spirited leadership of the seminarians the singing began to improve. Gradually, members of our own community appeared who had leadership skills, so that we did not any longer need outside help. Outstanding among them was Patrick Mahoney, whose talent with banjo and guitar and wonderful sense of rhythm had the power to get everybody singing.

Although hymns in new folk styles were being composed, our leaders found that most of what appeared in response to the Council's invitation was shallow in its ideas and musically weak. But Pat, and others who came to join the group, searched out the best, adding new ones as they were released, and collected them into loose-leaf booklets, which were constantly disappearing from the pews for use in some less advantaged parish! Pat even composed a few pieces himself which everyone liked and sang with gusto.

Father Giguere and I and the other priests who said Mass at St. Ann's found the spirit of these folk Masses refreshingly spontaneous. We would often vie for the opportunity to celebrate these Masses because we enjoyed the warmth of the congregation and the sheer pleasure of the excellent singing.

There was another group in the community that was equally enthusiastic about the more formal music of the St. Ann's choir. Eric Schwandt, a graduate student in music who had been the organist for several years, was joined by Bill Mahrt, also a graduate student in music, and Bill Pohl, a professor of mathematics. Together they became soul-mates in their determination to revive the rich classical tradition of music in the Church and to increase the level of musicianship.

Gregorian chant, which they had been using on a small scale, now became their prime interest, and was performed with a perfection not to be found elsewhere in the diocese. They also introduced the polyphonic music of the Renaissance to the repertoire of the choir. Before long other singers, not all of them Catholic, who had a serious artistic or academic interest in these areas were joining our choir.

Still another liturgical change introduced by the Council and now permitted by the diocese was the "altar facing the people." For many centuries the altars in most Catholic churches were built against the end of the nave, so that the priest stood with his back to the community, "facing God" while saying Mass, except when he went to the pulpit to preach. Now, in response to the work of many theologians, it was recognized that the Mass was first of all a community meal, like the Last Supper from which it had originated, and that the symbolism of the community facing each other took precedence over that of the sacrificial posture.

This change of symbolism and mood in most parish churches was attempted by putting a narrow table on the edge of the altar platform, across which the priest would speak to the people and present to them the bread and wine for Communion. Although I favored this arrangement in principle, we found it unattractive: the temporary wooden table was artistically out of balance with the permanent marble altar. Unfortunately, this was one of several worthy changes promoted by the Vatican Council which would take time to reach a satisfactory form.

Liturgy, the first area to be addressed by the Vatican Council, was the only one to be brought to a conclusion while Pope John lived. His death at the age of eighty-one during the summer of 1963 came as no surprise, for the progress of his cancer had been the subject of world news for several months. His brief four years as Pope had been a wonderful springtime for the Church, and now I, like thousands of other forward-looking Christians of all denominations, felt his loss as a great tragedy. From the pulpit at St. Ann's, and wherever I went among students, the death of Pope John was a topic of conversation—as had been the death of President Kennedy the previous year.

Soon the papers were full of pictures and accounts of those cardinals considered most likely to succeed him. My principal fear, and that of my community and colleagues, was that whoever his successor would be might fail to carry on Pope John's joyous spirit. Quickly, and predictably, the selection of the new Pope fell upon the Cardinal Archbishop of Milan, who took the name Paul VI. He promptly announced that there would be no change in the agenda of the Council. The bishops of the world reconvened in October, and during their three remaining sessions, produced fourteen major documents, of which those dealing with the nature of the Church and its place in the modern world were most significant.

The abundance of information in the press concerning the bishops' debates, as well as the theological treatises produced, opened up many questions for public discussion. Never before had the proceedings of a Roman Council been accessible to the press, and the opportunity to hear about and discuss them was, for most Catholics, a new, exciting experience. I took advantage of the Council's open spirit to introduce in my sermons such topics as the meaning of Mary's role and her virginity, the way in which God can be three and one, the meaning of the two natures in Christ, and the sense in which papal infallibility is to be understood.

Generally, I found people able to accept new interpretations of doctrinal matters. However, I discovered that when the topics touched on morality—especially sexual morality—many people in the congregation became anxious and resistant. After Mass when we all gathered on the plaza, I was told by some that the Church's moral laws, burdensome as they were, provided a firm framework for life, particularly in teaching their children. They found it upsetting for me to suggest that these teachings could be changed. However, I insisted that these questions concerned an essential part of life and could not be evaded. Accordingly, they had to be the subject of sermons from time to time.

Yet I began to dread the reaction from the conservative members of the congregation. Bill Mahrt, our choir director, for example, often took me to task for what he perceived as my taking liberties with Catholic doctrine—my implication that the Church's teachings sometimes might be wrong. Professor Tostado, a good friend who had been a graduate student in chemistry and a member of the Newman Club when I had been a student at Stanford, would confront me after Mass whenever in my preaching I suggested that conscience might take precedence over the Church's authority.

One of the most sensitive issues in the moral field was birth control, which the Church had constantly condemned as contrary to Divine Law. For many years in counseling people I had suffered with those married couples who felt an urgent need to limit the size of their families but were prohibited by the Church from using contraception. I had read every article that seemed to suggest that a "morally acceptable" method would be found, and shared this hope with those I counseled, but I was much disappointed that "the Pill" had not received the approval for which its originators had hoped. Accordingly it was exciting now to read that several of the major cardinals had raised the question on the floor of the Council, and that the new Pope Paul had appointed a large international commission of lay and clerical experts to make an intensive study of the question.

Then, one day in conversation with a young woman chemist from Stanford about the religious teaching of her children, a topic quite peripheral to contraception, I suddenly realized that there was nothing immoral with birth control as such. The pieces of the puzzle which had been troubling me for so long finally fitted together: what was wrong was not a technique, but rather irresponsible parenthood or conversely the irresponsible refusal of parenthood! I saw that the Church had simply been misled in its teaching by the limited knowledge of human physiology and psychology available in the past.

So I began reading the long historical study by John Noonan on the subject. I learned that there had been other matters of supposedly Divine Law where the Church had radically reversed its position, albeit very slowly. The condemnation of usury—the taking of interest on loans—had been abandoned during the early mercantile period beginning the sixteenth century. And it was not until the nineteenth century that the Church had ceased to insist that religious dissent was a danger to be suppressed wherever possible. Although the Church had only relatively recently declared the absolute immorality of birth control, I concluded from my reading that birth control could also find acceptance by the Church even after only a few decades. The papal commission, consisting of men and women in a variety of learned professions, must surely take into consideration new psychological and demographic information and, as a result, recommend that the Church accept birth control in principle.

With the general ferment about moral problems, the consciences of some Catholic people in our community were also turning to the problem of racial separateness even in the Church. St. Francis Parish in East Palo Alto nearby was largely black, but there was very little interaction with these Catholics. Some of the middle-class white Catholics who attended St. Ann's told me that they were involved in the formation of a Catholic Inter-racial Council. These included Edda Ritson, a faculty wife, Mary Ash, and Joan Abrams.

I was delighted to hear of their intentions and to announce the meetings from the pulpit. I saw this as dealing with an issue with which I had been concerned ever since my visit to New York and my work in the racially-mixed parish of Sacred Heart in Oakland.

The group began meeting at the Vallombrosa Retreat Center in Menlo Park; Earl Douglas was the first chairman of the "CIC" and the director there, Father Eugene Boyle, was appointed by the Archbishop as chaplain. The CIC's purpose was to promote friendship and understanding between Catholics of different racial backgrounds. Through St. Francis Parish in East Palo Alto, the CIC invited the participation of black Catholics at their meetings.

Those black people who attended the meetings of the CIC became friends with me—as the only other priest who became involved in the organization—as well as with the lay people. Some of these people began to attend Mass at St. Ann's, where they felt they were welcome. Among them were Barbara Mouton, who was many years later to be mayor of that community, and Henry Organ, a member of the staff at Stanford.

Besides the many issues which affected my public ministry, there were also some which affected my personal life. One of these was the use of the Divine Office. Like all seminarians in my day, I had accepted it an inescapable fact of the priesthood. The Office was always a pressing obligation that meant a daily commitment of one hour, a duty "under pain of mortal sin." Even after all these years the burden of the recitation had never diminished.

My release from this dreary task came suddenly, like a reprieve from prison. My savior was Godfrey Diekmann, a Benedictine liturgist from Minnesota whose writings were responsive to the open mood of the Vatican Council. Although many articles had been written that rationalized ways for reducing the burden of the Office, his article was different. Appearing in a theological journal in 1963, it stated quite simply that the obligation of the Office must be understood solely in the light of its purpose, namely to aid in our spiritual development. Failing that, it could not be imposed as a duty. If it would serve better in English than Latin, then English should be used, regardless of what the law said. And if the parts of the Office designed for each section of the day could not be said at that time, they should not be accummulated but simply skipped.

Why had it taken twenty years for me to realize this, and why did I have to hear it from a distant scholar? In any case, Diekmann's well thought-out thesis changed my life almost instantaneously. Never again did the Office lie on my shoulders as a burden. I immediately began reciting it in English, omitting those parts which would not fit comfortably into the schedule of my work.

I felt that through the scholarship of Godfrey Diekmann, I was participating in the awakening of the Church. No longer would laws have to be taken at face value. The Holy Spirit, at work in the debates of the Council, was pointing the way to a new understanding of law, and throwing new light on what it was to be a priest and to be a Christian.

By the fall of 1964, the community built around the Mass was clearly becoming the focus of religious development at Stanford Newman Center. The Newman Club model had never really worked and was now abandoned, although the term Newman Club was retained for purposes of classification at the university. In its place, a liturgically based community was emerging with the help of the changes made by the Vatican Council.

Rather than the slate of officers with a weekly meeting that was important to the old model, the Sunday Mass served to bring together all segments of the community where they could share in worship, hear about activities of interest to them, and take spiritual refreshment from the music and the sermons. I prepared a weekly bulletin containing announcements of all programs of the community, outside events that might be of interest, and reports on what had already occurred.

This growing community included graduate and undergraduate students, faculty members and university staff; it included alumni, not only of Stanford, but of other universities, and many townspeople from Palo Alto and beyond. However, the undegraduate students continued to be a source of concern to me. I felt that they were a major responsibility. With their youth and inexperience and the fact that most of them were without transportation, I feared that they would be less inclined to make sure that their needs were met.

And I knew that as long as they were not coming to St. Ann's, many of them would not attend Mass at all.

In spite of this concern, my Sunday mornings were the highlight of the week. The schedule was very full, and I loved greeting people as they arrived. The popularity of the folk Masses, now at nine and ten o'clock, meant more people and more Communions, more time for singing, and a longer time required to empty the church. As a result, the Masses were beginning to run into each other—particularly the second folk Mass, which was the most popular hour, delaying the start of the High Mass at eleven o'clock.

The High Mass choir began to resent being delayed and felt that the folk Masses were receiving too much support from the clergy, as well as too much popularity among the lay people. In contrast to the ebullient spirit of the ten o'clock crowd, the congregation at the High Mass every Sunday was now made up increasingly of those people who loved the traditional music and prized the atmosphere of quiet devotion.

The choir director, Bill Mahrt, came to me from time to time to remonstrate that the classical group deserved a better deal. He insisted that they were preserving an authentic and precious tradition, compared to which the folk music was but a passing fad.

Much as I enjoyed the folk Masses, I sympathized with Bill's position because I respected the choir's musical and liturgical ideals and felt badly that these people, who were so dedicated, were being inconvenienced. Moreover, I was proud that we were able to maintain a classical choir at St. Ann's when practically all other parishes had given up trying to do so. I also felt that the Bishop would have greater respect for our work with the folk music if he could see that we were also valuing the traditional side of the Church's liturgy.

But as the number of people attending the folk Masses continued to increase, they kept insisting on more time, and I eventually yielded. The High Mass was transferred to the less desirable hour of noon, and even, for short experimental periods, to other hours. However, I was not fully comfortable with these scheduling changes.

While we were trying to work out these adjustments in our Sunday routine with respect to music, I felt that the changes concerning the altar—also stemming from the Vatican Council—were not working. I thought that the experimental altar did not convey the majesty and permanence which belonged to the altar, which was central to every liturgy as the place of sacrifice and Divine presence.

It occurred to me that with Mrs. Luce as our patron, we might be able to replace our old marble altar with one which would be facing the people, as the Vatican Council requested, and which would, at the same time, have all the dignity and beauty of the old one. Accordingly, I wrote to Mrs. Luce asking if it would interest her to finance this change. When she made her next visit in January, she stated frankly that she had no interest in these liturgical reforms, but that I might find Henry Luce, her husband, willing to sponsor the project. So I wrote him immediately, and to my delight received a prompt and generous response.

With this architectural project before me, I was glad to have an opportunity to visit the new Cathedral of San Francisco, which was receiving considerable attention as an example of contemporary church architecture. My classmate Tom Bowe, who was now the pastor, had offered the rectory as the location of our annual class reunion.

Every year on the anniversary of our ordination, my thirteen classmates had faithfully met for an evening to renew our friendship, to reminisce, and to exchange news. This took place in earlier years at some resort or restaurant, but as the members of the class became pastors, each one took a turn playing host to these celebrations.

I drove to San Francisco on a windy afternoon. The new cathedral rectory, grey and squat as a fortress, lay in the shadow of the towering, austere new church. This modern building had replaced the old cathedral I loved, with its old wood and incense smells, where I had been ordained, where I was baptised, and where my mother sang in the choir when I was a baby. The old brick church had burned in 1962.

I parked and rang the bell, which echoed with a hollow sound deep within the building, and waited in the wind-swept entry way. A servant opened the door, and I went down the long, deeply carpeted corridor toward the sound of laughter and voices; almost all our class had arrived, gathered by the fireside in a large common room.

Because the time of our anniversary fell during Stanford's spring vacation, I had been missing reunions for the last few years, being instead in the mountains hiking or skiing. Jim Maher, who was always the convener of these gatherings, welcomed me warmly. And it was a delight to see this group of old friends again: Geno Walsh, now pastor of St. Leonard's in Fremont; Hart Doyle, director of social services for the new diocese of Stockton; Walt Albrecht, from the northern Sacramento Valley . . .

Before dinner, Tom Bowe gave us a brief tour of the church. Its massive stone altar table stood on a square platform several steps above the level of the floor, under the soaring vault of the central tower. The building gave a sense of enormous space and openness

137

which I liked, but the expanse of marble and glass seemed cold. As a result, I decided that I wanted the warmth of carpet in St. Ann's new sancturary rather than a bare floor.

Since I had last been with my classmates three years before, quite a few priests had left the priesthood, including some around our age. The atmosphere of freedom created by the Vatican Council made it possible for a priest to leave for marriage, vocational dissatisfaction, or some other reason without incurring the stigma of disgrace.

However, our class had lost no one, and it was a pleasure to see this group of old friends as we gathered around the dining room table for a hearty meal. But it was a surprise to me to find that most of them they looked rather middle aged. Although I was now forty-eight, I was usually surrounded by young people, and felt as if I were one of them.

I was also disappointed to find that my group of contemporaries were voicing cautious distaste for the results of the Vatican Council. Any mention of the new liturgy released a chorus of complaints from Vic, Tommy, Leonard, and whoever else could get a word in: "It upsets the people. . . they don't know what they're supposed to believe. . . you just get used to one thing, and along comes another change. . . I'm for the good old Latin: I don't want to hear the Mass in Japanese or Zulu. . . people get the idea there's nothing really certain—nothing really right or wrong. . . "

I made attempts to convey my experience of success: the lay people loved the changes and came to St. Ann's in increasing numbers. But all I would get in return was arguments that made me feel naive: that I was a foolish optimist. I heard from several of them, "You're working down there with the college students. . . they like everything new. . . that's not the real world." I was hopelessly outnumbered.

Once away from the disturbing mood of my class reunion, I quickly regained my confidence in the spirit of the Second Vatican Council. I promptly wrote to the Archbishop to tell him that Mr. Luce was willing to pay for a permanent altar facing the people at St. Ann's chapel. I quickly received the approval of the Building Committee, and was instructed to procede with the hiring of a good local architect. I selected Bill Sexton and explained to him my main objective, which was to have a large stone altar table as the focal point of the sanctuary. The design he created involved not only the altar itself but the space around it, eliminating the altar railing and terracing the whole sanctuary area.

138

The period of construction was a nightmare of dust and disor-
der, but the results were magnificent. The new altar table was
indeed massive, one great slab of granite standing on four pillars. It
stood near the front of the terraced sanctuary, allowing ample space
for the priest to move about behind the altar. Deep blue carpeting
covered the terraces, replacing the old grey concrete. The whole
atmosphere of the chapel was changed: warmer, larger, and more
inviting for participation.

One Sunday soon after the new altar had been completed, I
thought of a way to make more seating at a ten o'clock Mass that was
especially jammed. I announced that the small children would be
welcome to come up and sit on the carpeted steps, leaving the pews
for the adults. They did so willingly, and within a few weeks adults
were joining them. Bob Giguere and I decided to place the oak
benches that were part of our original dining room furnishings
around the curving walls of the sanctuary for still more seating.
After a while the whole space was a sea of people, seated or standing,
completely surrounding the altar.

The scene of children and adults massed around the altar,
singing together and smiling happily, was beautiful and strikingly
different from the usual appearance of a congregation at Mass. Children would sit underneath the altar and untie my shoelaces, or hang
from its edges peering over the top at me. When Bob Giguere, who
was quite short, was celebrant, he seemed almosty engulfed by the
crowd. Newcomers walking into St. Ann's were generally amazed
with this spectacle of unity and intimacy.

Another factor which served to develop a strong and spirited
community was a new sort of retreat. This began with my discovery
of an ideal location and grew with the introduction of a new retreat
model by some men in our community. The location was a YMCA
camp in a secluded redwood canyon known as Jones Gulch in the
Santa Cruz Mountains. The facilities consisted of an old lumber
mill, surrounded by little cabins scattered through the woods. I had
been fortunate enough to find this place through being guest
speaker there for a Presbyterian retreat.

The new model was the "cursillo," a three-day weekend of
Christian instruction and fellowship which had been developed in
Spain for the purpose of recapturing for the Church the many
unchurched males in the population. Imported into California, it
had already taken hold as a consciousness-raising experience. I
began meeting with Ken Copenhagen, Dick Glass, and Bill
Schumacher; these men who had made a cursillo helped me work
out a special version which would fit the needs of students in partic-

ular. We concluded that it had to be only two days in length, and that both men and women would be included.

Our first Jones Gulch retreat was a great success, in spite of heavy rain. A large number of students arrived, gathering in the warmth and light of the old rustic building, where a good meal was served by the YMCA staff. We were made cordially welcome and shown the way to our little cabins in the dark forest.

The retreat began with everyone sitting on the floor in a circle by the fireplace, each one introducing him or herself at considerable length. And as I listened, I gained an ever greater respect for and interest in the varied people who made up my community. After three hours together, we went off to our cabins to sleep; it was almost like camping, except that we had a roof overhead. Participants were aroused by song in the early darkness and had to walk through the wet woods to the restrooms and to the big hall for breakfast. Briefings and discussions followed.

At this first retreat, the leaders—the men who brought us this model—seemed to me a bit too anxious to get everyone into the spirit. They would watch to be sure everyone was joining in the discussions and at ease with what was happening. I also felt that the doctrinal content was too heavy and somewhat out of date. In spite of these weaknesses, our first cursillo-style retreat was exceedingly worthwhile. The returning students were enthusiastic about the beauty of the place and the comradeship they experienced.

After the weekend, some of the leaders, as well as some of the participants, formed a committee to plan future retreats, and they reviewed our recent experience to improve our model. The Jones Gulch retreats became a regular feature, usually twice each year, and did more than any other one factor to create a continuing source of leadership in the Newman community at Stanford.

It was a source of joy to me to witness the increasing vitality of the Catholic community at Stanford which was being fed from many sources. Among the large number of people making up our congregation, who formed a coherent community when gathered around the altar, there were many differing interests and needs. Several groups developed to serve them.

There was a group of parents who decided that a baby-sitting cooperative was needed on Sunday mornings; they used the Newman library and, during good weather, the gazebo in the garden. The garden was easily accessible from the chapel, and children who were attending Mass with their parents could conveniently run outside and play safely if they grew restless. For the older children, a Sunday school was established; in the beginning, the downstairs rooms of the Newman Center served the different grades; later, needing more space, St. Ann's arranged to use the nearby facilities of the Presbyterian Church.

Another group consisted of Catholic women who were secretaries in various departments at Stanford University. They began holding bag-lunch meetings on the campus, and I met with them whenever possible to discuss current religious questions which they brought up.

The Catholic members of the faculty attempted to form an organization of their own, and held monthly meetings at the Newman Center to hear lectures on new developments in the Church. However, the novelty of this diminished after a year, and, although many of these people remained active at St. Ann's, they did not maintain a permanent organization.

The Christian Family Movement, which had been my first supportive group at Stanford, continued to flourish, with its membership drawn increasingly from Stanford's new married-student housing known as Escondido Village. They held twice-monthly meetings, rotating from home to home, discussing family-related matters in the light of their faith.

Another group, consisting mostly of townspeople, created a different sort of fortnightly event: a home liturgy, followed by food and fellowship. They called themselves Mass at Somebody's House (MASH), and their meetings proved to be a fine way of assimilating new people into the St. Ann's community.

Several individuals who had participated in the trip to Mexico in 1962 continued their friendships in that country. One of these was Kathleen Costello, who played a major part in establishing a connection with Bishop Ruiz of Chiapas. He invited her and our group to come into his area. Among these people, Dr. Don Prolo and Father Jim Morrissey remained involved for an extended period and were able to create a permanent organization. Called Chiapas Relief and Educational Organization (CREO), it has continued to provide help to Mexican villages which lack sanitary water supplies.

The single Cathollic men and women who were alumni from various places banded together to form their own rather large group. The organization which they developed was more truly a club than other groups at St. Ann's and became federated with the Catholic Alumni Clubs of America. At their request, I served as their chaplain and soon introduced backpacking to their schedule of activities. I acted as their mountain guide on a long series of annual Labor Day weekend trips, which gave me the chance to explore new territory and to teach neophytes about the outdoors.

I welcomed the opportunity to take these extra trips with my Newman community because my mother was no longer able to go backpacking; Bob and I had taken Mother and Dad on their last pack trip in 1964 into the beautiful Green Lakes Basin; with us were Bob Nowak, a Stanford student, and my San Jose friend Fred Vertel and his young wife, Louise.

Now at seventy-seven she lacked the energy for a strenuous vacation, although she and Dad continued going to Silver Lake. But Bob and I took a couple of backpacking trips together, leaving them at our Camp Shadow on the Rock. On one of these trips we started from Florence Lake, where we had rented the burros for our very first packtrip in 1939.

It was an opportunity for companionship which we seldom had enjoyed. Bob was resident chaplain of O'Connor Hospital in San Jose. Hospital work was quite different from Newman or parish work. Every day for five years, he had patroled the corridors, pipe in hand, wearing his long black Cassock while visiting each room and each nurse's station. He was very dedicated to his work, and I was very proud that he had established himself as a very special friend to every member of the hospital community.

We traded stories of people we met in our work—generous people, funny people, the interesting ones and the crazies. However, we could not avoid discussing the painful topic of Mother's aging. She was a source of anxiety for both of us. She was becoming increasingly fretful and discontented at being unable to hike and sing. We knew how much it bothered her, for she had always dreaded the loss of her powers in old age.

During these years into the mid-1960s, when the Newman community was developing its self-concept and spawning many groups and projects, my own daily pattern was a fairly constant and satisfying one. I would get up about 7 a.m. and, after opening the chapel, go to the sunny breakfast room for a hearty meal with the students as they came and went. Mrs. Brown, our cook, presided cheerfully in the big, well-lighted kitchen, taking food orders and offering conversation.

By eight o'clock I would be at my office desk for a couple of hours of work, writing sermons and letters or reading and taking phone calls. My desk was just inside a sliding door to a balcony beneath the branches of a big oak tree. I could glance up from my work and watch the numerous birds and squirrels going about their own affairs.

Then I would dress in my clericals and ride my bike to the campus through the lovely fragrant eucalyptus forest that Senator Stanford had created to separate his university from the world outside. I sometimes had appointments with students at some office provided by a sympathetic dormitory director or outside by the fountain in White Plaza.

Once a week I joined the students at the free lunch served in the old Clubhouse building near the student union. This activity, one of the last things organized by the Newman Club when it was still functioning, had proved to be a lasting and very successful program. The noon hour was a convenient opportunity for me and the students to meet each other informally and without loss of time. The lunch was provided by women volunteers from St. Ann's who liked to meet the students and serve them in return for their welcome at the chapel.

In the mid-afternoon I would return to Newman House, sometimes to a convert instruction or pre-marriage interview, followed by the celebration of the 5:20 daily Mass. Then came dinner around the big oak table, with most of the household present. It was a fine meal and formed a highpoint of the day.

My "family" was fourteen in number with all assembled and consisted of a mix of older and younger students and members of many academic departments. It had been a struggle to break the sex barrier, for Mrs. Brown had resisted, fearing that women would criticize her cooking. But now our household was fully integrated.

Two or three evenings a week there would be meetings for me to attend. I was always at the meetings of the Catholic Alumni and the MASH group. Some meetings did not require my presence but I wold attend occasionally to give encouragement, for example, choir meetings, Sunday school committee, and the CREO group. Sometimes there were informal gatherings, such as a birthday party or a musical event. I would often return to the campus in the evening to visit a dormitory or a faculty home, and sometimes to attend lectures and student theatricals. On other evenings, I accepted social invitations from people in Palo Alto who belonged to our community.

In the later evening I would be up in my room reading and listening to records. I no longer felt I must recite the Divine Office, which had never been a form of devotion suited to my life and my make-up. My room was a peaceful place, even with the house full of students. The thick walls and long corridors muffled the cheerful sounds of student life which continued late into the night.

I often felt proud as I went to and from the Stanford campus that I was part of the university life in a place of such prestige and vitality. No year passed without new buildings sprouting on the campus and new names of distinguished scholars appearing on the faculty list.

Dr. Sterling, as president of the university, had brought many outstanding men and women to the faculty and had won the hearts of the alumni with his warmth and his vision for the future of the university. As a result, large grants were found to support both research and teaching.

The Department of Engineering, always important at Stanford, had grown from a small group of men, who were mostly friends of my grandfather Duryea (from Cornell), to a large school that included many divisions. Electrical engineering in particular was taking on worldwide preeminence, and several new buildings were being constructed.

At the same time, the whole university was growing. The School of Medicine moved from San Francisco to a vast new hospital complex north of the main campus. The Graduate School of Business, soon to be world famous, was built, and a little later, Art, Law, and Music each acquired its own building. There were several new libraries, including the enlargement of the Hoover Institution around its central tower. Unfortunately, the architectural uniformity of the original sandstone buildings was not preserved; but the red tile roofs continued to predominate.

Each of these new facilities was part of a master plan which required the gradual removal of many old campus houses and roads. The quiet elm-lined streets and square wooden homes of the early faculty which were familiar to me had been set in a rural environment with wide fields of grass and flowers surrounding the central Quadrangle. My grandparent's home stood three doors from the Engineering corner of the quad on Alvarado Row. Aunt Minna, who had lived in the house since 1892, was still living there during my first years as chaplain at Stanford. Unfortunately, her home was one of those that had to be removed to make way for the construction of the new Meyer Library.

During our frequent family dinners at Minna's home, we discussed the problems of her coming move. On several occasions, we assisted her in going through the old three-story house, sorting out what to keep and what to give away. There were many beautiful pieces of furniture and art, rugs and books, that had to be distributed among the relatives.

144

"I hate to see the old place go," my mother reminisced one Sunday afternoon as she and Minna packed some of the china. "I was only four when we moved in." She stopped for a moment, and turned to Minna, "Remember the morning of the earthquake? I ran through the upstairs hall with Hecky barking in my arms, and books flying off the shelves on either side!"

"Yes," Minna rejoined with a little chuckle. "And remember the Japanese student who lived in the attic? We were all out on the lawn, and he came strolling out fully dressed, remarking that this was nothing to him. And a little later," she added with her twinkly smile, "while he was sweeping the porch, there was an aftershock, and he came flying off the porch with the broom, like a witch, all in one bound!"

Although I knew it was hard for Mother and Minna to see the old home torn down, they were enjoying their reminensces as always. On Sunday afternoons Dad and I often sat quietly listening while Mother and Minna fondly recalled the early days at Stanford and the personalities that belonged to that period.

Always stiff-backed and dutiful, Minna accepted her move as unavoidable. "Mr. Glover has been very kind," she said. "The university will find me an apartment at Kingscote Gardens. I'll be right next to the Faculty Club any time I want to get meals there. They even sent over a photographer to take pictures of the house as it is, so that I can have a record of it." We were delighted to hear that she would be only a few blocks away. Kingscote was a charming old-style building in a lovely wooded hollow near the campus lake.

During another Sunday Minna and Mother were going through an old trunk in the attic. I stood in the doorway to the storage room watching them as Minna seized a marvellous old hat with delighted cry. "Look at this, Minna," Mother exclaimed, holding up a handwritten manuscript which had lain at the bottom of the trunk. "It's father's diary! And hardly faded at all. I'm going to edit this. I'll bet the Sierra Club will publish it in the Bulletin."

She stood up and came to the door where I stood. I felt excited to hold in my hand these sheets of paper which had been written by my grandfather so long ago. In this diary he described a trip to Yosemite during the summer of 1871 before he entered the University of California, which was then located only at Berkeley.

A few weeks later, my parents helped Minna move into her apartment with what belongings she could take with her. The collection of netsukes in their glass cabinet became part of my parents' living room; Dad's sister Anne took the rosewood dining table. The glass-fronted old bookcase came to the Newman Center and stood in the hall outside my room.

That year I was on the campus a great deal, not only in visits to my aunt in her new residence but for many students gatherings. I did not mind the distance between the Newman Center and the campus. The bike ride was exercise and recreation for me. But for many students, this distance—two miles, sometimes in wet or cold weather—could be quite a deterrent to attending Mass. And even those who came faithfully to Mass were less inclined to ride in the dark woods for a meeting or lecture in the evening.

The only real solution to this problem appeared to me to be the use of some campus facility for all student activities, including Mass. At this time, we were already using the Clubhouse for lunches, and I also found I could hold student meetings and even small liturgies in some dormitories and other residences. But there was no place to say Mass on campus for a large gathering because of the interpretation of Mrs. Stanford's will with respect to denominational services. From time to time the question was raised about using Memorial Church, but this was considered officially impossible.

Not only Catholics but many others felt that the Memorial Church would serve Mrs. Stanford's purposes better if it were available for everyone to use. During the fall of 1965, there were two students on the staff of the *Stanford Daily* who were determined to find a solution to this problem. Kirk Hanson, the editor, who lived at the Newman Center, and Bruce Campbell, a reporter, took on the challenge. Week after week the *Daily* carried articles and interviews on the subject of the history, rationale, and possible adjustments in Stanford's religious policy.

Members of the Religious Studies faculty were interviewed, as well as the chaplains for various denominational groups and members of the university administration. I was more than happy to give my views on the policy of exclusion, which had affected my ability to serve the community well.

I felt from what I had heard of Mrs. Stanford from my family that she was a woman of unusual vision in the matter of religious tolerance. Whereas many universities and colleges in the United States were themselves denominational and had chapels of their own faith, Mrs. Stanford, a deeply religious woman, wished that all religious groups should have equal treatment on her campus. Accordingly, I felt that her church would have been open to the services of all religions, had there been priests and ministers designated at the time to hold such services. As it was, the only service conducted had been by Dr. Charles Gardner, who, although he was Church of England, conducted these services in such a manner as to serve, if possible, all the students.

Over a number of months, the *Stanford Daily* continued to publish material on the issue. Most of the writing led to a conclusion similar to the one which I espoused: if Mrs. Stanford's purpose had been to prevent sectarianism, the goal would be achieved just as well by admitting all denominations as by admitting none.

Many members of the faculty and students of the university became interested in the subject, and President Sterling was asked to present the matter to the Board of Trustees. It was the right time for them to make this decision; in the wake of the Vatican Council the whole world was very much aware of religion and receptive to its importance. Toward the end of the year, the new policy was announced: the Memorial Church would be open to all religions. In the fall of 1966, I was free to begin saying Mass regularly on the campus.

Along with this policy change, a new position, Dean of the Chapel, was created and Dr. Davie Napier was brought from Yale to assume responsibility for the now broadened functions of Memorial Church, outranking Robert Minto, the chaplain, who was now approaching retirement.

I was looking forward to saying Mass there, and the place was already familiar and comfortable to me: I had often gone there to visit Chaplain Minto; sometimes I went inside for a few quiet moments of meditation; and even when I was in the seminary, Geno and I enjoyed listening to the organ when Vince Kelley obtained per-mission to play there. The church itself was very large, with balco-nies on either side. Mosaics in the Byzantine style covered much of the wallspace, depicting scriptural scenes and figures; and the sanc-tuary stood eight marble steps above the floor of the apse. The very size and grandeur of the place created problems: the acoustics were dreadful, and it was impossible to gain the feeling of closeness that people enjoyed at St. Ann's. But it was worth it!

Every Sunday I made a point of standing in the drafty arcade outside the church doors to meet the young people as they came. A few faculty and townspeople came too, but it was predominantly a young congregation; there were many whom I was unable to see in any other way. When I said Mass it was immensely satisfying to stand at the top of the marble stairs, looking out over a sea of stu-dent faces and feel that here I was in contact with a substantial pro-portion of my community. Pat Mahoney and other members of St.

Ann's folk group agreed to provide their guitars and their leadership so that the campus Mass could have music.

In addition to enjoying the use of the Memorial Church, I was now free, as were the other chaplains, to use office space in the Clubhouse building if we desired it. I loved having a base on the campus where I could keep books and files and where I could arrange office hours for counseling.

To my surprise, I discovered that the Catholics were the only group to take advantage of the church on a regular basis. "Mem Chu," as the students called it, proved too large for most others. Moreover, Rabbi Familant did not feel that the church, with its crosses and its explicitly Christian images, was suitable for his use; he requested and was granted permission to hold Sabbath worship in the Clubhouse.

But I found it wonderful to have a majestic and beautiful place available every Sunday afternoon where the student population could gather for Mass. Without the need to travel into town and without worrying about dressing up, they approached in groups of three and four, streaming from various directions across the Quad and down the corridors—several hundred all together.

8. A Changing Newman Community

With Mass now available to the whole student community at
Memorial Church on campus, St. Ann's became increasingly like a
parish church. Even the Chancery Office seemed to have tacitly
accepted this by listing my name among the pastors in official documents. Although a substantial number of campus people still continued to attend the chapel, crowding was reduced, and I could stop
worrying about whether there was room for the students at St.
Ann's. Also the conflict over the timing of the High Mass was settled,
and the choir could resume singing at its preferred hour.

St. Ann's continued to be full at almost every Mass. With more
townspeople attending, the income for the St. Ann's Newman Center accordingly increased, even though—to the amazement of visiting priests—I never mentioned money or even passed a collection
basket. Contributions were made by dropping them into a slotted
box just inside the door of the chapel.

I felt that we could now afford to hire a full-time secretary to
answer the phone when I was out and to do the bookkeeping and
copying. Kari, a member of the choir who sometimes directed in the
absence of Bill Mahrt, became my first secretary. Her desk was on
the broad landing at the head of the stairs outside my office. It was
soon impossible to imagine how I had managed at all without her
help.

In the fall of 1967, I also added a part-time lay assistant to my staff, Donna Myers. She had come to Palo Alto to live with a friend and fellow member of the Grail, a society of Catholic lay women dedicated in part to promoting the dignity of women, and was interested in trying her hand in campus ministry. I thought that she would be very helpful in extending the contact of Newman into the dormitory life on campus, and with her excellent organizing ability and a deep interest in the liturgy, this proved to be the case. Aware that many women lacked confidence in our patriarchical society, she also offered them counseling, thereby reaching some who might not want to talk to a male priest.

With the continuing development of the community, I thought that I might also benefit from the creation of a lay council which would help me govern the parish and would represent its many potentially competing interest groups. The concept of this parish council flowed from the Vatican Council document on the nature of the Church. It saw the Church as a community of people equal before God from whom are derived the priests and bishops who are to serve them, rather than the traditional authority system in which the power flowed through a chain of command from the Pope down to the people. At this time, even the Archdiocese was experimenting with democratic structures by creating a Senate of Priests to assist the Archbishop in the implementing the work of the Vatican Council. My brother, who was now pastor of St. Peter's in Pacifica, was chosen by the priests of the area as their Senator.

To create the parish council, I asked several people representing different elements of the community to begin meeting once a month. (After that, elections were held annually, making sure by a quota system that the students would have adequate representation.) The Council met around the table in the dining room of the Newman Center, and other members of the community were welcome to attend; all were welcome to bring up new business of any kind. I wanted the council to help me not only by bringing me information on the various activities of our community but also by making decisions I would otherwise have to make alone. I would ask their advice on liturgical developments, the allocation of our facilities among various groups, and the sponsorship of outside charitable activities.

One of the issues the council was called upon to consider early in its work was the influx of townspeople who were technicially residents of neighboring parishes. I had heard that a few concerned pastors were complaining to the Archbishop that I was poaching, accepting their parishoners in what was meant to be a student chapel.

While the council and I discussed this issue, two pastors, Dan Shea from St. Thomas Aquinas just a few blocks away and Ed Moss from St. Joseph's in Mountain View, came to see me in my office. I was surprised by their visit, for few parish clergy came to the Newman Center. After a few perfunctory pleasantries, Ed, who was always loud and blunt, came to the point. "John, you know Jack Tierney and I were good friends. Jack made it a policy to keep the Newman Center for students, and that's what it's supposed to be. I don't think you should let the adults from the surrounding parishes come here." And Shea complained, "And you're too close to St. Thomas. A lot of my best people are coming over here for Mass."

I listened quietly to all that they had to say. There was no way that I could tell them the things that people said: that they were bored with bad sermons, depressed by financial scoldings, or turned off by unkind personal treatment. Some of their parishioners had even told me that St. Ann's was the only place they were willing to go to Mass.

I knew I had no hope of making them understand my reasons for welcoming people from outside the Stanford community, but I wouldn't back down. Trying to avoid the unpleasantness of a confrontation, I turned to Shea, whose objection seemed to have more weight, and said firmly, "Father, I haven't invited or encouraged your people to come here. They just come. I believe it's their right to decide where to go. They seem to like the music here and the informal atmosphere. I won't try to drive them away. But you are free to win them back in any way you choose."

Since I gave the pastors no assurances, they abruptly got up to leave. Ed, as he stalked out of the room, sneered, "We'll see that the matter is taken care of!" Standing by my desk, I felt the weight of their hostility. As I reviewed the conversation, I became more and more depressed.

Feeling threatened, I turned for support to my parish council when they met that night. They agreed with me, that what I had said was proper, and we decided that I should seek confirmation from the Archbishop for my policy: to respect the right of every Catholic to worship wherever he or she felt spiritually nourished. I would also ask his advice about how to handle the objections of the pastors.

One of the advantages of having a council was that I could use their collective voice instead of speaking simply in my own name in dealing with the Archbishop. In this controversy, I was able to say to him that the parish council had felt that we should welcome those who, in attending Mass at our chapel, had found a wholly new religious experience: that going to church had ceased to be a duty, and was in fact a pleasure. He listened attentively to my case, and simply responded in his rumbling voice, "Well, if they come to you, take care of them." After receiving the Archbishop's support, I stopped worrying about the issue. I heard nothing more from the neighboring pastors.

Another area, which was somewhat more difficult for me to handle with the Archbishop, was the content of what I preached and wrote. From time to time the Archbishop would forward to me a letter of protest which had come to him from someone who had heard me speak, usually an out-of-town visitor complaining of heretical views or moral laxity in my sermons. This might occur when I stated from the pulpit that theologians did not all agree about something, such as the mode of Christ's presence in the Eucharist, or the Church's stand of birth control.

When the Archbishop did include a covering letter, he would simply suggest that I be more careful about what I preached. Only when my views were published would I receive a long letter from him, in addition to the offending text, objecting point by point to what I had written. This occurred most often with my column in the monthly newsletter of the Catholic Graduates Club. He could find a dozen heresies in any one of my paragraphs! Although he could have been much more severe, his way of handling these complaints, like his disappointing talk at Stanford four years earlier, showed me that his primary concern was always to protect orthodox teaching and strict morality rather than to promote the openness which had been generated by the Vatican Council.

In order to forestall such complaints, my tactic was to present both sides of every theological question, giving more weight to the progressive side, but not openly advocating it as my own. Since my sermons were now being taped, edited, and then duplicated for everyone who wished a copy, I only had to send the Archbishop a copy of a sermon that had drawn a complaint. I also discovered that he would be satisfied if in writing I expanded on my statements, supporting them with quotations and placing them within a larger context.

Another technique that I learned in dealing with the Chancery Office was to post all correspondence between us on the bulletin board at St. Ann's. It gave me the feeling that I was not engaged in a lonely contest with authority, but rather that I was defending the freedom of the community and was supported by it. Although I saw some people shaking their heads in quiet disapproval at my boldness, most who read these exchanges enjoyed them as a contest of wits and voiced their approval of what I had written.

The time when I felt the most threatened by the Archbishop was when I thought that I should uphold the rights of lay people as they came in conflict with the laws and policies of the Church. At Sacred Heart in Oakland, there had been such conflicts, but I had merely presented the cases and regretfully accepted the decisions of the Chancery Office. While in San Jose, I had sought certain permissions which required continuous pressure on the Chancery Office to obtain.

I now saw clearly that many of the Church's laws failed to recognize that lay people even had any rights: that they were not merely passive subjects of authority to be guided to salvation by means of obedience. As I read more and talked with the young priests in the house, I understood more deeply what the Vatican Council's new democratic image of the Church implied: that priests and lay people were already members of the Kingdom of God, and therefore should always have free access to the Sacraments and the other services of the Church. If I saw that individuals were being oppressed by arbitrary rules which stood between them and the grace of God, I felt that I should fight for their cause.

One such cause was that of Philip, a graduate student planning to marry a non-Catholic. At that time, certain "promises" were required in mixed marriages, namely, that all children were to be raised exclusively as Catholics, and a very explicit printed form had to be signed by both parties. Philip and his fiancee took seriously the responsibilities of marriage and were trying to work out a plan for the raising of their family, but they were not willing to exclude the knowledge of other religions. They could not conscientiously bring themselves to sign the form.

Using their own phrases, they wrote a statement that they would raise their children Catholic, which I submitted to the Chancery Office. What I received in response was a summons to appear before one of the Chancery officials, a notice which hung over my head and spoiled my peace of mind for a week. Upon arrival, I was greeted by Ray, a priest younger than myself whom I had known in the seminary. I was pleased to see him because I felt that he would be sensitive to my pastoral concern. I spent an hour with him, trying to make him understand that Philip's intention was the same as what the law intended. But he kept insisting that I should abide by the rules as stated. I left feeling depressed that he could not listen with his heart, that his role as a canon lawyer made it impossible for him to understand me. The couple's request was not granted.

After many frustrations, I began to realize that the only way I could serve the needs of some Catholics wishing to marry was to bypass the legal structures of the Church. In the case of divorced people, this frequently occurred if I could not find the technical grounds or evidence for annulment of prior marriages in the terms of Canon Law. Being unable to celebrate their weddings myself without jeopardizing my position, I would help them to deal with the problem of conscience in having their weddings elsewhere.

I explained that the marriage laws of the Church were not only unfair in their application but were not rooted in Sacramental theology. This theology affirms that the essence of marriage lies in the couple's committment to each other before God, which is intrinsically sacred. So I began recommending such people to sympathetic Protestant ministers nearby who would celebrate their weddings. I also assured them that they would still be Catholics and should feel free to continue receiving Communion.

Garden weddings were also forbidden in the Archdiocese, a rule that seemed too trivial to worry about. I wished to enable people to be married in the manner most congenial to them while maintaining reverence. Hence, when some garden weddings at the Newman Center garden were reported in the newspapers, I would receive a reminder from the Chancery Office that this was contrary to the rules. My answer was that if our garden was holy enough to use for overflow Masses, it was good enough for weddings too! I continued to receive reminders occasionally, but the weddings continued also.

I frequently found myself siding with the people not only against the Chancery Office, but also against the unkind treatment they had sometimes experienced from other priests when arranging for weddings, funerals, and baptisms. They had encountered dogmatism, unnecessary paperwork, empty promises, and evasions, to the point where I wondered why they had not responded with righteous anger instead of meekly leaving, feeling hurt and even guilty. In such cases I felt it was my duty to point out to them that they were innocent of any fault, except that of being too passive in the face of injustice.

As the Vietnam War escalated, I began to give support to some members of my community in a different area—a secular one. An increasing proportion of my counseling was with young people who came to me with conscience problems about the draft. Even high school students were struggling to understand the moral implications of what was happening in Southeast Asia and to decide for themselves what they could or could not do. I had to explain to them that the Church did not either approve or condemn war in general principles, but taught that everyone must judge the morality of every decision in life, including the justification of a given war.

Even when their consciences were firm in condemning the war, they still had to translate their convictions into legal terms for their draft boards. Quakers and Jehovah's Witnesses condemned war universally, and their members could use this authority to support their claim to conscientious objection. But Catholics who saw the Vietnam War as immoral found themselves without such unambiguous authority with which to confront their draft boards.

Most of my counselees were Stanford students, and I used my campus office to interview them. I wrote many letters to the draft boards supporting the claim being made that their conscientious objection rested upon religious grounds. I pointed out that, although a "just war" was at least theoretically possible in the past, the circumstances of modern warfare, where little or no distinction was made between combatants and civilians, rendered a just war impossible. Most for whom I had written letters reported that they had been granted the status of conscientious objector.

There were others, however, who were refused this status or who decided that they did not wish to apply for it. Some of these young people told me that they had decided not to cooperate with the draft system in any way, for they were totally frustrated with the obvious inequity of the whole thing. This radical stance was taken by an increasing number of students as the war dragged on, including one Newman member who was a close friend. Having been denied a "CO" status even on appeal, he refused induction and, for several years, lived under the threat of indictment. I supported him and others in whatever conscientious position they took.

Not only did I become concerned with the government and its unpopular war in counseling, but also during my daily trips to the university, which was now plastered with posters and graffiti. Everywhere I went around the campus I met friends—Protestant and Catholic alike—who were involved in protest and educational teach-ins. I usually attended the rallies being held in the plaza at noon every day to find out what was going on. A few times, as a representative of religion, I was asked to speak about the moral issues of war and military service.

On the fringes of every anti-war gathering, there would be members of the politically conservative group known as the Young Americans for Freedom (YAF), who were usually fraternity men and athletes. They would try to intimidate the participants if possible by their sheer size, or by pointed questions about cowardice and patriotism. One or two of these "Yaffers" attended Mass at St. Ann's regularly, and usually made a point of attacking any statement that I made in a sermon which was contrary to their conservative principles.

Much as I disliked both the radical rhetoric and the heckling of the YAF, I shared with the radicals a complete detestation for the war and the government policy that supported it. I could imagine no circumstances, given the modern military machine, in which a war could be just or could produce more good than the harm it did.

On one occasion, I was invited to participate in a peaceful march to the gates of Moffett Field, a nearby Naval Air facility. I joined a large group of men and women, young and old, led by an elderly Quaker carrying a huge poster saying "Veterans Against the War." It was startling to find the military fully armed, perched on the roofs of buildings prepared to defend the air base against our invasion. We sang a few songs, waved our banners, and marched peacefully away.

Another time I was invited to attend a meeting of clergy in Berkeley to discuss a form of nonviolent resistance to the war, the sanctuary movement. Drawing upon medieval Christian policy whereby criminals and refugees would be safe within the walls of any church, the group wished to manifest its support for servicemen unwilling to go back to Vietnam by welcoming them to seek protection. We approved the concept in principle that day, and a number of Catholic and Protestant churches decided to participate in this witness. St. Ann's was invited to a later meeting to work out the details, and the student representatives from Stanford were Tom Peterson and Peter Spain, a Maryknoll priest living at Newman at the time.

A group of churches, mostly in San Francisco, agreed to offer their facilities; St. Ann's and nearby Palo Alto First Presbyterian were the only ones in our area to join this coalition. This was not done in the hope of thwarting the arrest of those seeking sanctuary, but rather that they might feel supported and might have a platform for the presentation of their moral choice to the larger community.

A few weeks later, a case was referred to us by the coalition: a young Navy man now in San Francisco who for moral reasons refused to go with his ship to Vietnam. He was a sailor, a Lutheran from the Midwest. He sought our support, and spent several days in each of the two participating churches in Palo Alto. As they brought him food, blankets, and company, many of the people in our congregations came to know and admire him as a courageous and high-principled person.

He was arrested after a week, but the case received excellent media coverage thanks to Tony Myers, a Jesuit living at Newman, who was a communications major. When the man's court-martial took place he received no punishment but simply discharge from the service as he desired.

Naturally, St. Ann's received a warning call from the Archbishop's office: we were in dangerous waters, and they would not come to our rescue if we were indicted for assisting a sailor absent without leave. However, this admonition seemed trivial, compared to our cause, and cowardly because it put the legal propriety of the Church above its spiritual purpose.

Particularly during these radical times, the young priests living in the Newman Center were a source of great support to me. There were always two or three in the household, sent to Stanford from many different religious orders to get higher degrees in anthropology, classics, English, history, engineering, and even religious studies. These resident priests became close and valued friends, with whom I could share the ideas I had and the anxieties I experienced.

I loved Henry Torres, a Jesuit from Mexico, warm-hearted and hard-working; the Maryknollers, Frank McGourn, Peter Spain, and Jim Morrissey, whose research sometimes took them away to Central America and drew them into the post-colonial struggles which were beginning there; John Carmody, soft-spoken and scholarly, the only priest in the Department of Religious Studies; Dino Cinel, a student of United States history, whose running battles with his order in Italy and with our parish conservatives were fun to watch.

While they studied at Stanford, the resident priests also helped me in my ministry as their time allowed, taking part to some degree in the social life of the house and in the liturgy of the chapel. Generally, they did not preach, except to give the short homily at the weekday evening Mass.

I wished that I had more personal support from the diocese and the diocesan clergy, particularly in dealing with such moral issues as war and social justice. But in fact, diocesan priests almost never came to see me, and I had little contact with any clergy except the ones who were Stanford students and shared my life at Newman. When I did attend any archdiocesan events, I felt comradeship mainly with the young men whose seminary training had been in the spirit of the Vatican Council.

Although my brother Bob and I shared many values and interests, we seldom had a chance to visit for we both felt that our time off belonged primarily to our parents. However, on one Sunday afternoon in 1968 when our family was having dinner with Aunt Minna at the Stanford Faculty Club—her apartment was too small for entertaining—Bob said that he would like to drop in on me during the coming week. He was still pastor of St. Peter's in Pacifica and was very happy there.

He came to my office at the Newman Center a few days later, looking very serious. He was barely seated in my comfortable office when he blurted out, "Jack, I have to tell you something. . . I have a son."

I was startled; I never had the slightest clue. I knew that he was very popular in Pacifica, and while he, like myself, was now grey, he was full of energy and his parish was a model of Vatican II renewal. I could not imagine him keeping this surprising news to himself all this time: a son! How incredible. I suddenly saw a whole new dimension to my brother.

Not wanting to increase the awkwardness he must have felt in sharing such a personal part of his life, I tried to maintain a matter-of-fact manner. But I could not help asking: "How old is the boy? . . . How are you managing? . . . Tell me about his mother: where is she? . . . How did you meet her?"

"His name is Paul," Bob stated, looking somewhat relieved. "We named him for the Pope. He is about three, and he stays with a family—good friends of ours—while Lu is at work. She's a nurse at O'Connor; that's where we met. She rents a little cottage in Los Gatos."

"Oh, Bob, it must be terribly difficult to live all the time with a secret. Don't you think the Archbishop will eventually hear about it from somebody? I just can't imagine having that cloud over me all the time?"

"I didn't want to resign," he replied. "I love my work, and we figured we could manage. Pacifica is pretty far away from Los Gatos, and there's no reason anybody should hear about it. We've been very careful. Of course I couldn't tell Mother . . . "

He felt that Mother, like most Catholics, was unprepared for the enormous change in consciousness among many priests at this time about being married. Celibacy, like divorce and the Divine Office, was one of the questions opened up in the wake of the Vatican Council. I had never felt celibacy as a burden myself, but its weight was evident in the loneliness of some other priests, manifested sometimes in excessive drinking and a dreary preoccupation with parish finances.

Newly aware of the Church as a community, priests were mingling more freely with lay people and with nuns. They were less on guard than formerly; and inevitably, some fell in love and wished to marry. As a result, they were leaving the ministry in ever increasing numbers. I regretted the loss of many colleagues, particularly in the progressive wing of the Church. Even Bernard Barmann and Henry Torres, who had lived with me at Newman, were now married and had gone on to secular professions, anthropology and law.

Whereas before Vatican II I saw the resignation of a priest as a misfortune, perhaps almost a disgrace, I now felt that they had every right to leave if they so desired. I knew that the Church had imposed the law of celibacy upon all priests for several hundred years, and took the official position that a priest did not have a right to withdraw from that commitment. My conviction now was that celibacy should always be freely chosen and continually reaffirmed as a means for spiritual growth, never simply required as a condition for the priesthood.

Therefore, I was indignant to hear of the way priests were treated by the Church if they wished to marry with the Church's blessing: the long, slow, unpredictable and humiliating process known as laicization, or "reduction to the lay state." These priests were subjected to numerous interrogations involving all their reasons for entering the priesthood. The aim to prove that the priest should never had been in the priesthood from the beginning. It seemed to me that the purpose of this procedure was to demonstrate that the celibacy law was right and the priest who wanted to marry was weak and unworthy of his calling.

Bob and I were in agreement about these issues. Since neither of us felt that celibacy was essential to the priesthood, we also agreed that it made no sense for him to abandon the priesthood because of his love. However, the danger of discovery would always lurk in the background, and I was anxious to give help and moral support to him and his family. We arranged for me to meet his wife, Lualan, in the near future. The hardest part for Bob and now also for me was the need to hide his situation from Mother and Dad.

The discovery of Bob's burden of isolation made me more aware of how little supportive companionship either of us had among the clergy of the diocese. Although Bob was an elected member of the Senate of Priests, he found that group frustrating, stifled in trying to do the work of the Council by the ponderous response of the Archbishop. I was a member of the Priests' Association, a group of young men and a few of my contemporaries trying to create an independent pressure group in the diocese, but unfortunately the energy faded. The young leaders became discouraged as they found no way to influence events in the diocese; abandoning the effort, many of them left the priesthood.

There was only one clerical group with whom I felt truly at home: the priests (and some nuns) involved in Newman work. I had formed bonds with many of them when I had attended in the 1950s four national Newman conventions—long before the Federation had lost steam and been disbanded. We Newman clergy still felt a strong need to support and inform each other and so created the Newman Chaplains' Association, with an office in Washington D.C. which sent out information and arranged meetings on a regional basis once or twice a year.

These gatherings meant more and more to me on several levels. They were a chance to renew good friendships; they were an occasion for reinforcement and criticism of plans and techniques; and above all, they were a place where my work was understood and my perceptions of the Church were not seen as dangerous or insubordinate.

I was one of the senior members of the Newman chaplains' community now, and I felt respect and appreciation for my ideas and for my successful ministry. With the four vibrant years of the Vatican Council past, these meetings were really the only place where I sensed energy and hope for the work of the Church beyond my own parish. We enjoyed lively discussions about how to make the liturgy and sacraments more effective instruments of our ministry, and about how to do so without incurring the displeasure of our bishops.

There was one additional element: travel. These meetings were the only occasion I had to drive or to fly to some distant place and spend a few days away from the routine of life at St. Ann's. One autumn, the meeting was at the lovely old Timberline Lodge at Mt. Hood in Oregon, where snow had already fallen. Another was at a retreat house near Tucson, Arizona at the edge of a real cactus desert. Once I rode the train to Laramie, Wyoming, for a mid-winter meeting under the auspices of the most conservative priest in Newman work—dressed like a cowboy! A meeting in Spokane, Washington gave me the exciting opportunity to fly past the white cones Mt. Adams and Mt. Rainier. Another meeting was at Redlands, California, where my great-grandfather Stillman had raised grapes and melons on a vast tract of land.

One of the special programs offered by the Chaplains' Association was an annual two-week training school for priests and nuns new to the work. This program had been held on the East Coast for several years, but on three occasions at the end of the 1960s it was also held in California. I was asked by Charlie Albright, whom I had known when he was a Newman chaplain at Berkeley, to plan and direct it.

I was delighted to accept this opportunity. I felt I had a lot to share, especially my experience of living with students in a cooperative household. Stanford, with its ample living facilities, was an ideal site. We would be able to house, feed, and instruct the participants under one roof, and the pleasant weather and semi-rural atmosphere would create an enjoyable experience.

The priests and sisters who would be attending were not only strangers to each other when they arrived, but were also unfamiliar with the questioning tone of student life, with campus radicalism, and with the liturgical experimentation which prevailed at the major universities around the country. It was our task to introduce them to these ideas and to the ecumenical collaboration which made our work more exciting.

Donna Myers, my associate in the Stanford chaplaincy, and David O'Brien, a Paulist priest then chaplain at the University of Texas, were my colleagues in putting on the program. David and I would take turns lecturing in the mornings about the basics of Newman work as we had known it: the history of the movement, our programs, difficulties met, and the solutions we had found. Donna, who had proved to be an excellent planner, helped work out the program. With the arrival of the group, she took care of registration and played the indispensable role of hostess.

Each year between twenty five and fifty priests and a few sisters attended. The atmosphere of the meetings was informal and relaxed, and the group soon gained strong feelings of unity.

In the evening or afternoons, we had a series of guest specialists on current matters of interest, including Robert McAfee Brown, from the Stanford Department of Religious Studies, and Eugene Bianchi, a former Jesuit now teaching at Emory University in Georgia.

Dr. Brown was an outstanding exponent of the ecumenical dimension in American religious life. An energetic speaker whose charm and wit always held his audience, he was a strong advocate of the insights which the Vatican Council brought to the whole Christian community, not just to Catholics.

The most memorable of the speakers was Kathy McHale, a former Stanford student, whose fiery red hair matched her radical political perspective. A born Catholic who had attended a Catholic college in Boston, she had a thesis to share with the participants: that the large number of Catholics in the radical movements of the day was the direct result of the strongly moralistic training they had been given as Catholics. She held them in the spell of her encyclopedic knowledge, and shocked them with her machine-gun delivery and colorful profanity.

In the summer of 1969, Donna Myers announced that she would be leaving the Newman Center. She was to be married to a Jesuit priest, Tom Ambrogi, whom she had met while attending a theological conference in San Francisco. I knew that when the fall term began I would miss the work she had been doing, especially her presence on the campus, where she had built a network of contacts among the students.

Then in August I had a call from an energetic young nun, a convert from Mormonism, who had attended our chaplains' training program the previous summer: Sister Miriam. She had heard that Donna was leaving and was hoping to fill her position. I hired her without delay. Soon after she arrived, she informed me that she was in the process of leaving the convent and would also need a place to live. After a few weeks, a vacancy occurred at Newman in September, and she moved into the house. Now that she was living in the house, I had ample time to explain to her the work that Donna had been doing.

As had been Donna's policy, Miriam began joining me at the meetings of the campus ministry group, which consisted primarily of those clergy who had offices at the Clubhouse. With the increasingly radical emphasis in student life at this time, much of our discussion dealt with the hated war and related social issues. Our group at this time included two men who were politically far left: Joe Hardigree, a Congregational red-bearded Maoist, and Paul Rupert, a Protestant seminarian doing campus internship. Paul, who was an articulate leader in student radical activities, reported whatever was happening on campus at the ministry meetings. Both Paul and Joe gave a Marxist analysis to all these events.

Although Miriam was very much impressed with their perspective, I was troubled by the exclusive emphasis on politics. I raised objections occasionally: that we were gradually forgetting all about the psychological health of the students and matters of theology and liturgy. But Joe and Paul were eloquent and convincing in presenting their concerns, and the conversation tended to follow their lead.

After these intense discussions, both Miriam and I found it satisfying to go home to the quietness of the Newman Center and to a good dinner around the big table. As people coming for the first time often remarked, Newman was truly "a peaceful place." The spacious, thick-walled building never seemed noisy in spite of the many people who lived there. It was a haven of friendship and sanity, a refuge from the pressures of academic work and from the distressing events of the political and military world. The enclosed patio and the wide lawns secluded from the street—all spoke of serenity and order.

Among the memorable personalities making up the household at this time was Jim Bela, who was a student of civil engineering and geology. Some people knew him best by his handsome black cat "Smokey," who as a kitten had ridden with him to Stanford in a bicycle pannier after Jim's summer in Alaska. Smokey was part of the Newman household and went everywhere with Jim.

Jim built, rebuilt, or improved almost every part of the Newman Center, always with meticulous care and infinite slowness, and always attended by Smokey. He spent weeks on the roof re-laying the Spanish tiles, sometimes until midnight. When Mrs. Brown required a new stove and a new refrigerator, Jim researched the possibilities and did the installation. On the occasion of my twenty-fifth ordination anniversary, Jim renovated the lovely Spanish patio, using my father's great bronze dragonfly as a fountain piece.

There was a large recreation room with a parquet floor in the Newman basement. We had used it for Sunday school, but one winter it had flooded and the floor warped. Jim laboriously lifted the floor and re-layed it, making it again a usable part of the house, especially for parties. At the other end of the basement hall was a large room where Miriam had her living quarters. It was well-lighted, and with her brightly colored posters and hanging plants, she made it quite attractive as a place for entertaining students from the household and other friends.

Assuming that Miriam would fulfill the same niche in the Newman staff that Donna had occupied, I did not attempt to direct her activities. However, she started out by making her own contacts on campus, and before long her time seemed to be almost entirely taken up with the political side of campus life. As far as possible, she attended all rallies and lectures on social and racial issues, and on the war; and she brought back to Newman reports that were valuable. I appreciated the fact that she was representing me and the Newman Center in an area that was less congenial to me than some others.

However, her increasingly insistent emphasis on political matters stood in sharp contrast to the general mood of life at Newman Center. The students (and I too!) began feeling that it was frivolous to discuss such things as friends, sports, philosophy, the great outdoors, and even the Church. Only politics mattered. Miriam's table talk was of napalm in Indo-China, the underpaid workers at Stanford Hospital, Black Panthers shot up in a Chicago flat, or the use of torture in Brazil. Her urgency and dedication made the rest of us feel guilty if we were not actively involved in fighting these evils.

Although I shared her ideals, a steady diet of protest and politics was not psychologically possible for me, nor was it for most of the students. As time passed, I found that I was beginning to avoid her. However, I arranged for her to give the sermon on a few occasions for she felt that it was part of her duty to bring the social problems with which she was concerned to the attention of the whole community at St. Ann's. Naturally, there were those in the St. Ann's community who did not like having an "official radical" on the staff, and they kept bringing their objections to me.

Meanwhile on campus, the intensity of student protest against the war was constantly increasing. Many concerned students held the university responsible for the fact that some of its trustees were executives in war-related industries and that Stanford held stocks in companies of that kind. Almost daily at White Plaza there would be speeches about the university's alleged complicity in the war.

I sometimes attended these rallies and teach-ins, and other members of the campus ministry were always either participating or attending. At one point, a group of radicals decided to protest by sitting in at a university building. The one chosen was the Clubhouse, the place where the campus ministry offices were located. It seemed strange to me that they selected the one building where they already had the greatest amount of sympathy and support. However, the ministry group concurred, and promised the administration to provide round-the-clock supervision during the sit-in.

The sit-in lasted for a few days. My turn to provide the supervision was at night, but I had little heart in it. My office was small, cold, and not furnished for sleeping. The lights were on all night, and the mimeograph was grinding away. Most of the students were still able to sleep, but I spent most of the night listening to the drug-induced rhetoric of a student drop-out with a very bad cold.

Following the sit-in, the ministry group allowed the Clubhouse to become somewhat of a sanctuary for the radical movement. People slept there as a means of maintaining solidarity; they left their equipment and literature there; clothing, sleeping bags, and food were everywhere. I gave up using my office; it would be like trying to meet with people in the city dump.

The campus was becoming increasingly a battleground, attracting not only serious demonstraters but also others such as students from nearby Palo Alto High School. It grieved me to go on campus and see areas roped off where windows had been "trashed" by those who felt that the university, because of its wealthy trustees, its investments, and its academic aloofness, was in fact a condoner and collaborator in the war. The university looked as if it had been bombed.

The university administration became seriously alarmed by this violence, and for the first time in Stanford history called for outside police protection. The riot squads were called to break up new sit-ins, and large groups of students were arrested. I hated seeing the heavily armed police everywhere.

One day Jim Morrissey returned from the campus and told us of a massive police round-up at the border of the campus in which not only marching students but innocent shoppers were caught. Jim, who was accustomed to sneaking through the jungles of Guatemala, had escaped; but Terry, who was our student cook following the retirement of Mrs. Brown, had been hauled off to jail, shouting out to Jim the menu for the evening meal as they carried him away.

Except for a few uneasy placard-bearing marches, I remained on the sidelines. I detested the violence, anger, and destructiveness. When I did take part, I often withdrew when the issues became clouded by hysteria and undirected rage. Later, I would visit some of those I knew who ended up in jail, but I never was arrested myself. Although I sometimes felt cowardly and separated from the "action," I just could not join in the strident defiance of the law. It was much the same as my relationship to Church authority. I could think very independently and resolve my own conscience before God, but I could not be openly rebellious. Even when directly confronted, I always tried to keep things polite and to seek areas of agreement.

The community at St. Ann's naturally included some conservative professors and students as well as many townspeople for whom swearing and throwing rocks were more obviously evil than the war. They took me to task for what involvement I did have in the radical student movement and for the sermons I gave in which I sought to interpret what was happening. Frequently they would confront me afterwards on the chapel plaza, some objecting that I was supporting the destructive behavior on campus, while others feeling that I had no right to take a position against the government's war policies. A few people walked out or even interrupted my sermon.

165

My sermons honestly expressed my own conviction that the war was unjust. However, in preaching on this subject, as on all others, I attempted to leave my listeners free to form their own consciences. To do so, I would present all sides of the issues from the pulpit; this satisfied no one, of course, but left the way open to deal with new developments as they arose. While conservatives felt I was being soft on the radicals, the latter saw my attitudes as typical of the liberalism they despised.

The tension created within the St. Ann's community by all this was very painful to me. However, within the household itself I felt support and affection. The residents were in a very real sense my family, and I did not feel separated from them by the difference of my age or by my clerical status. I enjoyed them as companions and conversationalists, and in many cases as fellow hikers in the mountains.

By the beginning of the 1970s, my Newman household and a growing number of former residents and other friends developed into a special community which remained together for several years and formed bonds which were to endure the test of time and distance.

Different members of the group had things to offer which enabled a deep comradeship to flourish. Jim Bela's series of marvelous musical slide shows were an example: he would spend endless hours in the basement recreation room with tape recorder and light table, working out the timing and dubbing in bits of unexpected humor to illustrate our adventures in the mountains and other incidents in the life of the household. After every mountain trip I would schedule a slide show of my own, arranged in a narrative style that gave an experience of the beautiful country we had seen and the natural history of the area. I did not prepare my shows with the same care as Jim, instead relying upon the richness of detail provided by my large Rollieflex slides.

Most students who had been on the trips would turn out for our slide shows, recalling the places and the incidents that appeared on the screen. Participants would recall funnny things, and Pam Oatis could get the whole room full of people laughing because of the heartiness and spontaneity of her mirth as she recalled.

There were also wonderful evenings of music with Pat Mahoney's banjo and guitar and Becky Ahman singing as we sat around the fireplace in the big front room. And there were spontaneous parties too, for birthdays and other occasions, usually late at night around the peach-colored table in the kitchen. Pam's roommate, Kathy Falk, was the quiet organizer of many such events.

Sometimes on mild moonlit nights we would drag our sleeping bags out onto the lawn under a tall deodar tree—which Kathy had named "Scotty Pine"—at the end of the garden. Most of the group fell asleep fairly quickly, but she and I would often lie there talking sleepily while the crickets chirped.

Underlying the exceptional closeness of this community was the common experience of the mountains. Other things contributed, of course, such as the music, the happy spirit of the liturgy, the shared retreats, and the day-to-day living in the house. But the tradition of backpacking trips was the outstanding factor.

Although there had been many shorter backpacking trips, this tradition really began when I led our first week-long trip—nearly eight years after my arrival at Stanford. Our party of seven included Jim Duran, whom I had known since early San Jose State days; Carl Friehe, who lived at Newman and was always helpful in the care of the center; and Barby Rusmore, a student at Santa Cruz whose parents lived in Palo Alto.

We started from the Kings River Canyon and headed up the Copper Creek Trail for Goat Mountain on the Monarch Divide. This was a place which had special appeal for me, since my grandfather Stillman and other Stanford faculty had gone there in the summer of 1896 from a base camp in Kings Canyon. My mother had been eight years old, the youngest member of the party, and the whole trip was a part of the family's lore.

Leaving our cars at the road-end near Zumwalt Meadow, we began the long climb toward Granite Pass. The trail zigzagged up the north wall of the canyon, and soon the river was far below. We made camp late that afternoon beside a steeply inclined garden of multi-colored wildflowers looking across the canyon to the isolated peak of Mt. Brewer.

The second day out we made camp by an alpine lake a mile off the trail. There were several hours of daylight remaining, and, although we had climbed 6000 feet from our starting point at the Kings River, four of us still had the energy to climb a small nearby peak for a view of the country we had come to explore. I felt the joy of being still strong and energetic, at age fifty-one, even after the long day's climb.

As we approached the summit, we strode up a long sloping meadow where scarlet, blue, and golden flowers shone in the afternoon sun. Barby's long blond hair was streaming in the wind. The scene, set against the distant view, seemed to represent the essence of freedom.

167

The importance of the freedom which the mountains gave me is hard to exaggerate, always providing an escape from pressure and worry and reviving the sense of joy and wonder. As John Muir often wrote in his journals, "Nature is so filled with God." Like Muir, I experienced a joy that was almost ecstatic. In the wilderness I did not feel any need to "give thanks" to God as I might in church; I just felt the sacredness of it all.

Reaching the summit, we spent a few minutes studying the immense panorama spread out in all directions. On the way back, I suggested we take a swim when we reached the lakeshore. Jim and Carl were eager to be in camp and went on. Barby and I stopped and went down to a point of rocks jutting out into the lake. Her off-hand query, "Mind if I take everything off?" made my heart jump; I had never seen a woman naked! Before I could answer, she had her clothes off and had dived into the water.

Startling as this was to me, being nude seemed to be one appropriate expression of the freedom I was feeling in this place. So I quickly stripped too and jumped into the clear, icy water. After a very brief swim, we dried off in the sun before returning to camp. We said nothing about what for me was a first experience, but I found it to be one of joy, liberation, and beauty.

Although I had preached previously that one can be free without being immoral, I now had experienced this truth for myself: that human bodies can be freely perceived as part of the goodness of nature, rather than being always a source of temptation to be avoided or concealed. The fear of sexual attraction, so insistently taught by the Church, seemed stifling and irrelevant in this environment.

There were several other opportunities to swim during the trip and to repeat this feeling of wholesomeness and liberation. On our last evening we camped by a tiny lake in which floated an iceberg. However, the sun was still warm, and I couldn't help suggesting a swim. Although some members of our group didn't participate, Jim, Carolyn and Barby joined me in the icy water. Jim remarked, "We anthropologists have no hang-ups!" When we came out of the back-country and saw people in bathing suits by the Kings River, we felt quite superior.

From this time on we scheduled several week-long mountain trips each summer in which considerable numbers of students and other friends took part. I made a practice of announcing the trips in church and taking sign-ups. All who desired to go were welcome if they were physically able.

The most memorable trips were not always the pleasantest, and none was more often recalled than the "Rain Trip." Expecting normal June weather, our large group, dressed for summer, slogged through rain and snow around Mt. Hoffman to the Ten-Lake Basin. During this trip, first-timer Terry Fitzgerald immortalized himself by the midnight wail from his soaked sleeping bag, "Why don't you priests DO something about this?"

In the golden sunshine of one September week, a large group decided to make an off-trail exploration of the northern wilderness of Yosemite National Park. Since we could not all start at the same date, we made an unusual arrangement: two groups of Newmanites would start from different trailheads and rendezvous at Peeler Lake. Before continuing the trip, we spent two nights at this choice campsite, for the lake lay in a glacier-polished granite bowl at the very summit of the Sierra.

We also began to schedule trips during spring vacation and available long weekends in the spring and fall. Early one spring we took a three-day off-trail hike up the Stanislaus River from a base at the cozy mountain home of Tom and Dottie Scheller, who had been married at Newman. Another time on cross-country skis we reached my family cabin at Silver Lake, where we had to dig six feet down to the door, and where Gary Lukis, a medical student who had climbed in Alaska, built an igloo nearby which slept seven. To enjoy the brilliant spring sunshine, we brought up folding chairs from the house to sit on the snowbanks where we could survey the wide white sweep of the lake. Another year we made a three-day trip in which four canoes full of students headed down the Russian River, enjoying perfect spring weather.

In the spring of 1971 my brother called me to say that he had been summoned by the Archbishop and had been informed that a rumor was circulating that he had "attempted marriage," to use the canonical phrase. Bob's ploy had been to assure the Archbishop that his parish and its people were being well served, so why listen to rumors? The Archbishop let the matter ride.

Although I had sympathized with Bob's situation and had told no one, I had been very uneasy about the secrecy. For a priest to be married was so extraordinary that people were bound to talk. No other priest that I had ever known had tried to continue his ministry after marriage. I wondered how Bob would handle further developments.

A couple of months later he told me that the Archbishop had discovered all the facts: that Bob had a wife in Los Gatos, who was a nurse, and a small son, Paul, living with her. Bob had been given until Easter Sunday either to resign his pastorate or extricate himself from this "illicit relationship." Bob had decided that he would remain in the parish until Easter Sunday and on that day would inform the parish of his removal. Bob had shared his circumstances with enough of his parishioners that there would be a minimum of shock and surprise when he made the announcement.

At this point Bob, of course, told our parents what was taking place. Mother, who was now weak and slightly confused, accepted the news quite passively. On the other hand, Dad's response was one of joy: he had a grandson! It was a relief to us that neither of them was upset or grieved by the situation.

Because Bob's last Sunday in Pacifica was Easter, I could not leave St. Ann's, but my secretary Karen drove Dad to Pacifica to attend Mass at St. Peter's. Little Paul, then age six, was given communion for the first time, and Bob introduced his wife Lualan to the congregation. Karen reported that they were greeted with applause, and after Mass with many hugs and kisses.

Soon after, I was pleased to learn that the parish council, in a very strong show of support, had notified the Archbishop that they would be happy to retain Bob as their pastor. It was highly unusual that they would do so. In addition, they invited the press to attend a special council meeting, so that their request would receive national news coverage. Much as I wished that the people's desire could be fulfilled, I was not surprised that their petition was denied. I knew that there were some countries—perhaps Brazil or the Philippines, or even Italy!—where the strictures of Canon Law were taken more lightly, and a married priest might be quietly tolerated; but in the United States such a thing was unthinkable.

Now Bob was able to begin living a normal family life in their little house in Los Gatos, where he started a small practice in counseling. They visited my parents as often as possible, and a very warm relationship developed. Lu was devoted to my mother and did much to make her comfortable in her weakened condition, and Dad often remarked to me how much he loved his new daughter-in-law.

About six months after Bob's dramatic exit from St. Peter's, Mother fell and broke a hip on Christmas Eve. After leaving the hospital, she went to a convalescent home because of continuing extreme weakness. When Dad and I would visit her there, she would open her eyes and smile, but go right back to sleep. Late one night I was called at the Newman Center and told that she had passed away in her sleep. She had not lived to enjoy her new family long.

Early next morning, I went to break the news to my father. Dad, who had always been devoted in his care for her, was heartbroken. His voice quivering, he said, "Oh Jack, I can hardly believe Dottie's gone. . . . I thought I would be bringing her home in a few days. . . ." Shaking his head in grief, he added several times, "I should have been there. . . ." I knew him as one who seldom showed emotion; it was hard to see and to share his sorrow.

The day after her death, I came down with acute laryngitis and did not recover my voice in time to celebrate Mass for Mother's funeral. The Mass was held at St. Ann's with Father Giguere as celebrant. I invited my brother to give the sermon. Characteristically, Dad carried his grief with quiet dignity. Mother was buried in Alta Mesa Cemetery in Los Altos, where Uncle Dan and several other members of Dad's family were also buried.

The grief I felt was mostly for Dad's loneliness. For myself there was a sense of relief because I had experienced so intensely my mother's distress in growing old.

I took the news to the rest home in Menlo Park where Aunt Minna was now living. She was inarticulate now, after having suffered a series of strokes. I could not tell whether she understood her sister's passing.

A few weeks after my mother's death something strangely beautiful and moving happened to me. I was at my desk in the Newman Center when I heard a violin being played downstairs. Since none of the residents were violinists, I was curious. I went down to see who the musicians were. There were two girls, strangers, by the piano. I sat down on a couch just inside the door to listen.

Almost immediately, they began another piece, the andante movement of Wieniawski's D-minor concerto. This was the piece which above all others my mother loved to play with me. I felt my mother's presence—it was a sweet feeling, a happy feeling. I listened to the girls as they finished and thanked them. As I went quietly upstairs, I felt that my mother had been trying to tell me something by this strange coincidence—"Jack, don't stop playing!" I had not touched the violin for some months.

During the year after my mother's death, I saw a great deal of my father. Sometimes I would invite him to dinner at the Newman Center with us; only now did I realize what a deep bond of affection I had for him. He kept very busy in other ways, too: visiting Bob and his family as much as possible and spending a lot of time visiting with old friends, in addition to writing letters to people at a distance, and cleaning up business dealings.

He even suggested that he would like to have one or two companions in the house, and I easily found two students who felt they had lived long enough at the Newman Center and would welcome more privacy. John Young, a priest who was getting his medical degree, and Ed Heffern, who was nearing the end of his training as a geologist, rented rooms from Dad and became very fond of him.

During the following summer, Dad spent nine weeks at Silver Lake. Bob and Lu and I were there when possible, but Dad did not mind being alone. There was work for him to do because the county had issued new regulations making it necessary for us to build a second cabin with running water and septic tank. Jim Bela, who as a fellow civil engineer felt much in common with my father, joined him for a month and helped to lay out the plans for the cabin. Smokey, Jim's black cat, was there too.

During a bright, clear week the next winter, I took Dad to Carmel, where he and Mother had courted. We went on several hikes together and walked along the white beach while Dad reminisced about those early days when my grandparents' cabin stood among the sand dunes in the pines nearby. He recalled Mother's prowess as a swimmer, when defying Carmel's reputation as a dangerous beach, she had gone far out beyond the breakers and was only able to return by swimming across to the point near Pebble Beach.

On the last day of January 1973, I drove Dad to my brother's home in Los Gatos. We all had a pleasant dinner together. Later, I drove Dad to the family home before returning to Newman. Next morning I was called by the two students who lived with him. They were concerned because he had not risen early as he usually did. I went over and found him sleeping heavily. Although I was not alarmed, I asked them to notify me of any change.

It was evening when they called again, this time urgently. I rushed over to find John giving him artificial respiration. It struck me immediately that this was not the right thing to do. He was dying, and I thought it would be wrong to try to revive him. He had lived a long and useful life; he had been lonely for a year; and there was no work now that he had to do.

His death was more painful than I could have expected, greater than the loss of my mother. Conducting my father's funeral was the most emotional experience of my life. During the weeks which followed, I felt an emptiness in my life. I no longer had a father. The strength and integrity and reliableness which he had always represented was now gone.

It was a great comfort to me that I had the strong community of students around me during that spring and summer after Dad died. They were a great support, the more so because so many of them had come to know and love my parents in the last few years. Besides Jim Bela, Kathy Falk was a frequent friend at the family home. And, of course, Ed Heffern had lived with Dad and shared his interests in engineering.

But that June, eight of the key members of the Newman community finished their work at Stanford and left the household for work or for other schools. These included Kathy Falk, who was going to law school in Wisconsin; Pam Oatis, who left for medical school in Ohio; Cheryl Messmer, who went to teach in Arizona; Rosemary Ellmer, who pursued higher studies in theology at the Graduate Theological Union in Berkeley; Ed Block, who was to be married and to teach at Marquette University; Dan Anzia, who was going into psychiatry; and Joan Meyer, who was entering medical school. While some of the group remained, these had been united by our love for the mountains, as well as being a group of devoted friends.

That June a tragedy struck. Karen, my secretary and a frequent hiking companion, on arriving home from the mountains was notified that her husband of only a few months had disappeared in South America. A medical student and an avid mountaineer, Gary Lukis had been Jim Bela's roommate at the house during the previous year. After completing his medical degree, he had gone on an expedition to Peru. While taking pictures of the mountain they were to climb, he had vanished. His companions had searched for him in vain, and it was concluded that he had been a victim of bandits. His body was never found. Jim as well as Karen took his loss very heavily.

During the fall of 1973, the spirit of the house changed. There were several new students at Newman, and they seemed more solitary, more serious, and more self-involved. There was less concern for the issues of social justice and of Church reform than there had been during the last few years. The new people did not seem attuned to the things which had made Newman life so warm and close. And few of them were interested in the mountains.

In spite of these changes, the chapel was as crowded as ever with enthusiastic worshippers, and the musicians constantly worked to improve their repertoire. The vitality of St. Ann's was still praised by newcomers and still enjoyed by its regular participants.

However, some of the energy seemed to have drained from my ministry. My thrust had been the building of a strong, vital commu-

173

nity. This objective had been achieved to a considerable degree, but now its vitality had faded and I lacked a clear sense of direction.

9. Eve

The year 1974 opened in the midst of the first great gasoline crisis. I, who would normally have been smugly riding my bike, was forced this time to endure the long lines, for I was still much weakened by a prolonged sinus infection. I had spent a few days in Stanford Hospital toward the end of 1973. Early in the new year, still unable to do much work, I decided to have a minor operation. These were the only two times I had ever been hospitalized.

They were interesting experiences. I had been so often a professional visitor to hospitals; now I was for the first time experiencing both the comforting security and the boring routine of being a patient. The boredom of hospital life was lightened by many visitors, among whom was my cousin Andy Browne. His mother, my dad's sister, was also in Stanford Hospital during my second stay. She was seriously ill and died soon after I was released.

During my absence from St. Ann's, my secretary, Karen, and Bob Giguere had taken care of things effectively. But it was very hard for me to lose so much time from work and to feel weak over an extended period. Moreover, I was forced to miss two cross-country ski trips, organized by Dan O'Reilly and Jim Bela, the current leaders of outdoor projects.

In March, Newman organized a potentially fine hiking trip of three days in the Saint Lucia Mountains south of Carmel, with many first-timers participating. The first night out, camped one thousand feet above the coast in a lovely valley full of glossy red-barked madrone trees, we were treated to a three-inch downpour, which brought everyone crowding into our small tents and left many people with wet clothes and sleeping bags. As a result, most of the party went home without waiting for a second night, and we did not attain Ventana Cone, the highest peak in the area, which was our objective.

In April there was another ski trip, which enabled me to get to Silver Lake while the mountains were still under their mantle of snow. A large group skiied up the lake with packs to my cabin and enjoyed the long days and the utter isolation of the whole wide basin. The cabin was a comfortable base from which groups went exploring in various directions; two of the girls reported that they celebrated the occasion by skiing shirtless up the length of the lake in the warm, golden afternoon. The whole scene was completely white, except for the dark pine trees, and the surface of the lake gleamed brilliantly in the spring sunshine.

Besides the loss of Aunt Anne, Dad's sister, I experienced another that spring. Aunt Minna, Mother's sister, died in April at the age of ninety-four. Always fiercely independent, she had often expressed the wish to die rather than be helpless. Now it was a joy to know that she was free from the age-burdened body of the last few years. Her series of strokes had gradually deprived her of her job, her apartment, her speech, and finally her mobility. During the last couple of years she had been angry at her humiliating condition and did not want to see anyone. With Dad gone and Bob too far away, it had fallen on me to visit her occasionally in the rest home in Menlo Park. It had been an increasingly painful task; her death was a relief.

Her service was at Memorial Church, and my brother Bob gave a superbly appropriate eulogy, bringing tears and laughter to all who had known her, capturing the wonderful mixture of stiff-backed rectitude and keen wit which had endeared her to Stanford people for a period of sixty years. At last she was free to grow, as in fact we had seen her grow during her seventies in all the ways that were so unique and charming about her.

The spring of 1974 was not only difficult for me personally; it also involved changes at St. Ann's. Father Giguere, after fifteen years of preaching on Sundays at the church, was now with us as a full-time assistant. The Archbishop had told him that his philosophy courses were too existential and his influence with the students too personal and magnetic. Bob Giguere was unable to make so basic a change in his style of teaching, so the Archbishop asked that the Sulpicians transfer him to a different seminary. Instead he left the faculty.

People at St. Ann's had long enjoyed and appreciated what Bob gave us; his sermons were well-known for their unusual topics, often based on popular songs and children's literature. Greatly valued as a part-time member of the staff, he was invited by the parish council to join St. Ann's as a full-time assistant. However, perhaps because of his difficult experience, I noticed that his sermons seemed to become more conservative: serious biblical themes replaced the lighter talks we were used to.

He also needed a place to live, but did not want to be part of a large household such as Newman. Since Dad's death my home, which was only three blocks away, had been vacant. When the extensive repair work that my brother Bob and I found necessary was completed, we decided to rent the house to Bob Giguere. We did not wish to sell, for we expected that my brother and his family would want to live there someday. Bob Giguere moved in with his huge white poodle, subletting a room to John Young, a priest and Stanford medical student.

That spring John held a party for the Newman crowd at their house, which I attended. It was strange to be going to my home and finding that the atmosphere there was so different. Bob's pictures on the wall were disturbing: the garish colors and words of Sister Corita's serigraphs seemed to me a poor replacement for the paintings and etchings of scenes and people which had hung there most of my life. I especially disliked the fact that a beautiful landscape of the Carmel coast, which Dad had commissioned to fit over the mantle, had been removed. But I enjoyed seeing the old place full of life and gaiety, as it had been when my parents were alive and well.

Pleasant as life in the Newman household continued to be, it lacked the unity I had so much enjoyed. Many good friends were leaving. Arni, who, when the house was crowded, had become my most recent roommate, completed his work at Stanford Research Institute and returned to San Diego. Others who left the house included Bob Colopy, who had grown up in the strange commmunity founded by Father Leonard Feeney of "Boston Heresy" fame; John Justeson, who had completed his work in Mayan anthopology; and Father Dino Cinel, an Italian priest specializing in the history of Italian immigration to San Francisco.

Jim Bela, in his fifth year at Newman and now our house manager, was involved in a running battle about hours and wages with the parish council, leaving him frustrated and sullen. Our increasing contingent of Chicano students, although delightful as a group, remained uninvolved with the outdoors and many other activities which had characterized the Newman house. I missed the closeness our household had experienced in recent years.

Another factor which diminished my enjoyment of life at Newman was Miriam's insistent concern with social problems. Without the close bonds of the old group to diffuse the pressure, I felt more compelled to listen to the projects in which she was immersed.

In addition, many people continued to complained to me that Miriam's work had no connection to St. Ann's or Stanford, and should not be occupying her time. Miriam was very much involved at this time with an interracial day-care center in Sunnyvale which was based on the political principles of Mao Tse-tung. Although Miriam was very dedicated to this form of social action, I too felt that the project was not sufficiently related to St. Ann's community.

By contrast, the Social Justice Committee of St. Ann's Parish Council, which was headed by genial, indefatigable Edda Ritson, was involved in an educational project appropriate to the Stanford community. They were raising and distributing money in the form of scholarships to disadvantaged black teenagers in nearby East Palo Alto.

These two contrasting approaches to social action produced a conflict that was wearing me down. Moreover, I was distressed by the daily need to deal with Miriam's tireless enthusiasm in the house. Confusion and indecision tormented me: how was I to handle these situations? I found myself trying to avoid Miriam's dominating presence on the one hand, and on the other evading those who wanted me to fire her as associate chaplain.

Amidst these differences and difficulties, I welcomed the opportunity to get away for our semi-annual Newman retreat. Unable to obtain reservations in our favorite location, Jones Gulch, we used a new site: the youth hostel at the Hidden Villa Ranch in Los Altos. Since it was late in the spring, the nights were fairly warm. It was delightful as always to sleep outside in the moonlight and to cook cooperatively over the wood stove. Many individuals said they gained personal insights from the retreat, but the numbers were less than usual.

As summer approached, a series of backpacking trips were planned for the High Sierra—a total of five. The first was to be an exploration of the canyons below Silver Lake, a trip chosen to avoid the exceptionally heavy snow that year in the high country. The second was to be an investigation of the trail-less granite canyon above Wishon Lake on the north fork of the Kings River. The last trip was scheduled for September and would bring a group of less experienced hikers into the wide meadows at the northern tip at Yosemite Park, scarlet at that time with dwarf bilberry.

As the days grew long and the sweet smells of flowers and freshly cut grass filled the air, I would spend as much time as possible in the Newman garden. With my clipboard on my lap, I would work on sermons or write letters while enjoying the singing of the mockingbirds and the warm sunshine. At such times, I would be filled with longing for the high mountains.

One day, in the midst of all this seasonal activity I received a phone call from a young woman who wished to take instructions. She had attempted to get these lessons from a priest at St. Thomas Aquinas but had been frustrated by his routine answers and his paternalistic style. A neighbor suggested she call me. We made an appointment for later that day, the third of June.

At precisely three o'clock, I heard her coming briskly up the stairs and greeting Karen at her desk in the hall. As soon as she came into the office, I arose from my desk and led her to the long couch at the end of the room where I often sat while giving lessons. She was quite different from most of the women who came. Slim and small, with big dark eyes, she wore a long skirt with a swirly pattern, a brightly colored short-sleeved blouse, and a red scarf tied around her hair. The effect was a gypsy style which I found provocative and unusual.

I learned that she had moved to Palo Alto a few months before from the Monterey peninsula and that she was an artist, primarily a painter. She had no religious training but knew the importance of the Catholic tradition in art. Moreover, while living in Carmel, she had loved to meditate in the chapel of the Carmelite Monastery near Point Lobos. She wished to take lessons in Catholicism. We had a second lesson a few days later, but after that no more for a while, for there were two mountain trips that took me away for the latter part of June.

It was not until early July that we resumed our instructions, and I soon found that it was impossible to follow a regular course of lessons. I usually would have covered an orderly series of topics: basic doctrine, the history and organization of the Church, and its moral and spiritual teachings. But she never gave me time to present my own material. Her interest in the Church and its history was lively enough, but her questions were unexpected and often puzzling, arising from the perspective of psychology, mythology, and art. She appeared very well read in these areas.

I sometimes was at a loss to understand the things she told me. On one occasion she recounted a long dream—more detailed than any I had ever experienced—in which my bathroom sink had overflowed uncontrollably, so that she and I (in the sitting room) had seen blood running out into the room where we sat. I expected that I should give advice, but she was not looking for an interpretation from me; she just wanted to share her dream. I didn't know what to say next. These situations were embarrassing, yet she attracted me.

During the following days, she often came to the afternoon daily Mass. Sometimes brought Leslie or Ariel, her children, who were then seven and four years old. I was always aware of her presence.

On the eleventh of July, she invited me to come to dinner with her and her two little girls at the house which she was renting a few blocks away. Like all clerics of my time, I had been taught to avoid being alone with any woman, unless she was "super-adulta" (i.e., old!); however, the children seemed to provide the required atmosphere of propriety, and I accepted. I loved sharing meals in the homes of the people I knew: it filled out my understanding of them and always provided surprises in matters of food and decor and in interests to be shared.

On that warm evening she came for me after Mass. We stopped on the way to visit a blind potter whom she knew. She admired the way he produced such beautiful vases and dishes without being able to see them. As we left there, she reached out and gently led me by the hand in a way that was unexpected, charming, and a little embarrassing.

Her little house stood towards the back of the lot under a big oak tree, with a wide lawn in front. There was only one real room; the kitchen was closet-size, and the children had a little space of their own to one side. I was amazed at how much was crowded into so small a space. Books and works of art were everywhere; there was hardly room to sit down, and the drafting table occupied the place of honor.

She went right away into the kitchen to continue her preparation of dinner. I stood in the doorway or wandered about as we talked, looking at the diverse paintings and drawings on the walls. I was acutely aware of my lack of artistic sophistication and found it hard to carry on a good conversation. She called my attention to a drawing of a dead bird, which elicited from me an exceptionally tactless reaction, "It gives me the willies!"

After having managed to insult one of her pictures almost immediately, I didn't do very much better with the dinner, which was one of her favorites, a bouillabaisse stew. "What's that?" I asked clumsily. I felt self-conscious—too much so to be aware of the effort she had put into the dinner. Later on, she led the conversation into areas of art, poetry, and myth where I felt very inadequate. In fact, I felt very awkward all evening; I was only at ease talking about myself or about the Church!

The children had long gone to bed and still we talked on. I began to be aware of the late hour and was trying to find a graceful way of bringing the evening to a close. This was hard to do: the conversation never seemed to reach a natural conclusion. But I managed I to hint that it was time that I really should go home.

After a pause she looked at me with a little smile, and said softly, "I wish we could be lovers." For me this idea was so startling that it took a while to penetrate my consciousness. As it did, I was embarrassed, attracted, frightened. Eventually I stammered in my confusion, "I have feelings too." I was shaking.

Here I was suddenly faced with the possibility of a sexual experience—the thought was like an electric shock! I had never been approached this way before and had assumed for forty years that an intimate relationship with a woman simply would not to be part of my life.

I was afraid: afraid of the strange, new feelings of desire and curiosity within me, and also of the changes that this would bring into my life. I was deeply reluctant to hurt her and sad at the deprivation I was imposing on myself, but I clumsily told her that a love affair was simply impossible, that I could not imagine living under the cloud of secrecy which such a relationship would impose upon a part of my life. I admitted that I was terrified of what it might ultimately do to my vocation as a priest and the security of my lifestyle. In spite of the rebuff, she tenderly walked me home.

I didn't go to sleep for a long time that night, trying to sort out my feelings. This was nothing like what I experienced in the mountains where the nudity I shared was never sexual; nor were these feelings as easy to handle as when, in a counseling situation, I had talked to other couples about their amours. Should I discontinue Eve's instructions and avoid close contact with her in the future? But no, I could not be so unkind, so cowardly. Moreover, she seemed to really want to learn from me as a teacher and a priest.

The succeeding months were exceedingly busy. Not only did mountains trips, with all their attendant preparations and subsequent slide shows, occupy a good part of the remaining summer, but I had a number of other out-of-town commitments that continued through the fall. There was a retreat for married couples at Vallombrosa in Menlo Park, which entailed several daily lectures and many hours of counseling over a long weekend, and another retreat for students in the fall. There was a three-day visit to the campus at Ashland, Oregon, where I was asked to evaluate the ministry of the sister who was Newman chaplain there. I took advantage of the trip to visit the McClains, my brother's close friends, at their ranch near Mt. Shasta, and another couple in Eureka whom I had married at St. Ann's. There were two Newman Chaplains' Association meetings — one in Three Rivers near Fresno, so close to the Sierra that I could not resist driving up to the snow line; and the other at Spokane, Washington, which enabled me to visit David Stronk, who had been one of my San Mateo boy scouts in 1944 and was later ordained, but was now married and teaching at the university in Pullman.

When I was at home, the Newman Center was swarming with visitors, some on organizational business, others for counseling of various kinds, and some simply to catch up on the news. The place was full of life. It was a happy, satisfying fall and provided me with ample distraction from the new and enigmatic relationship I had developed with Eve DeBona. However, when I was in town she visited me. She was no longer seeking regular instruction; rather, her questions were personal, relating religion to her own experience.

One day she came to my office after a visit to the chapel. It had been deeply disturbing, for she had sensed a hostile presence there. I did not know how to advise her; most people did not recount such experiences, certainly not in church. Was the whole thing a fantasy, due to some psychological disturbance? Or was there some genuine diabolic spirit that had sought to oppress her?

I was at a loss to know how to respond. Characteristically, when people came to me with a problem I would feel that I should offer a solution to it or show that the problem did not exist. But as always, she was an enigma to me.

In spite of her charming personality and my efforts to remain business-like, these sessions were fraught with anxiety for me. She didn't ask the questions that I expected people to ask, she didn't say the things I had often heard people say, and she didn't react in the usual way to my explanations.

I tried to receive her as I would any other client: kindly but with professional detachment. Nonetheless, I was appalled by the strong feelings of hurt and anger she would suddenly direct towards me if I was cold and unperceptive. But equally disturbing was her love for me, which I felt I had done nothing to deserve. Her mercurial moods were as strange and alarming to me as her questions were unusual, and I was forever suspended between dread and anticipation.

I was also concerned by the outward appearance of her visits, their frequency and their free and easy style. She came to visit me a bit more often than others would and with a little possessiveness in her manner. I realized that her social and religious background carried no taboo against wooing the affections of a priest, but the need for caution weighed upon me. I was afraid that my secretary, Karen, would pick up something unusual as Eve entered and left my office.

One day Eve came in with a little surprise. She handed me a caligraphed manuscript which she had beautifully illustrated in color. It was the first chapter of a fairy tale entitled "Little Red Lips and the Three Priests." In this first installment, she described the enigmatic experiences of Little Red Lips in dealing with the first two priests, and her rapturous response to number three, who clearly was myself. I read it over and over trying to discover the message hidden within. What I found was that it offered me a mirror in which to study my conflicting motives, and it helped me to understand her mystifying emotions.

On subsequent visits, Eve brought me other episodes, which one by one, unfolded her relationships with the priests, ending with a soul-satisfying union with the third priest. Up to this point, I had been quite successful in ignoring her sexual attractivess; I had, after all, many years of practice in doing so with other women. But from her story I gained an insight into the beauty and power of human love that made me question my clerical assumptions about the negative effect intimate relationships would have on priests.

Once during the fall, she signed up for a Newman hike at Big Sur River below Carmel. Although she was formally just a member of the party, she was frequently at my side, sometimes holding my hand and asking many questions about the natural world around us. I felt protective towards her, and I wondered if the closeness I felt would be noticed by others in the party, in particular Karen, my secretary who was also on the hike.

Soon after that, on the twenty-fourth of October, I was again invited to dinner in her home. This time I was aware in some way that my acceptance of the invitation would mean an acceptance of herself. On my way to her house, I was filled with anticipation and warmth. Later that evening after dinner, before I left to walk home in the quiet night, we spent some time together in bed, an experiment in intimacy that told me that this relationship was something sweet and free from evil.

Some two weeks later she suggested that we go together to see a movie. She was raised in Hollywood and, unlike me, knew films very well. She had chosen a light but sentimental one, "Harold and Maude." I loved it; and when I took her home, I invited myself in. For the first time we really made love, and it was joyous and natural from the start. However, later that night alone in my narrow bed in Newman, I slept poorly, filled with the anxious question: where does all this lead? Is it only going toward a blind alley which will bring her grief in the end?

From that evening onward, our communication improved, and by Christmas we felt, at least at times, that we were really a couple. However, it was only at times: often I was haunted by the ambivalence of attraction for her and fear of a relationship. This conflict made my feelings ebb and flow and caused frequent fluctuations in my behavior, keeping Eve forever in suspense. I could not imagine giving up the priesthood; and when we talked of marriage, it was far off, after my retirement. I finally shared my feelings with Karen when the opportunity arose and learned that she had already sensed that Eve was beginning to occupy a special place in my life. She seemed happy for me.

I continued my priestly work and my parish social life as always, but quite insensitive to the difficulty that Eve had in maintaining her hidden role. "You come over here at night, as if you were doing me a big favor," she said angrily on one occasion. "At the end of an evening! Everybody else has first claim on your time. You never suggest anything for us to do. What am I supposed to do—just wait for your gracious arrival! I have my art work, and the kids, yes—but I'm tired of being your closet woman." I felt she was unfair: after all, she had started the whole thing, and I had my work to do. Her anger left me devastated and confused.

The happiest times Eve and I had were in the outdoors. The day after my fifty-seventh birthday, the two of us went to Henry Coe Park alone for a glorious day of sunshine, wildflowers and sparkling water. It was a delight to reveal to her the wonders of nature, which had been such a focus of my own life, and to share with her the beauty to which she was so responsive. For me, these excursions were a glorious relief. The wilderness setting seemed to sweep away the clouds of fear and anxiety which belonged to the Church-world: here I could be my true self, anonymous, and young at heart.

Early that February, Richard Thesing, president of the parish council, came to tell me that the council was planning to deal with whether Miriam should remain on the staff and, if so, what her role should be. The meeting was set for March 10, and as the time

184

approached, I heard that Miriam was gathering support for herself on campus and elsewhere. The meeting was obviously going to be large and controversial. The council decided that it should be held in the chapel so there would be room for everyone.

That night the church was packed. I sat with the council members looking out into the crowd from the stage of the altar; as during Sunday Mass, many people were sitting on the steps of the altar, including Eve, who was quite near me. In the congregation, I could see the faces of many people who were unconnected with our community. Richard presented the problem which had been developing: the community had become painfully divided over the appropriateness of having a person on its staff whose work was primarily concerned with radical politics. As a result, the tension was becoming too much to bear.

Some members of the community spoke on either side of this issue. Those who wanted to remove her from the position of associate chaplain were divided themselves. Many felt that the work she was doing was not serving St. Ann's community and therefore should not be paid for by that community. Others felt that she related too abrasively to those who did not share her political perspective. Some felt that radicalism implied the use of violence and therefore was incompatible with a Christian community.

Miriam and her supporters set forth their case: that St. Ann's was failing in its spiritual mission to speak to the needs of all the people. Being unwilling to accept the radical implications of Miriam's ministry, St. Ann's was trying to rid itself of her witness.

All over the church people were trying to speak. As a result, the issues were increasingly confused. Finally, the council called a halt to the discussion and left briefly to vote. Upon their return, Richard announced that their decision was to let Miriam go. Many people there were greatly angered by that decision, and the meeting ended full of bitterness and misunderstanding.

For the next few days, I stayed away from Newman. Upon my return, Eve confronted me with how badly the affair had been managed. I realized that long before the issue had reached such an intensity of feeling, I should have made it clear to Miriam and all others concerned that we must work together in such a way as to remain a community. I was the one responsible for making the changes necessary to achieve teamwork. The more I thought about what Eve had said, the more deeply I regretted the way in which I had allowed the matter to be decided. I felt more unhappy and guilty about my indecisiveness and the resultant damage to the community than any other failure in my life.

These parish problems made me more aware that Eve and I should not remain so isolated. We needed to have friends in common and places to go where we could share such stress and anxiety, as that evening had created, as well as the joy and fun of being together as a couple.

Eve was too new in Palo Alto to have friends to whom we could turn. Up to this point, it had been impossible to broach the subject to anyone; it amounted to presenting myself in a completely new and unfamiliar role. I expected people to greet my revelation with amazement, if not horror. I was even shy and reticient to tell our story to my brother and his wife, who now lived in Los Gatos.

As I began to look for some local friends who would accept us as a couple, Jim Duran and Gerry Colby came to mind. Their countercultural lifestyle assured me that they would accept us. Both were old friends of mine from the San Jose days and later at Stanford. We took them to dinner in Saratoga. It was a great evening. They were our first married confidants.

In April of 1975, I finally overcame the hesitance I felt about talking to Bob and Lu. I went alone to tell them, feeling more self-conscious about it than I should have been, considering that they had been through a parallel experience. Their first reaction was loving and supportive, and I was relieved. But within a few minutes, as I told my story of who Eve was and how we met, their attitude seemed to cool, although they listened attentively. They cautioned me about the problems that might lie ahead and suggested that I not act hastily. Driving home that evening, I tried to dismiss the feeling that all was not well, that they did not entirely accept or trust my new relationship. When Eve asked me about the visit, I was ashamed to share with her the anxiety I felt.

In June, just a year after we had met, I took Eve and her children for the first time to the Sierra to my beloved Silver Lake. For me it had the feeling of a pilgrimage: it brought together my new love with what had been the most continuous thread in my whole life. It also gave me my first taste of being a parent.

Heavy late snows kept boats off the lake, so we had to carry our supplies to the camp along a mile of snowy trail. Ariel, who was only five, soon grew tired, and I had to carry her part of the way. We settled in to the new wooden house that had been built to conform to county requirements. However, it was the old stone cabin that fascinated Eve, for it was an expression of my father's artistic spirit. It seemed so sad that she and Dad could not have known each other.

After the arduous hike in, we had the whole world to ourselves, peace and privacy, sunshine, the songs of nesting robins, and the fragrant pines. Eve and I climbed to the top of the granite ridge behind our camp which was clear of snow for a view of the lake. An open area of water off our shoreline permitted us to use the canoe for short trips, but mostly we stayed inside or on the deck of the house.

It was only a month after this that the world began falling apart for me. Earlier in the year I had accepted my brother's invitation to share a few days with his family at Silver Lake, as had been usual since Dad's death. Two months had passed since I had told them about Eve, but as the time approached they did not include her in the invitation. In fact, they made no effort to meet Eve or her children. This was both painful and puzzling to me, but I was loath to admit to myself that they might be distrusting my judgment and not accepting our love.

However, I continued with my plans to go, knowing that Eve had other projects and feeling that she would not care anyway. At the last moment, Eve told me that she was frustrated over my willingness to go without her. It hadn't occurred to me that she would see it as an act of disloyalty and abandonment. But in any case it was too late, I wasn't going to back out now. Peter Spain and I drove up together in his car.

I did not question Bob about why Eve was not included. On the second day, I went on a hike with Peter. On my return to camp, an urgent message was waiting to call Eve. I hiked down to Kay's Resort at the end of the lake to phone her, and learned that she was in bed with spasmodic back pain; she needed me. I felt caught between her needs and mine: what could I do? That night, I began to run a fever. Lu, although a nurse, did not know what was wrong with me and lacked what was needed to take care of me there, so she advised me to go home.

Peter drove me home. Hastening anxiously to Eve's little house, I found her flat on her back in great pain. We tried to comfort each other, feeling not only sick but sad about what had happened. Then I went home to Newman, where for a week I ran a high fever twice daily. From there I was transferred to Stanford Hospital, where my condition was finally determined to be mononucleosis, a disease that belongs reputedly to the young.

Lots of people visited me in the hospital, of course. Eve was up now, and every night, late enough to miss the other visitors, she would come with gifts of flowers and posters to brighten my room. She was always sparkling and unpredictable. Once she even came in a mask. Every night I waited eagerly for the encouragement and love which she brought me.

The doctor said that I would need a week in bed and a month of more of quiet recuperation after leaving the hospital. So for the first week Bob and Lu invited me to stay at their home, where Lu could give me good nursing care. I saw no alternative; to stay at Eve's house, so near to St. Ann's, did not seem possible. I accepted their invitation, although torn by the realization that Eve would be feeling cut off from me while I was there. Despite their love and care, I was unhappy because I felt her sense of exclusion.

After that week of separation, Eve picked me up and we, together with the children, drove south to be with Eve's mother and stepfather at their home near San Diego, far from any curious well-wishers. However, after a few happy sunny days, my disease recurred; we drove home, exhausted and worried. The doctor's word was clear: back to bed.

This time I accepted Eve's loving hospitality. It was not to the tiny cottage of our first romantic meetings that we went, but to a four-room flat in a large house on Addison Avenue which Eve's mother had bought as an investment. With the help of some students from Newman, Eve had moved there while I was in the hospital, but she had barely unpacked. The lower floor was her home, and she would rent the upper, an arrangment which seemed good on the supposition that several years would pass before we could settle down as a family.

Upon our hasty return from southern California, we moved in as best we could. I lay in a fold-out bed all day, surrounded by the chaos of furniture, books, papers, and art supplies. For a month, I was too weak to be any help at all; and my hearing was impaired for several months, a great frustration to all of us. In spite of the extra work it created for her, Eve enjoyed having me there and preparing strengthening, healthy meals for me. Leslie and Ariel seemed to accept me into the family; and Sophie, the grey kitten, lay all day on my chest.

Through it all, I felt like a concealed refugee, especially before we got curtains! When Eve interviewed potential tenants for the upper flat, she had to be sure they didn't know me. We also worried about Marie, a single parent whose children Eve had loved at St. Ann's. She belonged to the conservative choir group at St. Ann's and was a former nun; so we didn't feel we could trust her with our secret. We were afraid that she would just drop in unexpectedly.

Once she did. The girls, without having been coached, unob-trusively removed any signs of my presence in the house, while I hid in the bathroom. I sat on the floor for more than an hour waiting for Marie to finish her conversation with Eve. The children could have easily done something to give away my presence, but they always seemed to understand the situation and to accept me into the family without reserve.

During my recuperation, I read dozens of books, and after a while was able to do so out in the sun behind the house. When I became strong enough to do a little work again, I would go back to my office at Newman, unobtrusively and by various routes, for a couple of hours a day to meet with committee heads, to make decisions about questions that had arisen, and to handle my mail. Karen was warned to tell no one where I was convalescing.

At first as I returned to work, people were aware of my weakness and deafness, and accepted my reticence about the circumstances in my convalescence. But as I got back to my normal strength, I felt increasingly awkward about my frequent absences. The impossibility of being open about my life interfered with maintaining normal relationships with the students or the other people at St. Ann's.

I found this whole atmosphere of secrecy extremely oppressive. I took part in the Newman fall retreat, and there painfully became most conscious of this lack of candor. I had always been up front with whatever I thought, but now I had to be guarded. The atmosphere of a retreat was always one of sharing and trust—and here was I, unable to share the one thing in my life that was the cause of the most joy and the most anxiety!

The only part of my life at St. Ann's that seemed normal and enjoyable was preaching. After all my reading and my constant self-questioning, I had a lot to preach about. For those who knew nothing, these sermons were simply an insightful series; for those who knew or guessed my secret, they told the story of my inner struggle.

One of these sermons was from a book *I Heard The Owl Call My Name*, the story of an Episcopal priest who, working among the Indians of the Northwest, was powerless to prevent the erosion of their culture. Having experienced helplessness during my own illness, I deeply empathized with the pathos of this story. Another sermon was based upon the movie *One Flew Over the Cuckoo's Nest*, a psychological drama about life in a mental hospital in which an ordinary man with no lofty ideals is forced by his own honesty to defy the system, until the system has no choice but to destroy him.

One by one, I selected people to tell about Eve; I just had to share. Many were entirely supportive, even sentimental, in their response to my happiness; others, although regretting the probable impact upon my ministry, affirmed my right to be in love. Before Christmas, we held a party for all who had come to know us as a couple—quite a crowd by then—and for the first time had the enjoyment of one aspect of social normalcy, the feeling of entertaining together.

As the days went on, some of these people attempted to persuade us that we should "come out." They thought it would be better than having the Archbishop pick up a rumor and summon me to explain; moreover, it would permit the community of St. Ann's to deal with its own response to the situation without haste. It was disturbing to learn from them that already there were others who either knew my secret or suspected it and were feeling abandoned and angry.

Still I did nothing. Life at St. Ann's was busy, as always, but I felt unspoken questions in everyone's greeting, and a sense of uncertainty and waiting filled the air. I was the celebrant of the Christmas midnight Mass, which was always crowded and festive. However, as a result of my internal confusion, the sermon which I gave was a mess, a fact which Eve pointed out to me emphatically. I felt miserable.

Two days later we drove to Carmel, where the children were to spend a week with their paternal grandparents. Eve and I walked along the beach, talking of the years when she had lived there with them as babies.

Eve had grown up in west Los Angeles. Her first six years, while her father, Joe DeBona, was a flier in the war, were spent with her grandparents. She was happy there, but as an only child, she had to find her companionship with the maids who looked after her. After the war, her parents returned to live in the same area. Her father continued to fly as a hobby; he was a successful insurance man, busy and popular, but with little time for Eve, who was interested in art.

She attended the fashionable Marlborough High School, and most vacations were spent at the beach among her parents' social circle. After a year of college, she was married young and elegantly to Baron Florian von Imhof, a marriage which lasted only a year. She became part of the Los Angeles art world, moving in a fun-loving, interesting group of people. In time she fell in love with Jim Gore, whose special talent lay in film animation. They moved to the Monterey peninsula, where the girls were born, and lived in the colony of artists—new age people among whom being poor was no disgrace. This relationship came to an end when Ariel was less than two, and Eve eventually moved to Palo Alto, a place where she had heard the children would find more stimulation.

Compared to the stability of my life, hers seemed to have been difficult and lonely, punctuated by many abrupt changes. But we both shared an early experience of the ocean, and in particular of Carmel Beach, where I had often gone with my family as a child.

Climbing up from the beach, we went searching for the site of my Stillman grandparents' little shingled house, which I remembered so vividly. It had stood on the white sands just across the road from the beach, and the smell of the sea and the pines and the roaring of the waves were among my pleasantest memories. Sadly, there was nothing to show where it had been.

As soon as we returned to Palo Alto, the problem of my love and my priesthood again weighed heavily upon me. The St. Ann's Parish Council meeting in early January of 1976 provided me with the opportunity to reveal my situation. I had been advised by some to make my situation known, and I wanted help from the council in deciding what to do. Should I come out in public or not? Should I tell the Archbishop?

There were some radical voices among the group who wished to defy the authority of the Church and retain me as their pastor regardless of what the Archbishop said. But they were a minority; most felt that the parish would have to come to terms with the fact that I would soon be removed from my pastorate. Nothing would be gained by further delay. I should go to see the Archbishop as soon as possible. I made an appointment to see him.

On the fateful day Eve accompanied me on the drive to San Francisco for my interview. Although I had long since resolved my conscience—not only about our intimacy but also about those of my beliefs which ran counter to official Church policy—I was terrified of this meeting. For Eve, my feelings were bewildering, and I found it difficult to explain that it was not my own uncertain future that frightened me so much as the Archbishop himself, the authority figure whom I had always found so intimidating.

We parked well away from the Chancery Office. I changed in the car to my black shirt, round collar and suit-coat. Eve asked if I wanted her to walk with me to the door of the Chancery building, but I said no. I was afraid to be seen together. I left and walked to the Office, alone, to beard the lion in his den. How could I hope to make the Archbishop understand?

I don't know what I expected: some time, at least; maybe a suggestion of some way in which I could continue to serve the Church. I just knew that I could not go on any longer hiding from the world the special relationship which had become central to my life.

I was ushered into Archbishop McGucken's office almost immediately. He welcomed me in his heavy, guarded way. He was a big man, with large unsmiling eyes and a deep rumbling voice. He smoked constantly. I got quickly to the point: I was in love, and would eventually wish to marry. What would this mean for me in terms of my position in the Church?

As soon as I stopped talking, the turgid waves of his rhetoric rolled over me. Not that he said very much: ". . . Well, priests have these ideas. . . mid-life crisis. . . you've been under a lot of stress and illness. . . men fall in love, but often they get over it. . . go away for a few months. . . a good retreat. . . " I felt like a young priest being given fatherly direction which had the weight of unanswerable authority. It wasn't his words that made me feel this way, but the whole ambiance, the old clerical assumptions of obedience, celibacy, and the separateness of a priestly caste.

I found I could not put my present reality into any language that would be meaningful to him. To him, Eve did not exist as a person! She was merely a danger to be avoided. After a few lame efforts at expressing the seriousness of my love, I gave up, and agreed I would think about what he had said. Then I got out of there, feeling completely defeated and helpless. Faced with authority, I was always inarticulate.

Driving home, I felt cowardly and disloyal to Eve. I had not succeeded in communicating to the Archbishop the real importance of Eve in my life. We talked about it on the way, and I decided to write him immediately, saying on paper in the clear air of my own world what I could not express in his presence.

The next day, Eve and I took the girls to San Gregorio Beach. It was a glorious, golden day, and the beach was all ours. A day of sunbathing and photography and picnicking,: a time of serenity and naturalness after the nightmarish unreality of the Chancery Office.

That night I wrote the letter, in which I made it clear to the Archbishop that I did not believe marriage was in any way incompatible with the priesthood; therefore, I would not resign. If he could not accept that, he would have to fire me. Moreover, I would not seek "laicization," since that too would amount to condoning the oppressive policy of enforced celibacy which was robbing the Church of so many young and talented men. I was notified by return mail that I would be suspended from my pastoral office immediately.

Bob Giguere was summoned the following day and told that he would be chaplain until further notice. He came over to Eve's house to tell us about it, and he was very emotional, assuring me that I was welcome to speak to the community on Sunday at all the Masses. That night I took Eve to Los Gatos to have dinner with Bob and Lu and felt in their warmth and in Bob's witty reminiscences the support and family unity I had been missing for so long. Next morning I went to the *Palo Alto Times* to give them my official story, for publication on Monday. Then I settled down to preparing my final talk at St. Ann's.

On Sunday, I gave my farewell sermon, with Eve there. Starting with a review of the years at St. Ann's, I explained how my vision of the ministry had changed, becoming increasingly a commitment to building a community which would embody the hope in Christ's message. "We are trying to become our fullest selves," I said, "joyful, loving, and free." I cited the fact that I had often done this in spite of, rather than with the help of, the Church. "Now at last I have done the one thing the institution will not tolerate: I have fallen in love. I might be a tyrant, a drunk, a miser, or a do-nothing, and gotten away with it; but love is not considered compatible with ministry, at least not the total, intimate, and committed love which we call marriage."

I spoke calmly, but it was immensely satisfying to speak openly to my community after all the months of concealment and evasion. As I continued into the liturgy, the congregation was quiet; I could not tell what their reaction had been.

After Mass the people swarmed around me, affectionate and supportive. To the great majority of people, it was a total surprise. Many had met Eve but did not know her. She had helped with the child care on Sunday mornings and had many friends among the young parents. This morning she was at my side to be introduced as the one I loved. But behind the kindness and well-wishing, I felt that many people felt cheated that I had been experiencing so much without letting them in on it.

However, there were also many, less evident in the after-Mass gatherings that morning, who were shocked and angry. They had seen me as contented with my life—I had said so emphatically in my birthday sermon only a year before—and they were unprepared for this sudden change. They variously felt robbed, abandoned, insulted, and deceived.

A few days later a reporter interviewed Eve and me at length and with obvious relish about our romance. He also asked our views on many questions of current interest to religious people, such as divorce and abortion, gay rights, feminism, and the general question of priestly celibacy. We enjoyed talking with him. His story, when it appeared a week after my final sermon, caused an uproar in the community. Although his story was entirely faithful to what we had said, it did not carry the churchly reticence to which Catholics were accustomed. Therefore, our words sounded startlingly bald and inflammatory.

Our friends' reaction was: "This is a disaster! Your reputation is ruined." For a few days we sat around wondering if we would have any friends left. People told us that many of the middle-class Catholics in the St. Ann's community who had until now supported us were shocked by our candor. Their question was "How will we explain this to our children?" Of course there were people— Quakers, ex-Catholics, Unitarians, gays, and hippies—applauded our honesty and courage. But the euphoric mood of my last sermon was gone.

In spite of these setbacks, Eve and I often discussed the question of how and when we would be married. For a variety of reasons, June seemed to be the right time, permitting us to deal with an assortment of other business. However, it was hard to decide the style. Would we go quietly go away to the mountains to be married with just a few close friends? Would we ask my brother to do the ceremony? Should it be well publicized, to allow all the friends from St. Ann's to come, or should we try to keep it small? We did not feel that we were ready to answer these questions yet, and decided to let the events of the next month or two guide us in our decision.

During the next few weeks, I continued to go regularly to the Newman Center. I spent several hours every day at my desk, preparing records for my successor and dealing with mail. I also made appointments to meet people there. Although I was gradually packing my books and furniture, I had no idea of severing my connections with St. Ann's. Eve and I continued to go regularly to Mass on Sundays and to visit afterward with the people.

We also received invitations from several families in the St. Ann's community to have dinner, who said they wished to talk about what my leaving meant to their involvement with the Church. For me it was a pleasure to introduce and show off the one I loved, but Eve thought that some of these people had the unspoken purpose of sizing her up. In some cases she even felt that they held her to blame for stealing their priest.

In the course of these conversations and appointments, I made a disturbing discovery. Much as they had applauded my preaching, many members of the parish had not truly accepted one of my most consistent messages. At one of the dinner parties, a woman said, "Father, as long as you were speaking to us with the Church's approval, I was able to accept all sorts of new ideas about religion and morality. But now that you won't be there, I feel that I'm out on a limb by myself, and I will have to duck back into the security of my old beliefs." One woman even said, in Eve's hearing, "Father, you should never have left us. Things will never be the same without you." I was very disappointed by these comments and others like them.

For many years, I had attempted to convince my listeners that each of us must form his or her own conscience, not simply obeying the commands of someone in authority. I had encountered resistance to this message from more conservative members of the community, but most people welcomed gladly the idea that every human conscience is fundamentally free. When speaking about a controversial question, I would present both sides, supporting each one with good authorities, and I would then tell the people that they must make up their own minds. Now it was brought home to me that this message had not been accepted at the deepest level: people felt I had been leading them down appealing but dangerous paths, which they could no longer follow if I was not there to lead. Obviously, the personal freedom of conscience which I had so constantly preached had not been internalized.

Although I kept going to Newman, I became aware of my changed status—that I was no longer pastor—only when I met Bob Giguere. At these times, he seemed to be ill at ease, and said very little; I felt like an outsider. After all, he was now officially acting pastor, and it must have also been difficult for him, after fifteen years of my being the leader there, to switch roles. My presence must have been a cause of anxiety to him, for I found out that he had suppressed the copies made of my last sermon.

However, Bob was only acting pastor for two months. Soon the Archbishop appointed a diocesan priest as permanent Newman chaplain. His name was Eugene Boyle, no relative to my former pastor Edgar from the days of Sacred Heart in Oakland. Boyle was a classmate of my brother and had been a companion on pack trips and a guest in my parents' home. In recent years, he had been actively involved with such social issues as farm-workers' rights and the black freedom movement, and loved to speak of his acquaintance with Cesar Chavez and Martin Luther King, Jr.

I welcomed his appointment. His sensitivity to questions of social justice in the secular world made me think that he would be interested in the reforms of the Church which had occupied us at St. Ann's and perhaps even in the question of new roles for married priests. I suggested that I introduce him to the people. However, he ignored my offer.

Eve and I were there to hear his first sermon. I was accustomed to his ornate style from the times when he had introduced couples' retreats which I was to conduct when he was director of Vallombrosa Retreat Center. This time, he started by introducing himself, letting the community know from the start that he had been significantly involved with the struggles for social justice during the 1960s. Eve did not lose five minutes in making up her mind—his talk could have been given to any audience; it showed no awareness of the special spirit of this community. She walked out and never went to Mass there again.

Soon we were coming to the chapel only to meet our friends after Mass. Boyle's greetings were hearty but impersonal. The picture became gradually clear to me: I was being quietly excluded. Nothing was ever said directly to me, but the chairman of the spring retreat was informed that I could say no Mass there, as had been planned by the committee. I was not offered any function at the center. Eventually I felt that I was really unwelcome.

Feeling increasingly alienated from St. Ann's, Eve and I went to the Memorial Church for the celebration of Ash Wednesday, and were entranced with the message and the style of Ernle Young, who was the chaplain for Stanford Hospital and Associate Dean of the Chapel. He was a Methodist, originally from South Africa. Avoiding theological abstractions, he spoke with the simplicity of scriptural narrative; his words were warm and personal and full of faith. Eve poked me as Ernle talked and whispered, "This is the one"—the one to officiate at our wedding. I gladly agreed, and we asked him the next day. To our delight, he accepted.

Meanwhile Eve and I and the girls were involved with the practical matters of daily living. The change in my way of life, adjusting to a home and a family, was not as difficult as I had expected. Family life was not entirely new; I had the life-long model of my own home, a very strong and happy one. I also had already experienced several months of living as a convalescent in Eve's home, where the children accepted me as their father without comment or problem.

The hardest adjustment was to the limited room and lack of order. Eve had no need for the order around her which was so vital to me. As long as things were clean, it did not bother her that every surface was piled with her papers, books, and works of art. In the crowded Addison flat, I had only a single card-table which was "my space," and I felt the need for more.

From the start, I assumed we would move, as soon as Bob Giguere and John Young could find other quarters, into my family home, where we would have much more space. The move, in early

March, was accomplished with the help of friends and turned into a festive occasion, complete with food and drink.

To save us money, they loaned vehicles and helped install appliances. Furnishings that had been in our families were assembled from Newman and from Eve's house. John Kiely and a strong crew rolled my grandfather's huge old bookcase from Newman on a handcart. Everything movable was stored in Dad's old studio until it could be assimilated with what was already in the house.

After the crowded but cozy rooms at the Addison house, the place did not immediately seem comfortable, in spite of the beauty of its architecture. It was strange to be there as head of a family, my own family, and to be making this place our home. For several months both Eve and I felt that we were my parents' guests, as if we should be asking their permission to make changes in the arrangement of things. And in bureau drawers and closets we kept finding mementos: my mother's wedding dress, an old comb she used to wear in her hair, Aunt Minna's reading glasses, and the set of carving tools that my dad used in his work. Not till summer did we feel fully at home.

In spite of the excitement and hard work of getting settled into our home, the long-range problem of how to make a living lurked in the background, softened by my six months severance pay from St. Ann's. I took some action by providing for the management of my savings and the money inherited from my parents so that we would get a small but steady income from it. We had also a cushion in the gifts collected for us by friends.

Although some council members were hoping to arrange for a permanent pension, another group of my most active supporters at St. Ann's felt that the possibilty could not be relied upon. Accordingly, they formed a committee to raise money for a retirement fund. Although this sum never became large enough to generate an income for us, the money was a great blessing during this transitional period.

This group asked that I say Mass for them. I was happy that they wanted me to continue serving them in this way. They were accustomed to occasional home liturgies, and my living room seemed a comfortable and spacious place for us to gather. We began to meet there on Friday nights, avoiding Sunday mornings so that we would not appear to be competing with Mass at St. Ann's.

Aside from my role as their priest, I felt quite helpless. I had never in my life "found a job." Eve and I had a number of schemes, the most promising of which involved running a hostel at the Addison house for people with cystic fibrosis who were out-patients at Stanford Children's Hospital. There was a community of these young adults who were looking for just such a facility near the Hospital, and we thought we might manage the house for them. However, their funding fell through, and the scheme was abandoned.

In April our whole attention was turned to another matter: an operation on Eve's shoulder, which had been severely dislocated a decade before in the southern California surf. Her right arm had continued to dislocate frequently, but she had postponed having an operation for fear of losing still more mobility. But recently a friend, Bernardine Frank, had convinced Eve that the surgery could be safely performed by a doctor she knew in San Francisco.

It was a busy time, with many trips to see the surgeon before and after the operation, and I had many hours of massaging Eve during the following weeks. Again, as when we had moved, many friends rallied around with meals all prepared for the family. Everyone knew that I was completely helpless in the kitchen!

In May, we began arranging for the wedding, which we had decided to have at the Stanford Memorial Church. Not only was Ernle Young, whom we had asked to perform the ceremony, associate dean there, but it was also a special place for me. I had said Mass there for the past ten years; and it was where my parents' wedding had taken place sixty-two years before. Moreover, it was close and large enough to hold everyone who might want to come.

We enjoyed telling our friends about the plans for the day, and asking them to spread the word. It would be a dignified church wedding, but in the informal style that was congenial to Eve and me; and the music would be provided by Pat Mahoney and his wife, Becky. Eve prepared an announcement for the occasion to be mailed to distant friends. We also handed out our announcement on the plaza at St. Ann's, enjoying the fact that we could do what we pleased. The official Church had no more power to stop us. The local paper announced the coming event.

The wedding day was glorious. While the large crowds were gathering, Eve and I wandered around the Church greeting our friends and relatives. When it was time to start, we walked back to the Round Room where Ernle was waiting in his robes and brought him out with us to the foot of the altar. Ascending together to the top of the eight marble stairs, we turned to face the community. Leslie and Ariel stood with us. Some of the people, including my brother and his family, came up and sat on the steps on either side.

Ernle opened the ceremony in his warm, quiet way and read from the scripture. Pat and Becky played and sang music which was especially moving because they had sung so many times with me at

St. Ann's. This day, they opened with the Cat Stevens' song "Morning Has Broken," which touched me deeply with its suggestion of the breaking of a fresh morning in the mountains and the dawning of a new life for me.

After the brief official exchange of consent, I gave a short speech in which I declared my love to Eve and invited the gathering to join in celebrating that love. I considered it to be a fulfillment of my priestly ministry and a coming together of all the rich heritage of faith, art, friendship, music, and the outdoors which we brought to the union. Eve, wearing a Romanian peasant dress, responded by reading a mandala poem, the inspiration for which came from the discovery in our garden of a stone carpet laid by my father long ago which had become slowly covered by the earth.

After the blessing, we walked down the steps to greet our friends. The reception, held at Shoup Park in Los Altos, was essentially a picnic. Eve and I brought wine and cake, and people brought whatever else they wanted to eat. An electric dishwasher was carried onto the green and presented to us. It made a fine place for cutting the cake!

Eve's mother, grandmother, aunt, and cousins were all present. My brother made a speech, as did Afton Blake, Eve's closest woman friend, who unexpectedly flew in from Los Angeles. It was a lovely June day, and it was hard to bring it to an end.

Arriving home after the party with a few of our closest friends and relatives, I found a letter from the Archbishop. It began pointedly, "Dear Mr. Duryea" and informed me that by virtue of the automatic action of canon law, my "attempted marriage" in the presence of a non-Catholic minister entailed excommunication. He asked that I spare other priests the embarrassment of refusing me communion. In the euphoric mood of that day, this letter, far from being intimidating, seemed too archaic and irrelevant to touch our feelings.

4 June 1976

Mr. John S. Duryea
405 Lincoln Avenue
Palo Alto, California 94301

Dear Mr. Duryea:

It is with deep sorrow that I am obliged to notify you that by attempting marriage you have incurred the automatic excommunication provided in Canon 2244 of the Code of Canon Law. In addition to the suspension which you have already received, under Canon 2244 you will be automatically excommunicated. Consequently, you are forbidden to celebrate holy Mass or to receive Holy Communion.

We have been saddened by the fact that many people are scandalized at St. Ann's Chapel when they see you approach the holy table. I hope that you will respect the provisions of the law of the Church and not place any priest who is celebrating holy Mass under the disagreeable obligation of refusing you Holy Communion.

Despite our sorrow over this situation, I assure you that we will keep you in our prayers, with the hope that through the grace of God you may be restored to full membership in the Church and priestly activities, through your obedience to the laws of the Church.

Yours sincerely in Christ,

Joseph T. McGucken
Archbishop of San Francisco

Q

June 7 1976

Joseph T McGucken
Archbishop of San Francisco
445 Church St, San Francisco, Ca

Dear Mr McGucken,

Your letter, graciously timed to arrive on my wedding day,
was so remote from the reality of the occasion that it could
hardly arouse anger, much less fear. It reads like a document disintered from the age of the Inquisition, complete
with stifling legalism, muted threats, and crocodile tears.
I ask you to consider which spirit is represented by such a
letter: the spirit of Christ, or that of the pharisees?

Your anxiety over scandal at St Ann's appears to be unwarranted.
Some 500 people attended my "attempted" marriage in the Stanford
Memorial Church. Most of them were practicing Catholics, and
they made their warm support very evident.

I will continue to minister in all available ways, and my conscience is entirely clear in so doing. I am and will remain a
priest; that is why I did not go through the procedure of laicization. I do not wish to be a layman. And I do not intend to
admit the rightness of the law which denies the option of Christian marriage to priests. There are countless Catholics--I meet
them daily--who are alienated by the rigidity and inhumanity of
the official church and its representatives. I am finding a
fruitful ministry among them.

Despite the hollow booming of your Automatic Canons, I am peacefully in communion with the universal Church, and shall receive
communion when I please. If priests are too intimidated, I am
sure the lay ministers will not be.

Sincerely yours

John S Duryea

10. New Directions

During the summer following our wedding, Eve and I made sure that I had sufficient time for getting into the wilderness. We were looking forward to the serenity of Silver Lake after the illness of the previous year and the great upheavals of the past six months. As soon as the children were out of school, we packed the car and headed for the mountains.

It was a lovely early-summer week, with the robins singing their nesting songs, the days long and the sun warm, and new growth sprouting everywhere. This year, the snow was light, lying only on the distant peaks, and near the lake wildflowers were already appearing. We walked along the shore and canoed over to the island, but mostly just stayed around the camp. The girls played board games in the cabin—games that Bob's family had left there, while Eve and I read a lot under the trees or lay on the rocks sunning ourselves in our bathing suits. Once in a while I would shoo the children out of the cabin to enjoy the fresh air.

One day, in the company of a visiting family, we hiked a mile downstream below the lake to what we called "The Potholes"—a place where the rushing waters had carved polished basins in the granite bedrock.

Later in the summer I went on three mountain trips without the family. Eve was well aware of the importance of the wilderness in my life and wished me to feel free to go. She had not grown up with the outdoor experience and did not want to share all my adventures, and the children were too young. With small groups of friends from Newman, I took two pack trips, one near Silver Lake, the other out of Florence Lake.

A couple of times that summer I was delighted to receive invitations from Dean Kelly to substitute as liturgist and preacher at the Stanford Memorial Church. I had made no plans about what shape my future ministry would take, but I knew I would not cease to be an active priest. According to all theologians my ordination as a priest was irrevocable: the Church by its excommunication could not change that. While its intention was to deny me the right both to give and to receive the Sacraments, it had no power to enforce that denial. Therefore, as I had told the Archbishop at the time of my suspension, I intended to ignore the prohibition, for I considered it to be an abuse of spiritual authority.

When I said Mass during the summer at Memorial Church, I enjoyed a mild feeling of triumph. Not only did I feel perfectly free to say Mass, but it was a real pleasure to be leading a congregation in public Sunday worship once again. However, I did not say Mass in my home during the summer as I had done in the spring. I needed to live a private life for a while with my family and to be as much as possible in the mountains.

During the intervals between trips, my energies went into putting Dad's studio into shape for Eve's art work. Since he had worked in iron and wood and copper, Dad had not designed the place to be clean or warm or air-tight. Spider webs and dust were everywhere. But it was a treasure house of his tools, and there were carvings to be sorted for preservation or discard. Eve pounced delightedly upon the huge file of animal pictures Dad had collected from magazines and books to use as models for his carvings.

We were assisted by several friends, especially Dave Duisenberg, a builder, whose ideas and tools and willing hands helped me over the harder parts of the project, such as setting in new windows and creating a decent bathroom. I learned much as I went along.

Late in the summer, my family and I returned to Silver Lake, but the weather was against us. We tried to keep busy in the cabin, but after several days of rain and cold, we gave up and came home.

The next day, Eve and I sent the children to their grandmother in southern California to enjoy the beach. This gave us a chance for a little honeymoon. We began by crossing the Sierra in an August snowfall; and, descending into the wide spaces of Antelope Valley, we drove to Smith thirty miles east in Nevada, where my cousin Georgia Fulstone lived. After a pleasant night and day with her family, during which the storm cleared away, we then drove back into California by way of Mono County.

Now that the sun was shining we drove without haste. While she snuggled close to me I pointed our the features of the country— the white desert poppies along the roadside and the lush green valley of Bridgeport as it came in view. Our peaceful intimate drive ended in the village of Bridgeport, which I had always loved as representative of the "East Side" country since my family had first visited it in 1929. We had lunch in one of the little cafes, and then drove up the bumpy road in Green Lakes Canyon.

At the road end, we shouldered packs and started up the trail into the Wilderness Area. This three-day backpacking trip was Eve's first real mountain adventure, and I was happy to show her the area where my parents had taken their last backpacking trip twelve years before. Like all beginning hikers, she found the pack heavy and the uphill miles long. The second afternoon I left her painting by West Lake, an alpine tarn encircled by ruddy cliffs, while I hiked back to the car for more supplies. Much as I loved being with her and showing her things, it was also fun to stretch my legs and hike the round trip of eight miles at top speed.

After we the trip, it was time to face the problems of my future ministry. Where I would be able to say Mass in the fall? I had used my home in the spring only as a temporary place; we had not found it comfortable. Accordingly, I asked the pastor at the First Presbyterian Church near my home about the possibility of Mass there. While awaiting an answer from him and his council, my friend Manfred Bahmann, the Lutheran campus pastor, called me one day about a mixed marriage problem he had to deal with. I seized the opportunity to ask him about celebrating Mass at his chapel. "John, we would love to have you!" he exclaimed in his hearty way. His unhesitating welcome was enormously encouraging, and I accepted his offer.

During the first week of September, some of my friends at St. Ann's reported that there was about to be a public council meeting. They, including some members of the parish council, had continued to work for what they felt I deserved, a pension or a continuing salary. Although I was not very optimistic about the result, I postponed plans for a regular Sunday liturgy until after that meeting.

I decided not to attend. If the lay people at St. Ann's wanted to suuport me or if they wanted me back in some capacity, I didn't wished to be involved in the decision: it should be theirs alone. A few friends came directly from the meeting to report.

They told us that several people had spoken warmly about what I had meant to them at St. Ann's, and their desire to see me employed in some capacity on the staff. However, they reported that a young layman, quite new in the community, had given a scholarly explanation of why St. Ann's could not do anything more for me. After he had spoken, Father Boyle reinforced this point by noting that my public wedding and my Masses constituted "civil disobedience" to the Church, and that I must be well aware that it would entail punishment. Unfortunately, no one knew how to oppose these arguments; the voices of my friends fell silent, and my case was dropped.

The next day I wrote to Boyle, offering him the chance to correct me if I had been misinformed about what he had said. I did not deny that I was "civilly disobedient" to the Church, but expressed surprise that he, who was so proud of marching with Martin Luther King in Alabama, should now line up on the side of the oppressor, supporting the bad laws against which my protest was aimed, and helping to administer my punishment. He did not reply.

With the matter at St. Ann's closed, I began holding a regular and public Mass at the University Lutheran Center the following Sunday. During the first few weeks of my Sunday liturgies the crowds were large, but the faces were constantly changing. Slowly as the months passed, the casual well-wishers fell away and a steady community took shape.

Early on, our group decided to incorporate the community as a church under the laws of California. In doing so we took as our title the baptismal name of Pope John XXIII, Angelo Roncalli, the man who best symbolized the spirit of the Church as we felt that it really should prevail in the world.

During the years in which the Angelo Roncalli Community has continued its services, the official Catholic Church has taken no notice of it. When Bishop John Quinn became Archbishop of San Francisco, I wrote politely to introduce myself, explain who and what I was, and what we as a community were doing. Although he replied kindly, he ignored all the issues which I raised, the legitimacy of the celibacy law, for example, and assured me that he would pray that I return to the fold.

Again when the new diocese of San Jose, which included our area, was created I wrote to the newly appointed Bishop DuMayne to inform him of our existence and the spirit of my ministry. DuMayne did not reply at all. So much for the official Church.

While I was disappointed that my overtures were rejected by the bishops, I was really surprised and hurt by the silence of my classmates. Of the thirteen who had gathered annually on March 20 to recall our ordination, only Geno Walsh ever communicated with me after my marriage.

Sometimes I still feel a little resentful at the Church's indifference, but for the most part I am grateful not to carry the burden of its countless regulations and organizational demands. It is a pleasure to me that I can now conduct the affairs of my church without having to deal with anyone in authority, and in the manner that seems suitable to the time and to the group.

The mood of our liturgy is quiet, informal, responsive. Each week I plan the service around some theme arising from my reading, from events in the world, or from my personal experiences. In selecting themes and readings, and in developing the style of our liturgy, I have profited immensely from the freshness and objectivity which Eve brings to my work. Not having the reserve most Catholics feel toward the clergy, and the assumptions with which religious people are commonly burdened, she quickly detects anything unclear or trite, clashing or inappropriate. I usually hear about it over breakfast.

Occasionally we invite a member or a guest to talk to us on some matter of their special knowledge or experience. Our service is unmistakably a Mass, and every Sunday a member of the community brings the bread and wine for the Communion. The fifty or sixty people who belong to the Community are Catholics for the most part, but ones who find themselves at ease with our irregular status.

I hoped for awhile that I might discover a network of communities like ours throughout the country. I joined the newly formed Federation of Christian Ministries, hoping that it would provide the tie between these scattered groups. However, this has not happened. Apparently groups like ours are all too few.

Important as the Angelo Roncalli community is in my life, it is not a full-time "job." Nor is it the full extent of my ministry. For one thing, I am invited to perform a great many weddings, averaging one a week over the year, with the largest number in summer. I have celebrated weddings in many places: at Kamiak Butte in the Palouse country of eastern Washington, at Glacier Point in Yosemite, near the top of Buena Vista Peak in the High Sierra, on the cliffs above Half Moon Bay, and by the tropical beach of Barra de Navidad in Mexico. The vast majority are in the homes or gardens of the couples or their friends; a few in Protestant churches.

I have found that many people, disillusioned with institutional religion, still desire to celebrate their marriages, their christenings, and other significant events in the context of faith and in the tradition of the ancient Catholic liturgy. I am happy to serve all these people, to provide them with spiritual counseling and with the Sacraments of the Church according to their particular needs.

This ministry of mine is quite different from that which was instilled by my seminary training. Priestly ministry, as I understood it at the time of my ordination, was very institutional. My duty was to keep all the "sheep" safely enclosed in the corral, protected against the perils of the outside world. As I saw it then, each convert whom I instructed and baptized; each fallen-away that I brought back to the Sacraments; each hospital case annointed and absolved in preparation for death—was an individual human being saved from sin and damnation, and marked with the "sign of salvation."

And similarly, failures were felt not just as a reduction of "Catholic statistics," but as a failure to fulfill a responsibility toward the souls entrusted to my care. Not to reach the hospital in time to annoint someone on the point of death or not saying the right thing to a fallen-away Catholic might cost that person his or her eternal life, or so I thought. What a burden to bear!

It was not until I left parish work in 1950 for the youthful world of the Newman apostolate that I began losing this sense of urgency. Then the sincere, insistent questions raised by students slowly softened my doctrinal stiffness and challenged my moral certainties, and my respect for non-Catholic colleagues changed my perspective. All of these developments proved to be a preparation for the freedom of spirit which came with the election of Pope John and the convening of the Vatican Council—and which is now at the heart of my priesthood as I seek to respect and serve the members of the Angelo Roncalli community and others who turn to me.

Outside of my religious ministry, there are three other communities that now occupy an important place in my life. One is the Briarpatch, a consumer cooperative in our area; another is Nature Explorations, a local environmental group; the third is Amnesty International, a human rights organization. Eve and I joined the Briarpatch when we were first married, partly as an inexpensive way to buy good food, but also because we liked the new age spirit of the people we met there. The following year I was elected to the board and served four terms, enjoying the chance to learn something about running a small business, and about the co-op movement. When a part-time job opened up, I went to work, mostly in produce, for three years, experiencing for the first time in my life what it is like to go to work each morning and draw a regular hourly wage.

The Briarpatch community, like the Palo Alto Coop which my grandmother Duryea had joined in the early days of its existence, were people who hoped that neither the bureaucracy of the political left nor the pressures of competition on the right would govern the economic destinies of society. Rather, this cooperative effort of people working together would increase the blessings of the world's bounty for all.

I discovered Nature Explorations as I looked for people who would share my love of the mountains. Although I had been a life member of the Sierra Club since the 1940s, I had never become active in the club at the local level because my need for outings was being well met within my church commmunity. Moreover, the Sierra Club had grown too large! Nature Explorations seemed just right for me.

Here was a Palo Alto based group with a strong emphasis on the spirituality of the outdoor experience. Without much persuasion, I agreed to lead a High Sierra pack trip, the first week-long one that they had scheduled. Soon I was invited to join their board, and have since then continued to lead summer high mountain trips and offseason hikes in the coastal mountains, as well as to give lectures and slide shows on the natural history of the country. I find among this clientele, no less than among students, a satisfying opportunity to communicate the love of nature and the respect all human beings should have for its innate sacredness.

The third group with which I have been involved is Amnesty International, which is committed to a worldwide struggle against all abuses of human rights as these were defined in 1948 by the United Nations. This is its sole purpose, and Amnesty maintains a careful policy of political neutrality.

Together with several members of my church, I joined the local group, feeling that it would provide a good cause in which our community could be involved, and I served as chairman for several years. The prime task of Amnesty is to work for the release of prisoners of conscience—anywhere. The cases referred to us have been researched by the headquarters in London.

This is discouraging work, for the results are usually hard to assess. We write countless letters to the appropriate officials, relatives, and sometimes even the prisoners themselves, but we seldom receive replies. However, once in awhile, we have the thrill of learning that "our" prisoner has been released.

And besides all these, there is, of course, my home.

Having lived since the age of eighteen in schools and rectories where there was a housekeeper, I was quite helpless around the house when Eve and I were married, competent only to wash dishes and sweep the floor. However, she urged me to try cooking; she would like a holiday from the kitchen now and then. So I timidly began doing the grocery shopping, which was eased by the congenial atmosphere of the Briarpatch, and cooking dinner once a week.

This domestication was speeded by the addition to our menage of a boarder whose example as a good cook provided me with further incentive. Tom Devine had lived at Newman for a while and was now occupying a room in our neighborhood. So we invited him to eat with us daily, and he remained virtually a member of the family for three years, during which time he took his turn cooking. After dinner he would play the piano and accompany me in reviving my enjoyment of the violin.

Besides producing her own work in the studio which had been my Dad's, Eve continued as a student until she completed her master's degree in painting at San Jose State University. It has been one of the great joys of these years to be constantly observing the development of new facets of her artistic skill and vision. I constantly marvel at the meticulous crafting of everything she does, not only painting, drawing, and sculpture, but also poetry and the teaching of art.

The children, who were so little when Eve and I were married, are now teenagers. Although they seldom go to church, I can see that it does not matter; they are loving and self-reliant, and their ideals are well formed. When someone asks them what their father does, they answer without hesitation or embarrassment, "He's a Catholic priest."

During a recent summer both Leslie and Ariel asked, for the first time, to go backpacking with me in the Sierra. I took them on a five-day trip into the West Carson basin—a place which I had never before explored—lying just north of Yosemite Park, with Tower Peak looming at its head. One whole day we spent crossing a series of ridges between two lakes finding our way without trail. The girls carried their packs without complaint, and when we were not hiking seemed content just to be in the beautiful places we found. They swam in the cold water, and slept well at night. Only the mosquitoes really bugged them.

It was deeply satisfying to me to see that they were perfectly at home in the wilderness! What I had shared with hundreds of other young people, I could now share with my own.

The wilderness has been an unbroken thread of continuity in my life—always a source of spiritual and physical renewal. My earliest memories of keen pleasure were of the white sands and piny woods of the Carmel peninsula, and of the morning sunlight creeping down the granite walls of the American River Canyon at Kyburz. The Sierra was where I discovered the world of trees and clouds and flowers. The wilderness was my secret refuge from the dreary abstracions of philosophical theology and the cold severity of semiary spirituality. The mountains were where I felt the most united to my parents and my brother Bob, and where we found the greatest fulfilment and peace. The wilderness also became, to an ever increasng degree, a tool in my ministry for the creation of a sensiive and caring community, and the place where I could forget the social restrictions of the priestly role and become simply myself.

The wilderness of the high Sierra remains all these things for me still. And it is a realm of order and uplifting beauty, a sign of liberation from human authority and an experience of the transcendent presence of God. When the Church, by the act of excommunication, had driven me out—like the sin-laden scapegoat of old—into the "wilderness" of the world, it little realized that this was no punishment, for the wilderness had always been my home.

Until the summer of 1976, my life was in a sense a dialogue with the Roman Catholic Church: obedience and resistance, support and fear, inspiration and disappointment, pride and shame. All these opposites existed within me as I lived my Catholic life, first as a student, then for more than thirty years as a priest of the diocese. With my marriage that dialogue came to an end.

The dialogue is now between myself and God within me. I more keenly feel God's presence in the people I meet and serve, and as always in the wilderness; but most of all, in the creative, tempestuous, intuitive, and loving presence of Eve, my wife.

About the Co-Author

Oso Bartlett is a man of varied and special talents. A native of Maine he received his Bachelor of Arts Degree in Physics from the University of Maine. After a stint in the Navy as a nuclear reactor operator he attended San Jose State University and obtained a Master of Science Degree in Cybernetic Systems.

Presently he is a lecturer at SJSU for such courses as "Systems, Society, and Technology" and "The Systems Age". He is also a senior research analyst consultant for Creative Strategies Research International, where he has been editor of *Technology Growth Markets and Opportunities* and manager of *Telematics Market Analysis Program.*

He has edited and authored numerous professional articles, as well as worked in collaboration on a book length documentary on Cambodian refugee camps. It is a great tribute to his teaching, communications, and technical skills that he introduced Father Duryea to the world of computers and word processing, and together they developed this manuscript on the publisher's computer.

On January 12, 1985, Father Duryea celebrated the wedding of Oso Bartlett and Ann Gila Russell.